Meaning in History

By

KARL LÖWITH

THE UNIVERSITY OF CHICAGO PRESS

CHICAGO AND LONDON

International Standard Book Number: 0–226–49555–8

Library of Congress Catalog Card Number: 57–7900

THE UNIVERSITY OF CHICAGO PRESS, CHICAGO 60637
The University of Chicago Press, Ltd., London

To the memory of
MY MOTHER

THUS the world is like an oilpress: under pressure. If you are the dregs of the oil you are carried away through the sewer; if you are genuine oil you will remain in the vessel. But to be under pressure is inevitable. Observe the dregs, observe the oil. Pressure takes place ever in the world, as for instance, through famine, war, want, inflation, indigence, mortality, rape, avarice; such are the pressures on the poor and the worries of the states: we have evidence of them. . . . We have found men who grumble under these pressures and who say: "how bad are these Christian times!" . . . Thus speak the dregs of the oil which run away through the sewer; their color is black because they blaspheme: they lack splendour. The oil has splendour. For here another sort of man is under the same pressure and friction which polishes him, for is it not the very friction which refines him?

—AUGUSTINE *Sermones,* ed. DENIS, xxiv. 11.

PREFACE

AFTER I had finished this small study of the large topic of *Weltgeschichte* and *Heilsgeschichte*,[1] I began to wonder whether the reader might not be disappointed by the lack of "constructive" results. This apparent lack is, however, a real gain if it is true that truth is more desirable than illusion. Assuming that a single grain of truth is preferable to a vast construct of illusions, I have tried to be honest with myself and, consequently, also with my reader about the possibility, or rather the impossibility, of imposing on history a reasoned order or of drawing out the working of God. History as a partial record of human experience is too deep and, at the same time, too shallow to put into relief the humble greatness of a human soul which can give meaning, if anything can give it, to what otherwise would be a burden for man. History no more proves or disproves the incomparable value of a single man's righteousness and heroism in the face of the powers of the world than it proves or disproves the existence of God. Of course, individuals as well as whole nations can be hypnotized into the belief that God or some world-process intends them to achieve this or that and to survive while others are going under, but there is always something pathetic, if not ludicrous, in beliefs of this kind.[2] To the critical mind, neither a providential design nor a natural law of progressive development is discernible in the tragic human comedy of all times. Nietzsche was right when he said[3] that to look upon nature as if it were a proof of the goodness and care of God and to interpret history as a constant testimony to a moral order and purpose—that all this is now past because it has conscience against it. But he was wrong in assuming that the pseudo-religious makeup of nature and history is of any real consequence to a genuine Christian faith in God, as revealed in Christ and hidden in nature and history.

More intelligent than the superior vision of philosophers and

v

theologians is the common sense of the natural man and the un-common sense of the Christian believer. Neither pretends to dis-cern on the canvas of human history the purpose of God or of the historical process itself. They rather seek to set men free from the world's oppressive history by suggesting an attitude, either of skepticism or of faith, which is rooted in an experience certainly nurtured by history but detached from and surpassing it, and thus enabling man to endure it with mature resignation or with faithful expectation. Religious faith is so little at variance with skepticism that both are rather united by their common opposi-tion to the presumptions of a settled knowledge. One can, indeed, as Hume suggested,[4] erect "religious faith on philosophical skep-ticism"; but the history of religious and irreligious skepticism has not yet been written. A man who lives by thought must have his skepticism—literally, a passion for search—which may end in upholding the question as question or in answering it by tran-scending his doubt through faith. The skeptic and the believer have a common cause against the easy reading of history and its meaning. Their wisdom, like all wisdom, consists not the least in disillusion and resignation, in freedom from illusions and pre-sumptions.

That man has to make here and now decisions which run ahead of his potential wisdom and therefore fall short of it goes without saying; but his planning and guessing, his designs and decisions, far-reaching as they may be, have only a partial func-tion in the wasteful economy of history which engulfs them, tosses them, and swallows them.

> They know and do not know, that acting is suffering
> And suffering is action. Neither does the actor suffer
> Nor the patient act. But both are fixed
> In an eternal action, an eternal patience
> To which all must consent that it may be willed,
> And which all must suffer that they may will it,
> That the pattern may subsist....

> —T. S. ELIOT, *Murder in the Cathedral*

CONTENTS

INTRODUCTION

THE term "philosophy of history" was invented by Voltaire, who used it for the first time in its modern sense, as distinct from the theological interpretation of history. In Voltaire's *Essai sur les mœurs et l'esprit des nations* the leading principle was no longer the will of God and divine providence but the will of man and human reason. With the gradual dissolution of the eighteenth-century belief in reason and progress, philosophy of history became more or less homeless. The term is still used, even more widely than before, but its content has been so diluted that any thought on history may call itself a philosophy. The label "philosophy," as it is nowadays so cheaply used ("philosophy" of life, of business, and even of camping), does not indicate a specific philosophy but merely public and private opinions. In the following discussion the term "philosophy of history" is used to mean a systematic interpretation of universal history in accordance with a principle by which historical events and successions are unified and directed toward an ultimate meaning.

Taken in this sense, philosophy of history is, however, entirely dependent on theology of history, in particular on the theological concept of history as a history of fulfilment and salvation. But then philosophy of history cannot be a "science"; for how could one verify the belief in salvation on scientific grounds? The absence of such a scientific basis and, at the same time, the quest for it caused modern philosophers and even theologians like Troeltsch to reject the prescientific treatment of history altogether, while accepting, in principle, the empirical method of Voltaire. Arguing that the philosophy of history from Augustine to Bossuet does not present a theory of "real" history in its finitude, wealth, and mobility but only a doctrine of history on the basis of revelation and faith, they drew the conclusion that the theological interpretation of history—or fourteen hundred years of Western thought—is a negligible affair.[1] Against this common

1

opinion that proper historical thinking begins only in modern times, with the eighteenth century, the following outline aims to show that philosophy of history originates with the Hebrew and Christian faith in a fulfilment and that it ends with the seculari-zation of its eschatological pattern. Hence the inverted sequence of our historical presentation.

This somewhat unusual way of developing the historical suc-cession of the interpretations of history regressively, starting from modern times and going back toward their beginning, may be justified on three grounds: didactic, methodical, and substantial.

1. While the abstention from any theological or metaphysical frame of reference, as advocated by Burckhardt, is in itself per-suasive to the modern reader, the theological understanding of earlier ages is, at first, foreign to a generation which is just awak-ening from the secular dream of progress which replaced the faith in providence but which has not yet reached Burckhardt's resolute renunciation. Hence the didactic expediency of starting with what is familiar to the modern mind before approaching the unfamiliar thought of former generations. It is easier to under-stand the former belief in providence through a critical analysis of the theological implications of the still existing belief in secu-lar progress than it would be to understand belief in progress through an analysis of providence.

2. An adequate approach to history and its interpretations is necessarily regressive for the very reason that history is moving forward, leaving behind the historical foundations of the more recent and contemporary elaborations. The historical conscious-ness cannot but start with itself, though its aim is to know the thought of other times and of other men, different from our times and ourselves. History has time and again to be recovered and rediscovered by the living generations. We understand—and misunderstand—ancient authors, but always in the light of con-temporary thought, reading the book of history backward from the last to the first page. This inversion of the customary way of historical presentation is actually practiced even by those who

proceed from past ages to modern times, without being conscious of their contemporary motivations.

3. The methodical regress from the modern secular interpretations of history to their ancient religious pattern is, last but not least, substantially justified by the realization that we find ourselves more or less at the end of the modern rope. It has worn too thin to give hopeful support. We have learned to wait without hope, "for hope would be hope for the wrong thing." Hence the wholesomeness of remembering in these times of suspense what has been forgotten and of recovering the genuine sources of our sophisticated results. To do this is possible not by an imaginary jump, either into early Christianity (Kierkegaard) or into classical paganism (Nietzsche), but only by the analytical reduction of the modern compound into its original elements. The outstanding element, however, out of which an interpretation of history could arise at all, is the basic experience of evil and suffering, and of man's quest for happiness. The interpretation of history is, in the last analysis, an attempt to understand the meaning of history as the meaning of suffering by historical action. The Christian meaning of history, in particular, consists in the most paradoxical fact that the cross, this sign of deepest ignominy, could conquer the world of the conquerors by opposing it. In our times crosses have been borne silently by millions of people; and if anything warrants the thought that the meaning of history has to be understood in a Christian sense, it is such boundless suffering. In the Western world the problem of suffering has been faced in two different ways: by the myth of Prometheus and by the faith in Christ—the one a rebel, the other a servant. Neither antiquity nor Christianity indulged in the modern illusion that history can be conceived as a progressive evolution which solves the problem of evil by way of elimination.

It is the privilege of theology and philosophy, as contrasted with the sciences, to ask questions that cannot be answered on the basis of empirical knowledge. All the ultimate questions concerning first and last things are of this character; they remain significant because no answer can silence them. They signify a fundamental quest; for there would be no search for the meaning of history if its meaning were manifest in historical events. It is the very absence of meaning in the events themselves that motivates the quest. Conversely, it is only within a pre-established horizon of ultimate meaning, however hidden it may be, that actual history seems to be meaningless. This horizon has been established by history, for it is Hebrew and Christian thinking that brought this colossal question into existence. To ask earnestly the question of the ultimate meaning of history takes one's breath away; it transports us into a vacuum which only hope and faith can fill.

The ancients were more moderate in their speculations. They did not presume to make sense of the world or to discover its ultimate meaning. They were impressed by the visible order and beauty of the cosmos, and the cosmic law of growth and decay was also the pattern for their understanding of history. According to the Greek view of life and the world, everything moves in recurrences, like the eternal recurrence of sunrise and sunset, of summer and winter, of generation and corruption. This view was satisfactory to them because it is a rational and natural understanding of the universe, combining a recognition of temporal changes with periodic regularity, constancy, and immutability. The immutable, as visible in the fixed order of the heavenly bodies, had a higher interest and value to them than any progressive and radical change.

In this intellectual climate, dominated by the rationality of the natural cosmos, there was no room for the universal significance of a unique, incomparable historic event. As for the destiny of man in history, the Greeks believed that man has resourcefulness to meet every situation with magnanimity—they did not go further than that. They were primarily concerned with the *logos* of the *cosmos,* not with the *Lord* and the meaning of *history*. Even the tutor of Alexander the Great depreciated history over against poetry, and Plato might have said that the sphere of change and contingency is the province of historiography but not of philosophy. To the Greek thinkers a *philosophy* of history would have been a contradiction in terms. To them history was political history and, as such, the proper study of statesmen and historians.

To the Jews and Christians, however, history was primarily a history of salvation and, as such, the proper concern of prophets, preachers, and teachers. The very existence of a philosophy of history and its quest for a meaning is due to the history of salvation; it emerged from the faith in an ultimate purpose. In the Christian era political history, too, was under the influence and in the predicament of this theological background. In some way the destinies of nations became related to a divine or pseudo-divine vocation.[2]

It is not by chance that we use the words "meaning" and "purpose" interchangeably, for it is mainly purpose which constitutes meaning for us. The meaning of all things that are what they are, not by nature, but because they have been created either by God or by man, depends on purpose. A chair has its meaning of being a "chair," in the fact that it indicates something beyond its material nature: the purpose of being used as a seat. This purpose, however, exists only for us who manufacture and use such things. And since a chair or a house or a town or a B-29 is a means to the end or purpose of man, the purpose is not inherent in, but transcends, the thing. If we abstract from a chair its transcendent purpose, it becomes a meaningless combination of pieces of wood.

The same is true in regard to the formal structure of the meaning of history. History, too, is meaningful only by indicating some transcendent purpose beyond the actual facts. But, since history is a movement in time, the purpose is a goal. Single events as such are not meaningful, nor is a mere succession of events. To venture a statement about the meaning of historical events is possible only when their *telos* becomes apparent. When a historical movement has unfolded its consequences, we reflect on its first appearance, in order to determine the meaning of the whole, though particular, event—"whole" by a definite point of departure and a final point of arrival. If we reflect on the whole course of history, imagining its beginning and anticipating its end, we think of its meaning in terms of an ultimate purpose.

The claim that history has an ultimate meaning implies a final purpose or goal transcending the actual events. This identification of meaning and purpose does not exclude the possibility of other systems of meaning. To the Greeks, for example, historical events and destinies were certainly not simply meaningless—they were full of import and sense, but they were not meaningful in the sense of being directed toward an ultimate end in a transcendent purpose that comprehends the whole course of events.

The temporal horizon for a final goal is, however, an eschatological future, and the future exists for us only by expectation and hope.[3] The ultimate meaning of a transcendent purpose is focused in an expected future. Such an expectation was most intensely alive among the Hebrew prophets; it did not exist among the Greek philosophers. When we remember that II Isaiah and Herodotus were almost contemporaries, we realize the unbridgeable gulf that separates Greek wisdom from Jewish faith. The Christian and post-Christian outlook on history is futuristic, perverting the classical meaning of *historein,* which is related to present and past events. In the Greek and Roman mythologies and genealogies the past is re-presented as an everlasting foundation. In the Hebrew and Christian view of history the past is a promise to the future; consequently, the interpretation of the past becomes a prophecy in reverse, demonstrating the past as a meaningful "preparation" for the future. Greek philosophers and historians were convinced that whatever is to happen will be of the same pattern and character as past and present events; they never indulged in the prospective possibilities of the future.

This general thesis can be substantiated by reference to Herodotus, Thucydides, and Polybius.[4] Herodotus' concern was to give a record of things that had happened, "in order that the memory of the past may not be blotted out from among men by time" and "that great deeds may not lack renown." The "meaning" of recorded events is not explicit and does not transcend the single events but is implied in the stories themselves. What they mean is simply what they point out by having a point. Behind these obvious meanings there are also half-hidden meanings, occasionally revealed in significant words, gestures, signs, and oracles. And when at certain moments the actual human deeds and events coincide with superhuman intimations, then a circle of meaning is completed, wherein the beginning and the end of a story illuminate each other. The temporal scheme of Herodotus' narrative is not a meaningful course of universal history aiming toward a future goal, but, like all Greek conception of time, is periodic, moving within a cycle. In the view of Herodotus, history shows a repetitive pattern, regulated by a cosmic law of compensation mainly through *nemesis,* which time and again restores the equilibrium of the historiconatural forces.

In Thucydides the religious background and the epic features of Herodotus' historiography, which never clearly defines the border line between the human and the divine, are definitely replaced by a strict investigation of the pragmatic concatenations. History was to him a history of political struggles based on the nature of man. And, since human nature does not change, events that happened in the past "will happen again in the same or in a similar way." Nothing really new can occur in the future when it is "the nature of all things to grow as well as to decay." It may be that future generations and individuals will act more intelligently in certain circumstances, but history as such will not change essentially. There is not the least tendency in Thucydides to judge the course of historical events from the viewpoint of a future which is distinct from the past by having an open horizon and an ultimate goal.

Only Polybius seems to approach our concept of history, by representing all events as leading up to a definite end: the world domination of Rome. But even Polybius had no primary interest in the future as such. To him, history revolves in a cycle of political revolutions, wherein constitutions change, disappear, and return in a course appointed by nature. As a result of this natural fatality, the historian can predict the future of a given state. He may be wrong in his estimate of the time that the process will take; but, if his judgment is not tainted emotionally, he will very seldom be mistaken regarding the stage of growth or decline which the state has reached and the form into which it will change.

Moreover, the general law of fortune is mutability—the sudden turn from one extreme to the opposite. Having witnessed the perishing of the Macedonian monarchy, Polybius thought it therefore befitting to recall the prophetic words of Demetrius, who, in his treatise on Fortune, had predicted what was to happen, one hundred and fifty years after Alexander's conquest of the Persian empire:

For if you consider not countless years or many generations but merely these last fifty years, you will read in them the cruelty of Fortune. I ask you, do you think that fifty years ago either the Persians and the Persian king or the Macedonians and the king of Macedon, if some god had foretold the future to them, would ever have believed that at the time when we live, the very name of the Persians would have perished utterly—the Persians who were masters of almost the whole world—and that the Macedonians, whose name was formerly almost unknown, would now be the lords of it all? But nevertheless this Fortune, who never compacts with life, who always defeats our reckoning by some novel stroke; she who ever demonstrates her power by foiling our expectations, now also, as it seems to me, makes it clear to all men, by endowing the Macedonians with the whole wealth of Persia, that she has but lent them these blessings until she decides to deal differently with them [Polybius *Histories* xxix. 21].

This mutability of fortune did not merely cause sadness to ancient man but was accepted with virile assent. Reflecting upon the fate of all things human, Polybius realized that all nations, cities, and authorities must, like men, meet their end. Relating Scipio's famous saying after the fall of Carthage, that the same doom will eventually be pronounced on victorious Rome (fragments of xxxviii. 21 f.), Polybius comments that it would be difficult to mention an utterance "more statesmanlike and more profound," for to bear in mind at the moment of greatest triumph the possible reversal of fortune befits a great and perfect man worthy to be remembered. Polybius and his friend Scipio, however, only restate the classical mood as expressed by Homer (*Iliad* vi. 448 f.) with regard to the fate of Troy and Priam. And wherever classical feeling is alive, the ultimate wisdom of the historian is still the same.[5]

The moral lesson to be drawn from the historical experience of alternating glories and disasters is, according to Polybius, "never to boast unduly of achievements" by being overbearing and merciless but rather to reflect on the opposite extremity of fortune. Hence he wished to instruct his reader how to learn from the study of history what is "best at every time and in every circumstance," viz., to be moderate in times of prosperity and to become wise by the misfortunes of others—a maxim which is as reasonable as it is remote from the Christian realization of sin and the hope in redemption.

The fact that Polybius felt no difficulty in prognosticating future developments indicates the fundamental difference between the classic and the Christian outlook and attitude in regard to the future. To Polybius, it was "an easy matter" to foretell the future "by inference from the past." To the Old Testament writers only the Lord himself could reveal, through his prophets, a future which is independent of all that has happened in the past, and which cannot be inferred from the past as a natural consequence. Hence the fulfilment of prophecies as understood by the Old and New Testament writers is entirely different from the verification of prognostications concerning historiconatural events. Though the future may be predetermined by the will of God, it is determined by a personal will and not by natural fatality, and man can never foretell it unless God reveals it to him. And, since the final fulfilment of Hebrew and Christian destiny lies in an eschatological future, the issue of which depends on man's faith and will and not on a natural law of pragmatic history, the basic feeling in regard to the future becomes one of suspense in the face of its theoretical incalculability.

Thus far Burckhardt's thesis holds true that what separates us most deeply from the ancients is that they believed in the possibility of foreknowing the future, either by rational inference or by the popular means of questioning oracles and of practicing divination, while we do not. We do not think it even desirable.

Whether we imagine a man, for instance, knowing in advance the day of his death and the situation it would find him in, or a people knowing in advance the century of its downfall, both pictures would bear within themselves as inevitable consequence a confusion of all desire and endeavour. For desire and endeavour can only unfold freely when they live and act blindly, i.e., for their own sakes and in obedience to inward impulses. After all, the future is shaped only when that happens, and if it did not happen, the future life and end of that man or that people would be different. A future known in advance is an absurdity. Foreknowledge of the future, however, is not only undesirable, it is for us also unlikely. The main obstacle in the way is the confusion of insight by our wishes, hopes and fears; further, our ignorance of everything which we call latent forces, physical or mental, and the incalculable factor of mental contagions, which can suddenly transform the world.[6]

The ultimate reason, however, why "for us" the future remains opaque is not the shortsightedness of our theoretical knowledge but the absence of those religious assumptions which made the future transparent for the ancients. Antiquity, like most pagan cultures, believed that future events can be unveiled by special devices of divination. It can be foreknown because it is preordained. With the exception of some philosophers, nobody in antiquity questioned the truth of oracles, ominous dreams, and portents foreshadowing future events. Since the ancients generally believed in a predestined fate, future events and destinies were only slightly hidden from them under a veil which an inspired mind could penetrate. It was therefore a common feature of Greek and Roman life to make decisions dependent on an inquiry into fate. This ancient trust in divination had never lost its reputation until the church uprooted it. But the church, too, believed in predestination, though not by fate, while modern man does not believe in guidance, either by fate or by providence. He fancies that the future can be created and provided for by himself.

Burckhardt's own predictions about the future of Europe do not contradict his thesis, for he never pretended to know the possibilities of the future as one knows definite facts of the past. But what about Tocqueville, Spengler, and Toynbee, who prognosticate future developments theoretically? Is it for them also an "easy matter" to foretell what will happen? Certainly not; for their belief in a historical destiny is not the result of a single-minded acceptance of natural fate; it is profoundly ambiguous because of their counterbelief in man's responsibility for history through decision and will—a will which is always directed to a future of indeterminate possibilities.

To Tocqueville the march of democracy has as much of irresistible fatality as of irresistible providence, for both those who promote and those who obstruct it are blind instruments in the hands of a power directing history. "The gradual development of the equality of conditions is therefore a providential fact, and it possesses all the characteristics of a divine decree: it is universal, it is durable, it constantly eludes all human interference, and all events as well as men minister to its development." To attempt to stop democracy would then seem "to be fighting against God himself"[7] and against providence. The reverse of this impossibility of stopping the march of democracy and its providential fatality is that its future prospects can be foretold. The contemplation of so irresistible a revolution produced in Tocqueville's mind "a kind of religious dread." And yet in the next paragraph and again in the last chapter of his work, Tocqueville wants this providential process to be directed and restrained by man's own foresight and will; for the fate of the Christian nations "is still in their hands," though it may not remain there much longer. This solution of the difficulty by a partial freedom within a partial fatality restates, though in weaker terms, the old theological problem of the compatibility of divine providence with free will.

Spengler, in the first sentence of *The Decline of the West,* boldly announces that he attempts "for the first time" the venture of predetermining history. The presupposition of his attempt is that the course of history is in itself determined by necessity. The significance of historical cultures resides in the fatal fulfilment of life-cycles, from growth and flowering to decay. Being directed neither by the will of God nor by the will of man, history has no goal or purpose. Its "sublimity" consists in this very purposelessness. Yet, when Spengler goes on to define his supreme concept of "destiny," he introduces the notion of a noncyclical, "historical" time, directed toward the future. The historical sense is, according to him, a "sense of the future,"[8] peculiar to the Faustian soul and Weltanschauung, which are dynamic and infinite, in contrast to the static finiteness of the classical Apollinian culture. Spengler, belonging himself to the Faustian culture, which arose at the height of the Middle Ages but independent of the Christian religion, which has no proper place in his system, is far from accepting with classical detachment the inescapable fate of decline. He challenges those who cherish illusions and, like Nietzsche, teaches them that they should will and love fate, even promote and fulfil it.[9] No ancient ever fancied that the fate of decline should be willed and chosen; for fate is either really fate, and then it is futile to decide upon it, or it is a self-chosen destiny, and then it is no unavoidable fate. Spengler does not solve this problem of natural fate and historical destiny. His pathos grows from the confusion of the will to a future, still open to possibilities, with the acceptance of a definite outcome. The sequel to *The Decline of the West* is, therefore, an appeal to the coming "Years of Decision"[10] in this last historical crisis. He wants the Germans to build up a "Prussian socialism," to be prepared for it. Far from seeing in history a historiconatural process, he concludes his work with the sentence (derived from Schiller and used by Hegel but originating in the prophetic view of the Old Testament): "The history of the world is the world's court of justice" (*Die Weltgeschichte ist das Weltgericht*)—a tribunal without a moral judge. Hence the characteristic wording of his first sentence, according to which the prediction of history is not the easy matter of following simply the appointed course of nature but an "attempt" and a "venture," namely, the venture of prophesying history's judgment. What to Polybius is a theoretical statement of fact becomes for Spengler an ethical imperative; for the Faustian soul cannot help interpreting fate in the perspective of an *eschaton*.

Similarly divided between the classic and the Christian traditions is Toynbee's historical consciousness. He, too, tries to establish a recurrent rhythm of life-cycles,[11] repeating a permanent pattern of cultural genesis and growth, breakdown and disintegration. At the same time, he wants to extract from this historico-natural process a definite purpose and meaning. The material universality of his comparative study of twenty-one civilizations or rather "societies" is focused on the history of our Western society. "The Decline of the West" is also Toynbee's ultimate problem. He is, however, less assertive than Spengler in forecasting history, for disintegration may look like growth and vice versa.[12] Moreover, what causes a civilization to run down its fatal course is not a cosmic law of recurring cycles but a self-inflicted destruction, since history is a perpetual environment-man transaction of "challenge" and "response." Despite the freedom and responsibility which are implied in man's response, Toynbee suggests, however, a determinism even more exacting than that of Polybius: the standard run of the disintegration rhythm is exactly "three and one-half" beats, and the West is supposed to have already undergone the experience of one and one-half beats!

History is more than a history of civilizations. It is also, and even primarily, a history of religion, and religions are to Toynbee not homogeneous expressions of cultures, as they are to Spengler, but they transcend their cultures. Hence Toynbee's special concern with Christian and pre-Christian savior-religions. They are the only creative means of escape from a disintegrating society.[13] They create a new clime and dimension and, thereby, a new kind of society, namely, a universal church over against the dominant minority of universal states.

The disintegration of a secular society, pagan or nominally Christian, provides the opportunity for the rise of a universal religion and for a history of salvation for the souls of individual men; but indirectly it also transforms society. Men learn through suffering, and whom the Lord loveth he chasteneth. Thus Christianity was born in the death throes of a collapsing Hellenic society, which served as a good handmaid to the Christian religion.

If, so far from its being the historical function of higher religions to minister, as chrysalises, to the cyclic process of the reproduction of civilizations, it is the historical function of civilizations to serve, by their downfalls, as stepping-stones to a progressive process of the revelation of always deeper religious insight, and the gift of ever more grace to act on this insight, then the societies of the species called civilizations will have fulfilled their function when once they have brought a mature higher religion to birth; and, on this showing, our own Western post-Christian secular civilization might at best be a superfluous repetition of the pre-Christian Graeco-Roman one, and at worst a pernicious back-sliding from the path of spiritual progress.[14]

Following Toynbee's scheme of the breakdown of civilizations and of the rise of religions, one would naturally expect that a new religion is on the horizon of our future. But nothing of this kind is in store. The scientific detachment of Toynbee's universal survey here suddenly reverses to a confession and a commitment which can only be called "parochial" if we judge it by Toynbee's own standards of scientific objectivity, comprehensiveness, neutrality, and detachment. As a Christian he cannot envisage a supersession of the Roman Catholic church, "with the spear of the Mass, the shield of the Hierarchy and the helmet of the Papacy."[15] Instead of leaving open the possibility of a new religion and church, Toynbee endeavors to show that Christianity is still the greatest "new" event in the history of man, while the eruption of democracy and science—the latest new events in Western secular civilization—is "an almost meaningless repetition of something that the Greeks and Romans did before us and did supremely well."[16]

But Toynbee is neither an empirical historian nor a good theologian. Instead of arguing with Augustine and all the Church Fathers that Christianity is the latest news because it is *the* good news and because God revealed himself in history only once and for all, he argues on astronomical grounds. Instead of demonstrating by the knowledge of faith that Christianity is true or by the standards of history that it was once young and is, therefore, now old, he refers to the modern scientific discoveries of geolo-

14

gist and astronomers which have vastly changed our time-scale, on which the beginning of the Christian era is an extremely recent date.

On a time-scale in which nineteen hundred years are no more than the twinkling of an eye, the beginning of the Christian era is only yesterday. It is only on the old-fashioned time-scale, on which the creation of the world and the beginning of life on the planet were reckoned to have taken place not more than six thousand years ago, that a span of nineteen hundred years seems a long period of time and the beginning of the Christian era therefore seems a far-off event. In fact it is a very recent event—perhaps the most recent significant event in history. . . .[17]

But how can one infer from an astronomical "fact" a historical and even religious "significance"? It is sheer belief, quite apart from astronomical evidence and likewise apart from an empirical study of history, which prompts Toynbee to assert that Christianity is still new and that it will not only survive our Western civilization but even become *the* world religion. He thinks that the technical unification of the modern world may serve its historical purpose "by providing Christianity with a completely world-wide repetition of the Roman Empire to spread over."[18] What may happen is that "Christianity may be left as the spiritual heir of all the other higher religions ... and of all the philosophies from Ikhnaton's to Hegel's; while the Christian Church as an institution may be left as the social heir of all the other churches and all the civilizations."[19]

Thus Toynbee's universal history of twenty-one civilizations issues in the ecumenical prospect of a progressive realization of a very particular church, in spite of his other concern with the empirical demonstration of recurrent cycles in man's secular fortunes. One wonders how these cycles can be integrated into that progression and how the dismal results of Toynbee's historical study can be harmonized with the hopeful assumptions of Toynbee as a believer.

Toynbee's belief has no bearing upon his historical consciousness, for he is much more under the spell of naturalistic and secular thinking than he realizes. It is mainly on this account that he cannot accept the Christian frame of reference in his historical investigations. He replaces the Christian idea of the continuous unity of universal history[20] by a process of partial unification and dismisses the traditional concept of a "Christian" Occident. Accordingly, he has to give up the Christian division of all historical time into an old and a new dispensation before and after Christ and, consequently, also the traditional periodization of Western history, which is derived from the Christian viewpoint.[21] The scientific ideal demands from him empirical evidence and neutral detachment from moral and other "prejudices," peculiar to one's own, incidentally Western, even British and Christian setting. And yet he cannot help being inspired by Western and Christian thinking. His eschatological outlook is clearly indicated by the three mottoes with which he has chosen to open his work. And behind the seeming neutrality of his scientific endeavor to find categories which are universally applicable (growth and disintegration, challenge and response, withdrawal and return, detachment and transfiguration), there is his personal concern about the future "prospects"[22] of our contemporary society. What seems, at first, a bewildering multitude of societies is actually seen from and concentrated in the disquieting problem of our own history, while the supreme law of history, the "alternating rhythm," refers, with a curious lack of discrimination, to such diverse authors as J. C. Smuts, Saint-Simon, Empedocles, Chu Hsi, and Goethe.[23]

But how can the "elemental rhythm" of yin and yang and the cycle of growth and decay be adjusted to the belief in a meaningful goal and a "progressive revelation" of divine truth in history? How can the "economy of truth,"[24] as Toynbee, with a phrase of the Catholic Newman, calls the masterly dispensation, be reconciled with Greek and Chinese speculation? Toynbee's answer is that the perpetual turning of a wheel is not a vain repetition if with each revolution it is carrying a vehicle that much nearer to its goal.[25] This simile, which seems to unite the classic cycle with the Christian *eschaton,* presupposes that the wheel is carrying a vehicle (religion) with a driver (God) who knows how to direct

16

the natural force of rotation to a supra-natural goal. "If religion is a chariot, it looks as if the wheels on which it mounts towards Heaven may be the periodic downfalls of civilizations on Earth. It looks as if the movement of civilization may be cyclic and recurrent, while the movement of religion may be on a single continuous upward line. The continuous upward movement of religion may be served and promoted by the cyclic movement of civilizations round the cycle of birth—death—birth."[26] Or, to put the same problem differently: How can the Faustian Spirit of the Earth (as conceived by Goethe and cited by Toynbee), who weaves an "elemental rhythm" in the welter of life and the tempest of action, weave "the living garment of the Godhead" if this Godhead is more than the pagan divinity of the universe, namely, a God incarnate in a human savior? Toynbee admits that he is not in a position to answer this question; at the same time, it is clear to him that we cannot afford to ignore it, since it holds the key to the meaning of the weaver's work. Thus Toynbee concludes the sixth volume of *A Study of History* with an open question and in the hope that the secret of history may still become unlocked and then give answer to the problem of the apparent futility and meaninglessness of so much labor and suffering.

Polybius was concerned with Rome's history, i.e., with past events progressing toward the present power of Rome. Modern historians who rank with him are concerned with Europe's future, when looking backward and searching into her history. The classic historian asks: How did it come about? The modern historian: How shall we go ahead?[27] The reason for this modern concern with the future is that the Hebrew and Christian faith has perverted the classic meaning of *historein* and, at the same time, invalidated the classical view of the future as something which can be investigated and known like a fact.

In the words of Hermann Cohen, freely translated:

The concept of history is a product of prophetism. . . . What Greek intellectualism could not produce, prophetism has achieved. In Greek consciousness, *historein* is equivalent to inquiry, narration, and knowledge. To the Greeks history remains something we can know because it is a matter of "fact" [*factum*], that is, of the past. The prophet, however, is a seer, not a scholar; his prophetic vision has created our concept of history as being essentially of the future. Time becomes primarily future, and future the primary content of our historical thought. For this new future "the creator of heaven and earth" is not sufficient. He has to create "a new heaven and a new earth." In this transformation the idea of progress is implied. Instead of a golden age in the mythological past, the true historical existence on earth is constituted by an eschatological future.[28]

The future is the "true" focus of history, provided that the truth abides in the religious foundation of the Christian Occident, whose historical consciousness is, indeed, determined by an eschatological motivation, from Isaiah to Marx, from Augustine to Hegel, and from Joachim to Schelling. The significance of this vision of an ultimate end, as both *finis* and *telos,* is that it provides a scheme of progressive order and meaning, a scheme which has been capable of overcoming the ancient fear of fate and fortune. Not only does the *eschaton* delimit the process of history by an end, it also articulates and fulfils it by a definite goal. The bearing of the eschatological thought on the historical consciousness of the Occident is that it conquers the flux of historical time, which wastes away and devours its own creations unless it is defined by an ultimate goal. Comparable to the compass which gives us orientation in space, and thus enables us to conquer it, the eschatological compass gives orientation in time by pointing to the Kingdom of God as the ultimate end and purpose.[29]

It is also only within this teleological, or rather eschatological, scheme of the historical process that history became "universal"; for its universality does not depend merely on the belief in one universal God but on his giving unity to the history of mankind by directing it toward a final purpose. When II Isaiah describes the future glory of the new Jerusalem, his religious futurism and nationalism are actually teleological universalism. "Mankind," however, has not existed in the historical past, nor can it exist in any present. It is an idea and an ideal of the future, the necessary horizon for the eschatological concept of history and its universality.

18

We of today, concerned with the unity of universal history and with its progress toward an ultimate goal or at least toward a "better world," are still in the line of prophetic and messianic monotheism; we are still Jews and Christians, however little we may think of ourselves in those terms. But within this predominant tradition we are also the heirs of classic wisdom. We are in the line of classical polytheism when we are concerned with the plurality of various cultures as such, exploring with boundless curiosity the whole natural and historical world for the sake of a disinterested knowledge which is quite untouched by any interest in redemption.

We are neither ancient ancients nor ancient Christians, but moderns—that is, a more or less inconsistent compound of both traditions. The Greek historians wrote pragmatic history centered around a great political event; the Church Fathers developed from Hebrew prophecy and Christian eschatology a theology of history focused on the supra-historical events of creation, incarnation, and consummation; the moderns elaborate a philosophy of history by secularizing theological principles and applying them to an ever increasing number of empirical facts. It seems as if the two great conceptions of antiquity and Christianity, cyclic motion and eschatological direction, have exhausted the basic approaches to the understanding of history. Even the most recent attempts at an interpretation of history are nothing else but variations of these two principles or a mixture of both of them. The elaboration of these reflections may profitably start with an analysis of Burckhardt's *Force and Freedom: Reflections on History* and then work backward to the Hebrew-Christian understanding of history by faith.

I

BURCKHARDT

THE proper purpose of Burckhardt's lifelong study and teaching of history was neither to construct "world history" philosophically nor to promote technical scholarship but to develop the historical sense. His course on history was intended as an introduction to the study of "the Historical," in order to stimulate the genuine appropriation of those periods of our history which may appeal individually. For to him history was not an objective science concerning neutral facts but "the record of facts which one age finds remarkable in another." As a record it depends on remembering, and each generation, by a new effort of appropriation and interpretation, has to remember time and again its own past unless it wants to forget it and to lose the historical sense and substance of its own existence. Such interpretation implies selection, emphasis, and evaluation. They are not regrettable or avoidable subjectifications of neutral facts but creative in regard to historical understanding as well as to historical facts; for it is only by selective interpretation and evaluation that we can determine which are, after all, the historically relevant, remarkable, significant, and important facts. "There may be a fact of first importance in Thucydides which will only be recognized a hundred years from now." Far from being neutral and therefore incapable of judgment, Burckhardt was the most consciously selective and critical historian of the nineteenth century. But he never pretended to be a philosopher.

From the beginning, Burckhardt declares that his *Reflections on History* cannot and will not compete with a philosophy of history. His task is more modest. He will merely "link up a number of observations and inquiries to a series of half-random thoughts." He rejects any attempt to form a "system" and any claim to historical "ideas." The philosophy of history is to him a contradiction in terms, inasmuch as history co-ordinates observations, while philosophy subordinates them to a principle. He dismisses likewise a theology of history. "The amelioration offered by religion is beyond our scope." The religious solution of the meaning of history belongs, he says, to a "special faculty" of man—to faith, which Burckhardt did not pretend to have.

He refers to Hegel and Augustine as the two who made the most outstanding attempts to explain history systematically by a principle: by God or the absolute Spirit, each working out his purpose in history. Against Hegel's theodicy, Burckhardt insists that the reasonableness of history is beyond our ken, for we are not privy to the purpose of eternal wisdom. Against Augustine's religious interpretation he says: "To us it does not matter." Both transcend our possible, purely human wisdom. Philosophy and theology of history have to deal with first beginnings and ultimate ends, and the profane historian cannot deal with either of them. The one point accessible to him is the permanent center of history: "man, as he is and was and ever shall be," striving, acting, suffering. The inevitable result of Burckhardt's refusal to deal with ultimate ends is his complementary resignation concerning ultimate meaning. He asks himself: "How far does this result in skepticism?" and he answers that true skepticism certainly has its place in a world where beginning and end are unknown and where the middle is in constant motion.

And yet there is some kind of permanence in the very flux of history, namely, its continuity. This is the only principle discernible in Burckhardt's *Reflections on History,* the one thin thread that holds together his observations after he has dismissed the systematic interpretations by philosophy and theology. The whole significance of history depends for Burckhardt on continuity as the common standard of all particular historical evaluations. If a radical crisis really disrupted history's continuity, it would be the end of a historical epoch, but not a "historical" crisis.[1]

Continuity as understood by him is more than mere going on, and it is less than progressive development. It is less than progressive because it does not imply the complacent assumption that the whole process of history has the purpose of leading up to our contemporary mediocrity as its goal and fulfilment. According to Burckhardt, man's mind and soul were complete long ago. And continuity is more than mere going on, because it implies a conscious effort in remembering and renewing our heritage, instead of merely accepting the cake of custom. Conscious historical continuity constitutes tradition and frees us in relation to it. The only people who renounce this privilege of historical consciousness are primitive and civilized barbarians. Spiritual continuity, as constituted by historical consciousness, is "a prime concern of man's existence," because it is the only proof of the "significance of the duration of our existence." Hence we must urgently desire that the awareness of this continuity should remain alive in our minds. Whether such continuity exists outside our historical consciousness, in a divine mind concerned with human history, we can neither tell nor imagine.

Thus continuity points out not merely the significance of formal duration but also the need of preservation. The value of continuity consists in the conscious continuation of history as a tradition, and the historical tradition has to be continued and preserved against a revolutionary will to permanent revisions. Burckhardt's basic experience was that, since the French Revolution, Europe had been living in the state of a rapidly disintegrating tradition; and the fear of a threatening break with all that is precious and costly in European tradition was the background of his understanding of his historical mission. The personal motive of his study of history and of his almost desperate clinging to continuity was a passionate reaction against the revolutionary trend of his age. He realized that the restoration from 1815 to 1848 was but an "interlude" in a yet unfinished "era of revolutions," which began with the French Revolution and which proceeds in our days to the Bolshevist, the Fascist, and the National Socialist revolutions. By defending the mission of the historical consciousness, he tried at least to retard the imminent dissolution; and he defended his historical creed against the

22

radical movement, in which some of his most intimate friends had taken an active part. He thought that a radically egalitarian democracy would not lead to individual liberty and responsibility but to a pretentious mediocrity and a new type of despotism. He feared that economic socialism would promote an over-developed state machine, which any bold demagogue might easily seize and exploit, combining social democracy with military dictatorship. This process seemed to him prefigured in the paradigmatic course of the French Revolution, for Napoleon's Caesarism was the logical consequence of the social revolution inaugurated by Rousseau and executed by the Jacobins. "The two claws of the pincers" between which so-called "culture" will then be caught are the emancipated working classes from below and the military hierarchy from above; for it is the emancipation of the modern masses from the ancient social hierarchy and religious authority which created on the Continent a nationalism and a corresponding militarism of a hitherto unknown thoroughness as the only remaining guaranty of social order.

Disgusted by contemporary history, Burckhardt escaped to Italy to write his *Cicerone* and to collect material for *The Age of Constantine,* which gave him a historical standard for an understanding and evaluation of contemporary events; for what happened in the third and fourth centuries, when the ancient world disintegrated, may occur once more: a radical change in the thoughts and hearts of men, from progressive optimism to ascetic pessimism. Feeling that minor amendments would not do when the whole social body is in anarchy, he resolved to retire into a sort of Stoic-Epicurean privacy. "Yes, I will escape them all: the radicals, the communists and industrialists, the sophisticated and presumptuous ... the philosophers and sophists, the state-fanatics and idealists.... You do not realize what tyranny will be imposed upon the spiritual life on the pretext that higher education be a secret ally of capital which has to be destroyed."[2] Thirty years after his first premonitions, Burckhardt became even more keen and specific in his prognostica-

tions. It is possible, he thought, that a few half-endurable decades may still be granted to us until Europe, after a series of
terrific wars and upheavals, will settle down into a kind of
imperium Romanum, centralized by a military-economic despotism to which liberal democrats and proletarians alike will
have to submit; "for this fine century [the twentieth] is de-
signed for anything rather than true democracy." The vulgarization and standardization of life seemed to him inevitable.
Instead of a liberal democracy, he foresaw the totalitarian state
governed by *terribles simplificateurs,* who will overrun old
Europe and rule with absolute brutality, scornful of law and
quite unconcerned with the people's freedom and sovereignty.
He writes in 1871 to a German friend:

> I have a premonition, which sounds like utter folly and yet which posi-
> tively will not leave me: the military state must become one great factory.
> Those hordes of men in the great industrial centers will not be left in-
> definitely to their greed and want. What must logically come is a fixed and
> supervised stint of misery, glorified by promotions and uniforms, daily
> begun and ended to the sound of drums.... Long voluntary subjection
> under individual *Führers* and usurpers is in prospect. People no longer
> believe in principles but will, periodically, probably believe in saviors....
> For this reason authority will again raise its head in the pleasant twentieth
> century, and a terrible head.[3]

But this new authority, by which nineteenth-century liberalism
will find an unexpected end, is no longer an authority of tradition but the result of a revolutionary reaction against nineteenth-
century makeshift provisions. Seen in this historical context,
Burckhardt's emphasis on continuity is certainly understand-
able and yet remains astounding because it is the only desid-
eratum (*Wünschbarkeit*) which he exempts from his devastat-
ing criticism of desiderata as standards of historical judgments.
Historical continuity and consciousness have an almost sacra-
mental character for him; they are his "last religion." Only in
regard to those events which have established a continuum of
Western tradition does Burckhardt retain an element of teleological, if not providential, interpretation.[4]

Our own historical continuity, he declares, was created primarily by the Hellenization of the East after Alexander, the political and cultural unification under Rome, and the preservation of the whole complex of ancient Western culture by the Christian church. Here we can discern a historical purpose on the grand scale which is, "to us at any rate," apparent, namely, the creation of a common world culture, which also made possible the spread of a world religion. Both were capable of being transmitted to the Teutonic barbarians of the *Völkerwanderung* as the future bond of a new Europe. He adds, however, that the Roman Empire was inaugurated by the most frightful methods and completed in rivers of blood. And the question as to whether the forces that succumbed were perhaps nobler and better cannot be silenced by reference to the fact that there is nothing more successful than success.

However creative great upheavals and destructions may turn out to be, evil remains evil, Burckhardt maintains, and we cannot fathom the economy of the world's history. If there is anything to be learned from the study of history, it is a sober insight into our real situation: struggle and suffering, short glories and long miseries, wars and intermittent periods of peace. All are equally significant, and none reveals an ultimate meaning in a final purpose. "Ripeness is all." The existence of the many is at all times and everywhere such that "it just compensates the trouble." The most grandiose decisions and efforts may result also in an ordinary destiny. The only sound conclusion to be drawn from this spectacle is not a consolation with a higher world plan but a more moderate "taxation" of our earthly existence. The historical greatness of a nation does not make up for the annihilation of one single individual, nor are nations as such entitled to permanent existence. The balance between fortune and misfortune in history is kept not by a providential design but by the frailty of gain as well as of loss, and we are at a loss when we try to assess the historical losses and gains.

At the beginning of his lecture on "Fortune and Misfortune in History" Burckhardt illustrates our average judgments as follows: It was fortunate that the Greeks conquered Persia; and Rome, Carthage; unfortunate that Athens was defeated by Sparta and that Caesar was murdered before he had had time to consolidate the Roman Empire. It was fortunate that Europe held Islam at bay, unfortunate that the German emperors were defeated in their struggle with the Papacy, and so on. But in the last analysis, Burckhardt says, all such judgments annul one another, and the nearer we come to the present, the more opinions diverge. If Burckhardt were alive today and were asked about his judgment of contemporary events, as a European he would probably say that the defeat of Nazi Germany was fortunate and desirable, the rise of Russia appalling and undesirable, though the first depends on the second. As a historian, however, he would refuse to predict whether the alliance and victory of the Allies is ultimately a "fortune" or a "misfortune" in this incalculable world-historical process.

It is obvious that, on the basis of such an outlook, neither a philosophy nor a theology of history can be constructed. The thin thread of mere continuity, without beginning, progress, and end, does not support such a system. And yet Burckhardt's is the soundest modern reflection on history. It is "modern," inasmuch as Burckhardt understands the classical as well as the Christian position, without committing himself to either of them. Over against the modern striving for social security, he praises the ancient greatness of passion and sacrifice for the sake of the city-state; over against the modern striving for a higher standard of living, he has a deep appreciation for the Christian conquest of all things earthly. At the same time he knows perfectly well that "the spirit of antiquity is not any longer our spirit" and that "from Christianity 1800 years are separating us." The Christian faith and hope in a moral purpose and meaning are toned down in Burckhardt's reflections to blind desiderata, "the deadly enemies of true historical insight." How different is this modern wisdom of Burckhardt's from all those philosophies of history—from Hegel to Augustine—which definitely knew, or professed to know, the *true* desirability of historical events and successions! They knew it, not as scientific historians, not even as philosophers, but as theologians who believed in history as a story of fulfilment.

BURCKHARDT'S VIEW OF CHRISTIANITY

At a time which appears to us as having still enjoyed stability, security, and freedom, Burckhardt considered himself already an uprooted refugee. "Set thy house in order," he warns a friend in the prosperous Germany of 1870; that "is the wisest thing to do for us in all of central Europe," for everything will radically change. Hence his deep understanding of that classical period of disintegration in which the followers of Christ opposed the pleasures and vices of a decaying society and conquered the souls of men. While the world and all worldly powers were corrupt, the Christian church spread charity, discipline, and asceticism, and even men and women of the Roman nobility gave away their possessions for the sake of the poor and resolved to live in the world without being of it. Others, still more radical, left the cities and went into the deserts or into monasteries. To Burckhardt these men were not unprofitable escapists but "heroes of the desert," who, after a tremendous struggle, had realized a profound need in an age of civilized barbarism. Without the extreme example of these early monks and hermits, the church would not have maintained its integrity and become the only spiritual institution which nursed and preserved all higher education. We, however, says Burckhardt, who take the pursuit of science and the freedom of intellectual work still for granted, like to forget how much we are indebted to the church of those "Dark" Ages for the cultivation of a knowledge which is not worldly and of practical purpose.

Likewise, Burckhardt's only hope for the future of Europe was in "ascetic men," i.e., in austere characters with the courage to abstain and to renounce, instead of getting along and ahead. In the face of Europe's progressive industrialization and vulgarization, it was Burckhardt's fundamental conviction that "the new, the great, and the liberating" can come forward only *in contrast* to power, wealth, and business. "It will need its martyrs. It must be a something which by its nature can keep its head above water in all catastrophes, political, economic, and otherwise. But what kind of something? There you overask me. It may be that we too shall not recognize it when it enters the world. In the meantime let us be assiduously listening and studying...,"[5] for in a very short time all intellectual interest may be in a dreadful dilemma, due to a general change in the way of life and the series of wars to come. And yet it was this very imminence of disaster which made Burckhardt hope that a fresh initiative of great minds might come to the scene in the twentieth century, "when times of pauperization and simplification" will make an end to material luxury and waste.[6] In the last analysis, Burckhardt thought that no liberal education will be able to save us from the great violation of the human soul which is now going on, but only religion, "for without a transcendent urge which outweighs all the clamor for power and money, nothing will be of any use."

To Burckhardt the model case for this prophetic vision was the rise of Christianity. In his view genuine Christianity is essentially "ascetic" because of being otherworldly, since its hope and expectation are in another world. With regard to the ways of this world, Christianity is a religion of suffering and renunciation. Through these modes of asceticism it achieved its spiritual freedom and conquest of life. Hence Burckhardt was not impressed by modern Christendom, which lives by compromise with the world, in order to remain acceptable. Though himself the son of a minister, he felt no vocation for this profession but quitted the study of theology. Some of his early letters to a theologian friend[7] explain the motives of his convictions, on which he stood firm through all his life. "How intensely religious," he once remarked, "were the ancient heretics as compared with modern Christians." In the religious restoration of the forties he saw an impotent reaction against "the gigantic course" and the inevitable consequences of the historicocritical treatment of the Bible. "Dogmatic theology is now in the highest degree disgusting," for "the whole range of possible theological standpoints has already been tried out.... If theology understood its own advantage it would rather be silent for the next thirty years." On the other hand, he held that a Christianity reduced to morality and deprived of its supernatural and doctrinal foundations is no longer a religion. Modern man cannot solve this perplexity by a sheer will to believe, for genuine faith is not only a commitment but also an overwhelming power which has to be experienced. Nor can he solve it by reducing the Christian ideal of the saint to that of a (Christian) gentleman.[8] He felt keenly that a Christianity which is watered down to a humanitarianism in which the priest is "first of all a *Gebildeter*," a man of the educated class, then a philosophizing theologian, and eventually a little bit of a timid man—that such a Christianity cannot appeal to the secular world as an inspiring religion. It is true, he says, the church still has a mission, but "that Christianity has outlived its great epochs is as evident to me as that two plus two make four." And he saw no prospects for a genuine revival because the modern spirit of unrestricted worldliness, of labor, business, and acquisitiveness, is unconcerned with personal salvation in a world to come and is decidedly hostile to any form of spiritual practice and pure contemplation. Morality is now emancipated from its religious foundation in a supernatural faith. "The modern mind aims at a solution of the supreme enigma of life independent of Christianity." A striking instance of this separation of secular morality from religion is modern philanthropy because it is motivated by optimistic and activistic premises. While Christianity taught unconditional charity by depriving one's self of one's possessions, modern philanthropy is far more "a concomitant of the money-making spirit," endeavoring to foster activity and to help man along to a better adjustment in his earthly career. Mundane life and its interests now outweigh all other considerations.

Primitive and genuine Christianity stands in complete contrast to the standards of the world. It is more extreme and exact-

ing than even "the strictest Christianity of our time" is ready
to admit. "The humble surrender of self and the parable of the
right and the left cheek are no longer popular." People want
to maintain their social sphere and respectability; they have to
work and to make money; hence they cannot but allow the
world to interfere in many ways with their traditional religion.
"In short, for all their religiosity, people are not disposed to
renounce the advantages and benefits of modern culture." Thus
the Calvinist countries produced the Anglo-American compromise between religious puritanism and ceaseless moneymaking,
while in the Lutheran countries the pastor has "the falsest position which has ever existed under the sun." Consequently, it
may be that modern Protestantism works unconsciously for the
benefit of the Roman Catholic church. These modern men,
believing, first of all, in the values of progressive civilization,
have great difficulty in believing or even in conceiving how
passionately distant peoples and ages have indeed had faith
in things invisible. Nowadays men do their duty far more
from a sense of honor and decency than from a religious motive.
To modern man Christianity is not a stumbling block and
foolishness but—if he is not hostile to it—a wholesome element
of secular civilization.

Modern Christendom wants to forget that Christianity has
always been at its best and most influential when it maintained
its divergence from worldly culture. In contrast to the polytheistic cults of classical paganism, the Christian religion was and is
not a cult consecrating a national culture but a transcendent
faith in a future redemption. It was hostile to the pagan gods
of nature and culture, as it must be hostile to the idols of modern
civilization. The moral strength of the early Christians consisted
not least in their unconcern with nature and culture; dominated
by an eschatological faith, the Christians of the apostolic age
could not have any real interest in them. "The end of the world
and eternity were at the door, and it was easy to turn away
from the world and its delights." But even the fact that Christianity soon entered the history of the world by adopting Greek

culture and Roman statecraft did not obliterate its original and permanent conflict with the *saeculum*. It would be undone if it were to forget that it is a faith in the glory of the Cross, a victorious religion of suffering, a faith for those who suffer. And in one way or another, Burckhardt was convinced, it will have to come back to its fundamental inspiration instead of accommodating itself to state, society, and civilization. "How, in the long run, the will to live and work in the world can be made compatible with that idea we cannot foresee"; and one may ask "whether the real test of the vitality of a religion does not, after all, lie in its venturing upon an association with culture."[9] Such association—no more and no less—was most splendidly achieved in the Middle Ages, when architecture, music, scholarship, art, and literature were indeed expressing Christian religion in the manifold forms of visible culture. This achievement of a Christian culture, however, was possible not because the church taught the world what the world knows already more clearly by itself, but because the church impressed on the world the otherworldly distinctness of a transcendent faith.

At a time when liberal optimistic Protestantism was in full sway on the Continent, Burckhardt called the nineteenth-century optimism "atrocious" and predicted its evaporation, while he insisted on the invincible strength of a genuine faith over against the principalities of the world. "In the twentieth century those amazing caricatures of so-called reformed pastors will no longer endure, for all this agitation will scatter like dust as soon as people fall into real distress." On the other hand, persecuting governments "might meet with a resistance of the strangest sort from Christian minorities who would not fear even martyrdom."

It is characteristic of Burckhardt's honesty that he did not offer any self-styled solution but only stated the problem. He was completely free of modern prejudice, in particular, of that of Hegel, who saw in history a cumulative process of progressive development, realizing more and more the idea of Christianity in the secular world of history. Instead of such progressive development, Burckhardt discerned in "modern" Christianity a contradiction in terms, because the evil genius of modern life, its *Erwerbssinn* and *Machtsinn,* the striving for power and gain, is downright opposed to voluntary suffering and self-surrender. This simple but basic insight of Burckhardt is the more remarkable because it is the insight of a secular historian of the nineteenth century and not of a neo-orthodox theologian of the twentieth.

II

MARX

WHILE Burckhardt, in his lecture course on history, was expressing the mature wisdom of an old European, Marx was preparing to publish *Capital*, in which all history is absorbed into an economic process moving toward a final world revolution and world renovation. Representing the revolutionary movement of the forties in its most radical form, Marx wanted not to retard but to hasten the disintegration of the bourgeois-capitalist society for the sake of a final consummation of the whole historical process. The fact that the author of *A Contribution to the Critique of Political Economy* and of *Capital* had "settled his accounts" with his "former philosophic conscience" and had definitely turned to the economic analysis of history as the "anatomy" of capitalistic society does not invalidate the thesis that Marx was, first of all, a philosopher with an immense historical sense. However, he is a philosopher of history far less in his historical studies (*The Class Struggles in France from 1848 to 1850, The French Civil War,* and *The Eighteenth Brumaire of Napoleon Bonaparte*) than in the *Communist Manifesto* and *Capital;* for the outstanding characteristic of the last two works is not the dogmatic emphasis on class struggle and on the relation between labor and capital but the absorption of all these categories into a comprehensive historical pattern. Like Hegel in philosophy, Darwin in biology, and Ferdinand Christian Baur in theology, Marx, too, resolved the problems of his special science into a historical problem.

The central significance of Marx's historical outlook appears first in his philosophical doctoral thesis of 1841 on the philosophy of nature of Epicurus and Democritus.[1] The leitmotiv in this brilliant analysis of classical materialism is the general question of the historical significance of epigonic philosophies. He compares the Epicurean, Stoic, and Skeptic schools, after Plato and Aristotle, with the modern schools of Feuerbach, Stirner, and B. Bauer, after Hegel, interpreting the historical significance of these subjective and moralizing sects as a necessary consequence of the preceding consummation of an objective philosophy of pure contemplation; for, if the abstract principle of a classical philosophy has been worked out to an all-embracing totality, as with Aristotle and Hegel, further progress in the traditional line is no longer possible. At such historical turning-points a new attempt has to be made by a definite break with the philosophical tradition. "This storm in which everything totters occurs with historical necessity at such a junction. Those who do not understand the necessity of a new beginning will have to resign or to copy [like the conservative pupils of Hegel] in cheap plaster what has been created in costly marble by the master." Only by accepting the necessity of a revolutionary change can one understand why a Zeno, an Epicurus, and the Skeptics could arise after Aristotle; why "bottomless poor attempts" of new philosophers could come into being after Hegel.

The half-hearted minds have in such critical times the opposite view of wholehearted generals: they believe that they might repair the damage by diminishing their forces ... by compromise and appeasement ... while Themistocles [i.e., Marx], when Athens [i.e., pure philosophy] was threatened by disaster, boldly advised the Athenians to give up their city completely and to found a new Athens [i.e., a new kind of philosophy] on the open sea, in another element [i.e., in the element of political-economic praxis].

The time which follows such catastrophes is an iron age, either marked by titanic struggles or merely imitating bygone epochs of historical greatness. This iron age is unhappy, for the old gods are dead and the new god is still invisible and ambiguous like the twilight, which may turn to utter darkness as well as to full day. The core of the unhappiness in such times of crisis is that the spirit of the age cannot sincerely accept any given reality, while its relative happiness consists in the subjective forms of

34

philosophical consciousness as represented by the private philosophies of late antiquity and late Christianity, respectively.
The "universal sun" has set, and what illuminates the darkness
is only the artificial light of "private lamps." But, since Marx
himself had already settled his accounts with the "German
ideology" of post-Hegelian philosophy, he felt confident in
anticipating the future philosophy which realizes the unity of
reason and reality, of essence and existence, as it was postulated
by Hegel. But, if reason becomes really realized in the whole
realm of material reality, philosophy as such is annihilated by
becoming a theory of practice. While with Hegel the world had
become philosophical, a realm of spirit, now, with Marx, philosophy has to become worldly, political economy—Marxism.

This "now" is the decisive "instant," to use a term of Kierkegaard, which divides all meaningful history, not into a pagan
B.C. and a Christian A.D., but, no less radically, into a "prehistory" and a future history which leads through the dictatorship of the proletariat from the realm of necessity to that of
freedom from all prehistoric antagonism; for the present capitalistic society is the "last" antagonistic form of the social process
of production, developing in its own womb the conditions for
the final solution of the antagonism between capital and labor,
between oppressors and oppressed. The bourgeois-capitalist society constitutes "the closing chapter of the pre-historic stage
of human society."[2]

In an early outline of the future society Marx describes this
earthly Kingdom of God thus: "In all history up to now it is
certainly an empirical fact that single individuals, with the
expansion of their activity to a world-historical scale, have become more and more enslaved to an alien power," i.e., to capital
or, more precisely, to the capitalist mode of production which
in the modern world represents the ancient fate. This fatal
power has become steadily more massive and apparently inescapable.

But it is just as empirically grounded that through the overthrow of the
existing social order, through the communist revolution, i.e., the abolish-

ment of private property, this power ... will be dissolved, and then the emancipation of every single individual will be achieved to the same extent that history transforms itself completely into world-history. ... That all-sided dependence ... of the world-historical coöperation of individuals (which characterizes the capitalist society) will be transformed by the communist revolution into a control and conscious domination of those powers that are born of the mutual reactions of men, and which have heretofore imposed upon them and ruled over them as powers completely alien.[3]

In a later essay of 1856 Marx describes more concretely this alienation of man from himself:

There is one great fact characterizing the nineteenth century which cannot be denied by any party: on the one side, industrial and scientific powers have developed which no former period of history could have fancied; on the other side, there are symptoms of disintegration surpassing even the well-known terrors of the late Roman Empire. In our time everything seems to be pregnant with its contrast. The machine is endowed with the marvelous power to shorten labor and to make it more profitable; and yet we see how it produces hunger and overwork. The newly emancipated powers of wealth become, through a strange play of destiny, sources of privation. ... Mankind becomes master of nature, but man the slave of man. ... The result of all our inventions and progress seems to be that material powers become invested with spiritual life, while human life deteriorates into a material force. This antagonism between modern industry and science, on the one side, modern misery and corruption, on the other side, this antagonism between the forces of production and the social conditions of our epoch, is a tangible, overwhelming and undeniable fact. Some parties may wish to get rid of the modern capacities in order to get rid also of the modern conflicts. Or they may fancy that such evident progress in the realm of production cannot be achieved but by a corresponding regress in the social political life. But we recognize in this antagonism the clever spirit [Hegel's "cunning of reason"] which keenly proceeds in working out all these contradictions. We know that the new form of social production, to achieve the good life, needs only [!] *new men*.[4]

One may wonder if Marx ever realized the human, moral, and religious implications of his postulate: to create a new world by creating new men, a new kind of man. It seems that he was completely blind to the prerequisite of a possible regeneration and was dogmatically satisfied with the abstract formula that the new man is the Communist, producing commonwealth, the *zoon politicon,* or "collective being," of the modern cosmopolis.

The matrix of this new man is, according to Marx, the most wretched creature in capitalist society, the proletarian who is alienated from himself to the extreme, by being forced to sell himself for wages to the capitalist owner of the means of production. Far from having an all-too-human compassion for the individual destiny of the proletarian, Marx sees in the proletariat the world-historical instrument for achieving the eschatological aim of all history by a world revolution. The proletariat is the chosen people of historical materialism for the very reason that it is excluded from the privileges of established society. Just as Sieyès, before the outbreak of the French Revolution, had postulated that the bourgeois was "nothing" and *therefore* entitled to become "everything," so Marx, fifty years after the victory of bourgeois society, postulated the universal mission of the proletariat which had developed from it. The proletariat has a total claim because it is totally alienated from human existence. Being an exception to existing society, by living at the fringe of it, it is the only class which has in itself the potentiality of becoming normative; for, though the disintegration of existing society is represented by bourgeoisie and proletariat alike, the latter alone has a universal mission and a redemptive significance because its uniqueness lies in a total privation of the privileges of the bourgeoisie. The proletariat is a class not within but outside existing society, and therefore it is the potentiality of an absolute, classless society. Concentrating and summing up the antagonisms of all social spheres in their human summit, the proletariat is the key to the problem of the entire human society; for it cannot emancipate itself from the bondage of capitalism without emancipating thereby the totality of society.

In *German Ideology,* Marx defines the universal significance of the proletariat thus: "Only the proletarians who are completely excluded from all spontaneous exercise of their human faculties are also capable of achieving a complete and not only partial emancipation by the appropriation of the totality of all means of production." Being completely alienated from himself by "the earthly question in actual size" (i.e., by the question of making "a living" by earning money), the wage laborer—this impersonal producer of commodities who is himself but a commodity for sale on the world market—is the only revolutionary force which can redeem society at large. The proletarian embodies modern economy as human fate in such a way that his particular interest cannot but coincide with the common interest over against the private interest of private property or capital. Only in this universal and eschatological perspective could and did Marx assert that the proletariat is "the heart" of future history, while Marx's philosophy is its "brain."

This philosophy of the proletariat as the chosen people is expounded in a document, the *Communist Manifesto,* which is scientifically relevant in its particular contents, eschatological in its framework, and prophetic in its attitude. It opens with the incisive sentence: "The history of all hitherto existing society is the history of class-struggles," i.e., of social antagonisms between freeman and slave, patrician and plebeian, lord and serf, guildmaster and journeyman, or, as Marx sums up, between "oppressors and oppressed."[5] This fight was carried on, now open, now hidden, in all recorded history; and it ended either in the revolutionary reconstitution of society at large or in the common ruin of the contending parties. The modern bourgeois society that has sprouted from the stump of feudal society has not done away with this class antagonism; it has only established new classes and thereby new conditions of exploitation and oppression; and yet, according to Marx, this epoch of bourgeois-capitalist society is not like others. It possesses a distinct feature: it has simplified the class antagonism by concentrating it into "two hostile camps," facing each other directly for a final showdown between bourgeoisie and proletariat.

This last and decisive epoch is characterized by the development of modern industry and of the industrial armies of the bourgeoisie, which during its rule of scarce one hundred years has created more colossal productive forces than have all preceding generations together:

Subjection of Nature's forces to man, machinery, application of chemistry to industry and agriculture, steam-navigation, railways, electric telegraphs, clearing of whole continents for cultivation ... whole populations conjured out of the ground—what earlier century had even a presentiment that such productive forces slumbered in the lap of social labor? ... It has accomplished wonders far surpassing Egyptian pyramids, Roman aqueducts and Gothic cathedrals; it has conducted expeditions that put in the shade all former Exoduses of nations and crusades.

The reverse of this stupendous advance of Western civilization is that it has put a definite end to all patriarchal and human relations:

Modern industry has converted the little workshop of the patriarchal master into the great factory of the industrial capitalist. Masses of laborers, crowded into factories, are organized like soldiers. As privates of the industrial army they are placed under the command of a perfect hierarchy of officers and sergeants. Not only are they the slaves of the bourgeois class and of the bourgeois state, they are daily and hourly enslaved by the machine, by the overseer, and, above all, by the individual bourgeois manufacturer himself. The more openly this despotism proclaims gain to be its end and aim, the more petty, the more hateful and the more embittering it is.

Modern industrial bourgeoisie has torn asunder the "natural" ties that bound man to his "natural superior." It has left no other nexus between man and man than naked self-interest, callous cash payment:

It has drowned the most heavenly ecstasies of religious fervor, of chivalrous enthusiasms, of Philistine sentimentalism, in the icy water of egotistical calculation. It has resolved personal worth into exchange value, and in place of the numberless indefeasible chartered freedoms, has set up that single, unconscionable freedom—Free Trade. In one word, for exploitation, veiled by religious and political illusions, it has substituted naked, shameless, direct, brutal exploitation. The bourgeoisie has stripped of its halo every occupation hitherto honored and looked up to with reverent awe. It has converted the physician, the lawyer, the priest, the poet, the man of science, into its paid wage laborers.

At this stage of its development modern society cannot exist without constantly revolutionizing the instruments and social relations of production:

Conservation of the old modes of production in unaltered form was, on the contrary, the first condition of existence for all earlier industrial classes. Constant revolutionizing of production, uninterrupted disturbance of all social conditions, everlasting uncertainty and agitation distinguish the bourgeois epoch from all earlier ones. All fixed, fast frozen relations, with their train of ancient and venerable prejudices and opinions, are swept away, all new formed ones become antiquated before they can ossify. All that is solid melts into the air, all that is holy is profaned, and man is at last compelled to face with sober senses, his real conditions of life, and his relations with his kind.

And, while the need of a constantly expanding world market for its products chases the bourgeoisie over the whole globe, drawing even the most distant and barbaric nations into its civilization, compelling them to adopt the capitalistic mode of production, this Western civilization conjured up such gigantic means of exchange and production as to become "like the sorcerer who is no longer able to control the powers of the nether world whom he has called up by his spells." The history of industry and commerce is becoming more and more a history of the revolt of modern productive forces against the social and economic conditions. It develops an "epidemic of over-production" because the conditions of bourgeois society are too narrow to contain and control the wealth created by them. The weapons with which the bourgeoisie has conquered the world are now turned against itself. Among these self-created deadly weapons which prepare the defeat of the bourgeoisie stands, first of all, the working class.

In proportion as the bourgeoisie, i.e., capital, is developed, in the same proportion is the proletariat, the modern working-class, developed, a class of laborers who live only so long as they find work, and who find work only so long as their labor increases capital. These laborers, who must sell themselves piecemeal, are a commodity, like every other article of commerce, and are constantly exposed to all the vicissitudes of competition, to all the fluctuations of the market.

If this class becomes class-conscious, organized, and politically directed, it will change the whole course of history "when the class struggle nears the decisive hour."

A first symptom of the imminence of this last judgment of history on the established society is that "a small section of the ruling class cuts itself adrift and joins [like Marx himself and many an intellectual today] the revolutionary class" as the only one that holds the future in its hands. "Just as, therefore, at an earlier period, a section of the nobility went over to the bourgeoisie, so now a portion of the bourgeoisie goes over to the proletariat, and in particular, a portion of the bourgeois ideologists, who have raised themselves to the level of comprehending theoretically the historical movements as a whole." They have understood that in the face of modern industry the other classes must decay, while the proletariat alone is a really progressive class with a universal mission, for

the proletarians cannot become masters of the productive forces of society, except by abolishing their own previous mode of appropriation, and thereby also every other previous mode of appropriation. They have nothing of their own to secure and to fortify; their mission is to destroy all previous securities for and insurances of individual property. All previous historical movements were movements of minorities, or in the interest of minorities. The proletarian movement is the self-conscious, independent movement of the immense majority. The proletariat, the lowest stratum of our present society, cannot stir, cannot raise itself up without the whole superincumbent strata of official society being sprung into the air.

The proletariat saves the whole of human society by bringing to the front the common interests of the entire proletariat, i.e., the communist character of the working classes in the different countries. At the end of this process the organized proletariat will not be a ruling class like the bourgeoisie but will have abolished its own supremacy as a class; and, in place of the old bourgeois society and its class antagonism, we shall have an "association" in which the free development of each is the condition for the free development of all. Eventually the whole realm of life's necessities will be replaced by a "realm of freedom" in a supreme community of communist character: a Kingdom of God, without God and on earth, which is the ultimate goal and ideal of Marx's historical messianism.

In the consciousness of Marx and Engels themselves the revolutionary discovery of the *Communist Manifesto* consisted, however, not so much in its historical pattern as outlined above. Rather, it consisted in the materialist thesis that in every historical epoch the prevailing mode of economic production and exchange and the social organization necessarily following from that mode form the *basis* upon which is built, and on which alone can be explained, the political and intellectual history of that epoch. This "basic" fact is expressed in the first sentence of the *Communist Manifesto,* which reduces all history to economic antagonisms. Whatever else appears in history is, consequently, to be understood as an ideological "superstructure," for it is always the mode of material production that determines the general character of the social and political, legal and spiritual, processes of life.[6] This materialistic interpretation is summed up in the well-known proposition that it is not the "consciousness" of men which determines their "being," but, on the contrary, their social-economic existence which determines their consciousness—a proposition which seemed to Engels so simple that it must be "self-evident to anyone who is not bemused by idealist delusions." And when in times of revolution the economic foundation undergoes a radical change, then the entire superstructure of legal and political, religious and philosophical, forms of consciousness is also more or less rapidly transformed. To judge, says Marx, such transformation by its own consciousness would be as superficial as to judge an individual merely by the opinion which he has of himself.[7]

If we apply this distinction between conscious thought and real driving force to the *Communist Manifesto* as it was understood by Marx himself, the result is rather curious; for, granted that legal, political, and spiritual history has, in its economic conditions, its "secret history" which does not coincide with its ideological reflections, the same can be said in the reverse with regard to Marx's materialism. For the secret history of the *Communist Manifesto* is not its conscious materialism and Marx's own opinion of it, but the religious spirit of prophetism. The *Communist Manifesto* is, first of all, a prophetic document, a judgment, and a call to action and not at all a purely scientific statement based on the empirical evidence of tangible facts.[8] The fact that "the history of all hitherto existing society" shows various forms of antagonisms between a dominant minority and a dominated majority does not warrant the interpretation and evaluation of this fact as an "exploitation" and even less the expectation that what has been hitherto a universal fact will necessarily in the future cease to be what it was. Marx may explain the fact of exploitation "scientifically" by his theory of surplus-value; exploitation, nevertheless, remains an ethical judgment, something which is what it is by being unjust. In Marx's outline of universal history it is no less than the radical evil of "prehistory" or, in biblical terms, original sin. And, like original sin, exploitation, too, affects not only the moral but also the intellectual faculty of man. The exploiting class cannot comprehend its own system of living except through a deceptive consciousness, while the proletariat, free from the sin of exploitation, understands the capitalistic illusion together with its own truth. As a supreme and all-pervading evil, exploitation is far more than an economic fact.

Even if we assume that all history is a history of class struggles, no scientific analysis could ever infer from this that class struggle is *the* essential factor that "determines" all the rest. To Aristotle as well as to Augustine the institution of slavery was one fact among many others. To the first it was a most natural fact, far from being repulsive; to the second a social fact, which should be alleviated by charity but which was not at all decisive for eternal salvation or condemnation. Only with the rise of an emancipated bourgeois society did the relation between rulers and ruled become felt and identified as exploitation, out of the desire for emancipation. It is a strange misinterpretation of Marx by himself when he insists on his being unprejudiced by moral judgments and evaluations and yet sums up his enumeration of various forms of social antagonisms in the challenging words: "oppressors and oppressed." The fundamental premise of the *Communist Manifesto* is not the antagonism between bourgeoisie and proletariat as two opposite facts; for what makes them antagonistic is that the one class is the children of darkness and the other the children of light. Likewise, the final crisis of the bourgeois capitalist world which Marx prophesies in terms of a scientific prediction is a last judgment, though pronounced by the inexorable law of the historical process. Neither the concepts of bourgeoisie and proletariat, nor the general view of history as an ever intensified struggle between two hostile camps, nor, least of all, the anticipation of its dramatic climax, can be verified "in a purely empirical way." It is only in Marx's "ideological" consciousness that all history is a history of class struggles, while the real driving force behind this conception is a transparent messianism which has its unconscious root in Marx's own being, even in his race. He was a Jew of Old Testament stature, though an emancipated Jew of the nineteenth century who felt strongly antireligious and even anti-Semitic. It is the old Jewish messianism and prophetism—unaltered by two thousand years of economic history from handicraft to large-scale industry—and Jewish insistence on absolute righteousness which explain the idealistic basis of Marx's materialism. Though perverted into secular prognostication, the *Communist Manifesto* still retains the basic features of a messianic faith: "the assurance of things to be hoped for."

It is therefore not by chance that the "last" antagonism between the two hostile camps of bourgeoisie and proletariat corresponds to the Jewish-Christian belief in a final fight between Christ and Antichrist in the last epoch of history, that the task of the proletariat corresponds to the world-historical mission of the chosen people, that the redemptive and universal function of the most degraded class is conceived on the religious pattern of Cross and Resurrection, that the ultimate transformation of the realm of necessity into a realm of freedom corresponds to the transformation of the *civitas Terrena* into a *civitas Dei,* and that the whole process of history as outlined in the *Communist Manifesto* corresponds to the general scheme of the Jewish-Christian interpretation of history as a providential advance toward a final goal which is meaningful. Historical materialism is essentially, though secretly, a history of fulfilment and salvation in terms of social economy. What seems to be a scientific discovery from which one might deduce, after the fashion of Marxist "revisionists," the philosophical garb and the relic of a religious attitude is, on the contrary, from the first to the last sentence inspired by an eschatological faith, which, in its turn, "determines" the whole sweep and range of all particular statements. It would have been quite impossible to elaborate the vision of the proletariat's messianic vocation on a purely scientific basis and to inspire millions of followers by a bare statement of facts.

The possibility of tracing back the inspiration of the *Communist Manifesto* to Jewish messianism and prophetism reminds one of a fundamental difficulty of the materialistic interpretation as such, a difficulty which Marx has recognized without solving it. Discussing it in regard to Greek art and religion, he asks: "Where does Vulcan come in as against Roberts & Co.; Jupiter, as against the lightning rod; and Hermes, as against the Credit Mobilier? ... Is Achilles possible side by side with powder and lead? Or is the *Iliad* at all compatible with the printing press and steam press? Do not singing and reciting and the muses necessarily go out of existence with the appearance of the printer's bar, and do not, therefore, the prerequisites of epic poetry disappear?"[9] But, he goes on to say, "the real difficulty is not in grasping the idea that Greek art and epos are bound up with certain forms of social development. It rather lies in understanding why they still constitute a source of enjoyment with us, and in certain respects prevail as a standard and model beyond attainment." Applied to our own attempt at illuminating the *Communist Manifesto* by its religious background, the corresponding question would be: How can ancient messianism still appeal and prevail as the spiritual pattern of historical materialism if the modes of material production—which since Isaiah have fundamentally changed—are the determining factor of all forms of consciousness? Marx's solution of this difficulty is by no means convincing. He simply states that Greek culture, in spite of the primitive character of its material conditions, exerts an "eternal charm" because we like to return in imagination to the beauty of "childhood." One may wonder if Greek tragedy and Jewish prophetism owe their abiding charm to their childishness. The right answer to Marx's wrong question might rather be that a single factor like the economic conditions can never "determine" history as a whole and that an interpretation of the whole historical process requires a frame of reference which cannot be found in neutral facts.

MARX'S CRITICISM OF RELIGION

The Communist creed, though a pseudo-morphosis of Jewish-Christian messianism, lacks the fundamentals of it: the free acceptance of humiliation and of redemptive suffering as the condition of triumph. The proletarian Communist wants the crown without the cross; he wants to triumph by earthly happiness. In contrast to the religious character of Russian nihilism and socialism of the nineteenth century, Marx was completely devoid of any genuine interest in and understanding of the problems of a religious consciousness. He did not even revolt against God to achieve his kingdom on earth by dictatorship. He was a scientific atheist, for whom the criticism of religion was an accomplished fact like the historical end of Christianity itself. In full agreement with Feuerbach, but also with Kierkegaard,[10] Marx points out the complete inconsistency of all the standards of worldly practice with all the fundamental teachings of the gospel and of the Church Fathers.

Does not every moment of your practical life give the lie to your religious theory? Do you think it is unjust to appeal to the courts if somebody cheats you? But the apostle says it is wrong. Do you offer your right cheek if somebody slaps your left cheek, or would you rather start a lawsuit? But the

46

gospels forbid it. Do you not ask for a rational law in this world, grumble about the slightest increase of taxes and become excited at the smallest violation of personal liberty? But it is said unto you that the sufferings of this *saeculum* do not matter in comparison with the future glory and that long-suffering and hopeful expectation are cardinal virtues. Does the greatest part of your lawsuits and civil laws not deal with property? But it is said unto you that your treasures are not of this world.[11]

Established Christendom is to Marx "the religion peculiar to capitalism," an ideological superstructure the very existence of which only indicates that the real problems of life have not yet been solved on earth by a change of the economic conditions.

The atheistic motivation of Marx's materialism appears most clearly in his doctoral thesis. There he considers Epicurus as the greatest ancient *Aufklärer* because he followed Prometheus, "the most noble of all martyrs in the annals of philosophy," by challenging as a mortal man the gods of heaven and earth. This challenge is now to be resumed in the face of the Christian myth and the idols of the modern world market, for the final liquidation of the religious consciousness is the prerequisite of man's mastery and control over his world. On the basis of this inherent atheism of earthly self-reliance, Marx undertook his radical criticism of the existing order with the purpose of changing it. His whole enterprise of changing the world by a world revolution has as its negative presupposition the denial of man's dependence on an existing order of creation.

The preparatory work in behalf of the destruction of the religious consciousness had already been done by the left-wing Hegelians—by men like D. F. Strauss, L. Feuerbach, B. Bauer, and M. Stirner. Marx's criticism of Hegel's *Philosophy of Right*[12] begins with the statement: "As to Germany, the criticism of religion is essentially brought to an end, and the criticism of religion is a prerequisite of all further criticism," to wit, of the nonreligious, real world which is but indirectly reflected in the illusions of supernatural and otherworldly religions. After Feuerbach's "discovery" that God is only an infinite projection of finite man and that the essence of theology is anthropology, the task now is to establish "the truth of *this* world." Referring to the Christian idea of the Kingdom of God and its relation to history, Marx says that he, too, believes in revelation through history and that in his judgment history is indeed "one and all" and of greater significance than even with Hegel. He rejects, however, the idea of a peculiar history of the Kingdom of God because it invalidates all real historical revelation. If there is a Kingdom of God, the eighteen centuries after Christ would be an absurd extension. "We reclaim the whole content of history, but we do not see in it a revelation of God but only of man."[13] When "the religious halo of man's self-alienation" has disappeared, one has to unmask its profane form, i.e., man's self-alienation not by spiritual sin but by material exploitation. Thus the former "criticism of heaven" changes into a "criticism of earth" and the criticism of theology into that of economics and political science.

Nevertheless, by advancing toward the criticism of man's material conditions, Marx does not simply leave behind the criticism of religion but rather resumes it on a new level; for though, on the basis of the social-political world, religion is but a false consciousness, the question has still to be answered: Why did this real world at all develop an inadequate consciousness? If we assume with Feuerbach that the religious world is only a self-projection of the human world, one has to ask: Why does the latter project the first and create a religious superstructure? Asking this, Marx is indeed more critical than Feuerbach, whose humanism was still a pious atheism. "It is," says Marx, "indeed much easier to discover by analysis the earthly kernel of religious fogs than to develop, the other way round, out of the real conditions of life its heavenly transformations." The latter method is, however, the only scientific, materialistic, and critical one. The task of historical materialism is therefore to analyze the particular contradictions and needs within the real world which make religion possible. Hence the following criticism of Feuerbach:

Feuerbach starts out from the fact of religious self-alienation, the duplication of the world into a religious, imaginary world and a real one. His work consists in the dissolution of the religious world into its secular basis. He overlooks the fact that after completing this work, the chief thing still remains to be done. For the fact that the secular foundation lifts itself above itself and establishes itself in the clouds as an independent realm is only to be explained by the self-cleavage and self-contradictoriness of this secular basis. The latter must itself, therefore, first be understood in its contradiction and then, by the removal of the contradiction, revolutionized in practice. Thus, for instance, once the earthly family is discovered to be the secret of the holy family, the former must then itself be theoretically criticized and radically changed in practice.[14]

It is not enough to state with Feuerbach that religion is a creation of man, this statement has to be qualified by the further insight that religion is the consciousness of *that* man who has not yet returned from his self-alienation and found himself at home in his worldly conditions. Religion is, in short, a "perverted *world*," and this perversion must necessarily last as long as the essence of man has not yet found an adequate existence in the Communist order and freedom—but no longer. Religion is the "illusory sun turning around man as long as he does not yet turn around himself." The annihilation of the "illusory bliss" of religion through materialistic criticism is only the negative side of the positive claim to "earthly happiness." Marx is sure that the final withering-away of religion will be caused by this will to earthly happiness, the secular form of the quest for salvation. A strictly materialistic criticism of religion consists neither in pure and simple rejection (Bauer) nor in mere humanization (Feuerbach) but in the positive postulate to create conditions which deprive religion of all its source and motivation. The practical criticism of the existing society can alone supersede religious criticism.

In consequence of this transformation of the traditional criticism of religion into a strictly materialistic one, atheism, too, changes its meaning. To Marx it is no longer a theological problem, i.e., a fight against heathen and Christian *gods,* but a fight against earthly *idols.* The outstanding idol of capitalist society is, however, the "fetish-character" of our commodities, brought

about by the perversion of useful means of production to objecti-
fied things, of concrete use-values to abstract exchange-values.
By this perversion, man the producer of goods becomes a product of his own productions. "As in religion man is dominated by
the creation of his own mind, so in capitalistic production by the
creation of his own hands." The commodity-form of all our
products is the new idol which has to be criticized and changed.
Furthermore, the modern world is only seemingly entirely
worldly. By its own inventions it has once more become superstitious. "Hitherto one believed that the creation of the Christian
myth under the Roman Empire was only possible because the
printing press was not yet invented. But it is just the opposite:
the daily press and the telegraph, which spreads the inventions
of the press in a few seconds over the whole globe, fabricate more
myths in a single day than could be produced formerly in a century."[15] Hence it is not sufficient to reduce, with Feuerbach,
theology and religion to the so-called "essence of man," but one
has to watch the rise of new idols and superstitions and make
them impossible by an ever renewed criticism of the real, i.e.,
historicomaterial, conditions.

Marx and Engels believed that they could fulfil the philosophy
of Hegel by revolutionizing the material conditions of social
life. Paradoxical as this may seem, it is not utterly nonsensical,
for the materialistic philosophy as intended by Marx himself is,
in principle, not only a negation but also the material "realization" of Hegel's idealism. The abstract principle of Marx is still
what it was with Hegel: the unity of reason (*Vernunft*) and
reality (*Wirklichkeit*), of general essence and individual existence. In a perfect communist commonwealth each individual
has realized his human essence as a common sociopolitical existence. In consequence of the acceptance of this principle, Marx
could say that Hegel was to blame not for having asserted the
reality of reason but for having neglected its worldly realization.
Instead of criticizing theoretically and changing practically the
whole established reality for the sake of reason, Hegel accepts
religious and political history as reasonable in itself. From the

critical and revolutionary standpoint of Marx, such acceptance is "crassest materialism"—and Marxism purist idealism![16]

In the same way the Marxist agrees and disagrees with Hegel's philosophy of history, which was the direct prerequisite of the new materialistic mode of thinking. "Abstract and idealist though it was in form, yet the development of his thought always proceeded in line with the development of world history ... the real [historical] content entered everywhere into the philosophy.... In his phenomenology, aesthetics, history of philosophy, this magnificent conception of history penetrates, and everywhere this material is treated historically, in a definite, even if abstractly distorted interconnection with history."[17] Here again, as in Marx's criticism of Hegel's *Phenomenology* and *Philosophy of Right,* the difference between the materialistic and idealistic positions is not a difference in principle but one of application. The historical source of Hegel's "idealism," however, is the Christian tradition. Like all German idealism, Hegel's philosophy of Spirit rests on Christian supernaturalism. It is the faith in Christ as the Lord and Logos of history which he translated into a metaphysical Spirit unfolding itself in the process of history. Since Hegel, however, identifies the history of the world with that of the Spirit, his understanding of history retains much less of its religious derivation than does Marx's materialistic atheism. The latter, in spite of its emphasis on material conditions, maintains the original tension of a transcendent faith over against the existing world, while Hegel, to whom faith was only a mode of *Vernunft* or *Vernehmen,* had, at a critical turning-point in his intellectual history, decided to reconcile himself to the world as it is: existing, real, and reasonable.[18] Compared with Marx, the greater realist is Hegel.

III

HEGEL

IN HIS Introduction to the *Lectures on the Philosophy of History* (1830) Hegel describes world history as it appears at a first glance:

> ... we see a vast picture of changes and transactions; of ... manifold forms of peoples, states, individuals, in unresting succession. ... On every hand aims are adopted and pursued. ... In all these occurrences and changes we behold human action and suffering predominant; everywhere something akin to ourselves, and therefore everywhere something that excites our interest for or against. ... Sometimes we see the more comprehensive mass of some general interest advancing with comparative slowness, and subsequently sacrificed to an infinite complication of trifling circumstances, and so dissipated into atoms. Then, again, with a vast expenditure of power a trivial result is produced; while from what appears unimportant a tremendous issue proceeds ... and when one combination vanishes another immediately appears in its place. The general thought—the category which first presents itself in this restless mutation of individuals and peoples existing for a time and then vanishing—is that of change at large. The sight of the ruins of some ancient sovereignty directly leads us to contemplate this thought of change in its negative aspect. ... But the next consideration which allies itself with that of change, is that change, while it imports dissolution, involves at the same time the rise of a new life, that while death is the issue of life, life is also the issue of death.[1]

The most effective springs of historical action and suffering seem to be human interests, passions, and the satisfaction of selfish desires, disregarding law, justice, and morality:

> When we look at this display of passions, and the consequences of their violence; the Unreason which is associated not only with them, but even (rather we might say especially) with good designs and righteous aims; when we see the evil, the vice, the ruin that has befallen the most flourishing kingdoms which the mind of man ever created; we can scarce avoid being filled with sorrow at this universal taint of corruption; and, since this decay

is not the work of mere Nature, but of the Human Will, a . . . revolt of the Good Spirit . . . may well be the result of our reflections. Without rhetorical exaggeration, a simply truthful combination of the miseries that have overwhelmed the noblest of nations and polities, and the finest exemplars of private virtue, forms a picture of most fearful aspect, and excites emotions of the profoundest and most hopeless sadness, counterbalanced by no consolatory result. We endure in beholding it a mental torture, allowing no defence or escape but the consideration that what has happened could not be otherwise; that it is a fatality which no intervention could alter. . . . But even regarding History as the slaughter-bench at which the happiness of peoples, the wisdom of States, and the virtue of individuals have been victimised—the question necessarily arises: to what final aim these enormous sacrifices have been offered?[2]

We all know this "panorama of sin and suffering" which history unfolds. It is the same that Burckhardt has in mind and that Goethe describes. History, Goethe says, is "the most absurd of all things," a "web of nonsense for the higher thinker."[3] "What one can observe on the whole," he writes in a letter to Schiller (March 9, 1802), with reference to Napoleon, "is a tremendous view of streams and rivers which, with natural necessity, rush together from many heights and valleys; at last they cause the overflowing of a great river and an inundation in which both perish, those who foresaw it and those who had no inkling of it. In this tremendous empirical process you see nothing but nature and nothing of that which we philosophers would so much like to call freedom." We encounter the same vision again in Thomas Hardy's great drama of the Napoleonic wars, commented upon by the choruses of the years, of the pities, of sinister and ironic spirits, and of rumor. The angels are only recording what happens. What Burckhardt, Goethe, and Hardy thus describe, is it not history as it is? And why not stop here, instead of asking Hegel's question: To what final purpose are these enormous sacrifices offered time and again? Hegel says that this question arises "necessarily" in our thinking. The implication is, however, that it arises in our occidental thinking, which is not satisfied with the pagan acceptance of fate.

After describing history as permanent change, wherein death

is the issue of life and life the issue of death, Hegel goes on to say that this is an "oriental" conception, representing the life of nature which, like the mythical phoenix, eternally prepares its own funeral pyre and is consumed upon it, rising from its ashes in a new life. This image, he says, is not occidental. To us history is a history of the Spirit; and, though it is also self-consuming, it does not merely return to the same form but comes forth "exalted, glorified," with each successive phase becoming, in turn, a material on which the spiritual history of man proceeds to a new level of fulfilment. Thus the conception of mere change gives place to one of spiritual perfection, though involved with the conditions of nature.

This occidental conception of history, implying an irreversible direction toward a future goal, is not merely occidental. It is essentially a Hebrew and Christian assumption that history is directed toward an ultimate purpose and governed by the providence of a supreme insight and will—in Hegel's terms, by spirit or reason as "the absolutely powerful essence." Hegel says that the only thought which philosophy brings to the contemplation of history is "the simple concept of reason" as the "sovereign of the world"; and this statement (which was so irritating to Burckhardt) is indeed simple if, as in Hegel, the historical process is understood on the pattern of the realization of the Kingdom of God, and philosophy as the intellectual worship of a philosophical God.[4]

Having discussed the defects in the classic concept of reason, Hegel deals with the Christian idea of providence. To him providence is a truth that consorts with his own proposition that reason governs the world. The common belief in providence, however, has the philosophical weakness that it is at once too indefinite and too narrow to be capable of application to the entire course of human history. The plan of providence is supposed to be concealed from our understanding. Only in isolated cases, in particular circumstances, is this plan supposed to be manifest— for example, when help has unexpectedly come to an individual in great perplexity. But in the history of the world the individuals are peoples and states, and therefore we cannot be satisfied with such a "peddler's view of providence."

The concept of providence has to be brought to bear upon the details of the great historical processes. "The ultimate design of the world must be perceived." And, if theology fails to explain these processes, then philosophy has to vindicate the Christian religion by demonstrating God's execution of his purpose in history.

Our intellectual striving aims at realizing the conviction that what was intended by eternal wisdom is actually accomplished in the domain of existent, active Spirit, as well as in that of mere Nature. Our mode of treating the subject is, in this aspect, a theodicy, a justification of the ways of God . . . so that the ill that is found in the world may be comprehended, and the thinking Spirit reconciled with the fact of the existence of evil. Indeed, nowhere is such a harmonising view more pressingly demanded than in Universal History.[5]

To harmonize the view of history, as it appears at a first glance, with the ultimate design of the world or the ways of God, Hegel introduces the idea of the "cunning of reason"[6] which works in and behind the passions of men as their agents. It is not by chance but of the very essence of history that the ultimate outcome of great historical actions is always something which was not intended by men. Caesar and Napoleon did not and could not know what they were doing when they consolidated their own positions. They fulfilled unknowingly a general purpose in the history of the Occident. The apparent freedom of their actions is the ambiguous freedom of passions pursuing, with an animal faith, a particular purpose, but in such a way that the pursuit of their individual interests is prompted and driven by an anonymous impulse, necessitating their will and decisions. The universal purpose and the particular intention meet in this dialectic of passionate action; for that which world-historical individuals are unconsciously driving at is not what they are consciously planning but what they *must* will, out of an urge which seems to be blind and yet has a wider perspective than personal interests. Hence such men achieve, with an instinctive comprehension, that which is intended with them. They act historically by being acted upon by the power and cunning of reason, which is to Hegel a rational expression for divine providence: thus the motives, passions, and interests in history are indeed what they appeared to be at first glance, namely, the human stuff of it, but within the framework of a transcending purpose, promoting an end which was no part of conscious intentions.

Peoples, like individuals, do not know what they are really driving at; they are tools in the hands of God, in obeying, as well as in resisting his will and his purpose. Thus the final results of historical actions are always both more and less than what has been intended by the agents; the ultimate design surpasses and even perverts the planning of man.[7] And now, after these preliminary statements, Hegel casts a second glance at the world, which, since it is now perceived with "the eyes of reason," presents, in turn, a reasonable aspect. This meaningful aspect, reduced to its bare bones, is somewhat as follows. The world's history began in the East and ends in the West. It started with the great oriental empires of China, India, and Persia. With the decisive victory of Greece over Persia, meaningful history shifted to the Mediterranean world, and it ends with the Germanic-Christian empires in the West. Europe is "plainly" the goal of history. In this East-West movement the spirit has been educated to the reality and consciousness of freedom, that is, of coming home after its intrinsic alienation from itself. In the Orient, only one—the ruler—was free in the sense of unlimited caprice; in Greece and Rome some were free—the free citizens as compared with their slaves; the Germanic world has realized, under the influence of Christianity, that man as such is free. The Orientals were the childhood of the world, the Greeks and Romans its youth and manhood, the Christian peoples are its maturity.

The inner limitation of the classical world was that the ancients were still dependent on external fate, which, through such means as oracles and divinations, shaped their supreme decisions. Christianity, however, liberated man from all foreign authority by establishing real selfhood in relation to the absolute. "With the setting in of the Christian principle, the earth is circumnavigated and, as it were, round for the Europeans." With Christ the time is fulfilled, and the historical world becomes, in principle, perfect, for only the Christian God is truly spirit and at the same time man. This principle constitutes the axis on which turns the history of the world. All history moves up to this point, and then on from this point.

In other words, the history of the world is to Hegel a history B.C. and A.D. not incidentally or conventionally but essentially. Only on this presupposition of the Christian religion as the absolute truth could Hegel construct universal history systematically, from China up to the French Revolution. He is the last philosopher of history because he is the last philosopher whose immense historical sense was still restrained and disciplined by the Christian tradition. In our modern universal histories and historical maps, the Christian time-reckoning has become an empty frame of reference, accepted conventionally like other means of measurement and applied to a material multitude of cultures and religions that has no center of meaning from which these cultures and religions could be organized, as they were from Augustine to Hegel.

What distinguishes Hegel from Augustine in principle is that Hegel interprets the Christian religion in terms of speculative reason, and providence as "cunning reason." "The process displayed in history," he says, "is only the manifestation of religion as human reason, the production of the religious principle under the form of secular freedom." He concludes the chapter on the rise of Christianity with the words: "The discord between the inner life of the heart and the actual world is removed. All the sacrifices that have ever and anon been laid on the altar of the earth are justified for the sake of this ultimate purpose." As the realization of the spirit of Christianity, the history of the world is the true theodicy, the justification of God in history.

With this secularization of the Christian faith, or, as Hegel would say, with this realization of the Spirit, Hegel believed himself loyal to the genius of Christianity by realizing the Kingdom of God on earth. And, since he transposed the Christian expectation of a final consummation into the historical process as such, he saw the world's history as consummating itself. "The history of the world is the world's court of justice" (*Die Weltgeschichte ist das Weltgericht*) is a sentence which is as religious in its original motivation, where it means that the world's history is proceeding toward its judgment at the end of all history, as it is irreligious in its secular application, where it means that the judgment is contained in the historical process as such.

Hegel himself did not feel the profound ambiguity in his great attempt to translate theology into philosophy and to realize the Kingdom of God in terms of the world's real history. He felt no difficulty in identifying the "idea of freedom," the realization of which is the ultimate meaning of history, with the "will of God"; for, as a "priest of the Absolute," "damned by God to be a philosopher," he knew this will and the plan of history. He did not know it as a prophet predicting future catastrophe but as a prophet in reverse, surveying and justifying the ways of the Spirit by its successive successes.

It would be easy to point out, a hundred years after Hegel, the limitations of his historical vision and the oddity of some of its applications—for example, to the Prussian monarchy and to liberal Protestantism.[8] His world was still the Christian Occident, old Europe. America and Russia, to whom he dedicated only a few pages, though pages of remarkable foresight, were only on the periphery of his interest.[9] Furthermore, he did not foresee the effects of the technical sciences on the unity of the historical world, united now by all means of rapid communication and yet much less universal in spirit than during the Roman Empire or the Middle Ages.

More decisive than the material limitations of Hegel's vision is the inherent weakness of his principle that the Christian religion is realized by reason in the history of the secular world— as if the Christian faith could ever be "realized" at all and yet remain a faith in things unseen! Far more true and more Christian is Burckhardt's view of the relation between Christianity and secular culture. Fifteen hundred years of Western thought were required before Hegel could venture to translate the eyes of faith into the eyes of reason and the theology of history as established by Augustine into a philosophy of history which is neither sacred nor profane. It is a curious mixture of both, degrading sacred history to the level of secular history and exalting the latter to the level of the first—Christianity in terms of a self-sufficient Logos absorbing the will of God into the spirit of the world and the spirits of the nations, the *Weltgeist* and the *Volksgeister.*

IV

PROGRESS versus PROVIDENCE

HEGEL'S formula of the production of the religious principle "under the form of human reason and secular freedom" is not peculiar to him. It is the common principle of all philosophies of history of the Enlightenment. What distinguishes Hegel from his predecessors and from his radical successors is that he restrained the optimistic view of the Enlightenment by reinterpreting once more the theological tradition according to which the time is already fulfilled. The use which he made of the rational principle of progress is not revolutionary but conservative. For him, progress is directed toward a final elaboration and consummation of the established principle of the whole course of history. To the typical rationalists of the seventeenth and eighteenth centuries, progress is an indefinite advance toward more and more reasonableness, more and more freedom, more and more happiness, because the time is not yet fulfilled.

J. B. Bury, in his study of *The Idea of Progress,* has shown how this idea emerged in the seventeenth century and developed into a common opinion. The belief in an immanent and indefinite progress replaces more and more the belief in God's transcendent providence. "It was not till men felt independent of providence that they could organize a theory of progress,"[1] and vice versa: as long as the doctrine of providence was undisputed, a doctrine of progress could not arise. Eventually, however, the very doctrine of progress had to assume the function of providence, that is, to foresee and to provide for the future.[2]

The assertion of progress, in particular of intellectual progress, arose at first in the famous *querelle des anciens et des modernes,* which was passionately discussed for more than a century by men like Fontenelle, Swift, and Lessing. The dis-

60

tinction between "moderns" and "ancients" apparently ignores the question of whether the moderns have progressed beyond Christianity also. A careful reading of these all-but-harmless discussions shows, however, that their crucial problem was the basic antagonism between antiquity and Christianity, between reason and revelation. And with the full development of the modern idea of progress into a sort of religion, the assertion of the superiority of the moderns was openly applied to Christianity. Modernity became distinguished from classical antiquity as well as from Christianity. With Condorcet, Comte, and Proudhon, the question of whether the moderns have advanced beyond antiquity is no longer serious; the problem is now how to replace and supersede the central doctrines and the social system of the ancient Christians. At the same time, they realized, though only dimly, that the progress of the modern revolutionary age is not simply a consequence of its new knowledge in natural science and history but that it is still conditioned by that advance which Christianity has achieved over classical paganism. Hence the ambiguous structure of their leading idea of progress, which is as Christian by derivation as it is anti-Christian by implication and which is definitely foreign to the thought of the ancients. While the starting-point of the modern religions of progress is an eschatological anticipation of a future salvation and consequently a vision of the present state of mankind as one of depravity, no similar hope and despair can be found in any classical writer describing Athens' or Rome's decay. The eschatological interpretation of secular history in terms of judgment and salvation never entered the minds of ancient historians. It is the remote and yet intense result of Christian hope and Jewish expectation.

1. PROUDHON

Proudhon had the keenest insight into the anti-Christian implications of the modern religion of progress.[3] He is the theologian of progress and, as such, the most radical critic of providence; for he understood that the recognition of and submission to either pagan fate or Christian providence is incompatible in principle with the faith in progress, which is essentially revolutionary and worldly. Christianity, "the great revolt against pagan fate," replaced impersonal fate by personal providence; the task of the modern revolution, according to Proudhon, is the *défatalisation* of the latter by taking into the hands of man and of human justice the direction of all human affairs. Man has to replace God, and the belief in human progress has to supplant the faith in providence.

At first, however, it seems impossible to reduce the working of God to the labor of man; for all traditional understanding of history depends on the distinction between the will of God and the will of man, between hidden designs and visible agencies, between prompting necessity and personal freedom of choice.[4] In the theology of history the hidden designs which work themselves out with providential necessity in the decisions and passions of man were referred to God; in Kant's philosophy of history, to a hidden design of nature. Proudhon tried to solve this antagonism by a sociological transposition. He distinguishes man as a social or collective being from man as an individual person. While the latter acts consciously with rational deliberation, society seems to be acted upon by spontaneous impulsions and to be directed by a superior counsel, apparently superhuman, driving men with irresistible power toward an unknown end. Hence the religious customs of questioning oracles, of public prayers and sacrifices, to safeguard historical decisions; hence, also, the philosophical explanation of history (Proudhon refers in particular to Bossuet, Vico, Herder, and Hegel) by a providential destiny presiding over the movements of men. Against these religious or semireligious interpretations of history, Proudhon argues that it is man's privilege to apprehend the apparent fatality as a social instinct, to penetrate its promptings, and to influence it. The providence of God is nothing else than the "collective instinct" or "universal reason" of man as a social being. The god of history is but man's own creation, and "atheism (i.e., humanism) the foundation of every theodicy."

This "humanitarian atheism" is the last term in man's intellectual and moral liberation, and at the same time it serves "the scientific reconstruction and verification" of all those dogmas which have been demolished by rational analysis, the "indefatigable Satan" who inquires incessantly.[5]

Far from being directed by providential destiny, history advances by revolutionary crises that give birth to new conceptions of justice. The first crisis was provoked by Jesus when he proclaimed man's equality before God. The second was inaugurated by the Reformation and Descartes, achieving equality before conscience and reason. The third began with the French Revolution and established equality before the law. The coming revolution, which is economic and social, will mark the end of the religious, aristocratic, and bourgeois age. It will bring about final equality by the "equation of man with humanity." To effect this ultimate advance, man has to take up the eternal fight between man and God and decide it; for God, or the Absolute, is the one great obstacle to human progress and the one great source of all kinds of absolutism—economic, political, religious.

While Voltaire and Condorcet were anticlerical and antireligious by temper and policy, Proudhon prides himself on being radically "anti-theistic." "The veritable virtue which makes us deserve life eternal is to fight against religion and God himself," for "God is *the* evil." As a providential creator-God, the Christian God is depriving man of his own creative power and prevision. Instead of saying with Voltaire: "If God did not exist, it would be necessary to invent him," Proudhon says that "the first duty of a free and intelligent man is to chase the idea of God out of his mind and conscience incessantly"; for, if he exists, he is essentially hostile to our nature. "We attain to science in spite of him, to well-being in spite of him, to society in spite of him: every progress is a victory in which we crush the deity."[6] By and by man will become the master of creation and thus equal God. Instead of man's being created in the image of a providential God, God is created in the image of man's power of foreseeing and providing. "Take away this providence and God ceases to be human." Eternal God and finite man are definite rivals in an irreconcilable competition, the prize of which is progress in the government of the universe by rational prevision. In this age-long fight of humanity against the deity to master its destiny, God has not intervened and abbreviated man's agonies but rather has tormented him as he did Job. God is "the ghost of our conscience," and all the attributes of divine providence, such as father, king, and judge, are nothing else than a caricature of humanity, incompatible with autonomous civilization and refuted by the catastrophes of history. God is essentially "anti-civilisateur, anti-libéral, anti-humain."

"Nobody shall tell us 'the ways of God are inscrutable,' for we have indeed scrutinized them and we have read in characters of blood the proof of his impotence if not malevolence. . . . Eternal father, Jupiter or Jehovah, we know thee: thou art, wert, and ever wilt be envious of Adam and the tyrant of Prometheus."[7] God is man's antagonist as Jehovah is Israel's. It is therefore false to reduce with Feuerbach theology to anthropology, thus deifying humanity; for what has to be demonstrated is that humanity is essentially *not* divine and that God, if he exists, is man's enemy. It is the privilege of man to be capable of finite and providential reason and to practice "the prophecy of his future," while perfect saintliness is contradictory to progressive perfection.

Eighteen hundred years ago a man tried, as we do nowadays, to regenerate mankind. The genius of revolution [Lucifer], the adversary of "The Eternal," thought he could recognize his own son in him, because of his saintly life, prodigious intelligence, and imagination. Pointing at the kingdoms of the earth he said to him: "If you are but willing to acknowledge and worship me, I will give unto you everything on earth." "No," answered the Nazarene, "I worship God alone." . . . The inconsequential reformer was crucified. After him Pharisees, publicans, priests, and kings reappeared, more oppressive, rapacious, and infamous than ever before, and the revolution was taken up twenty times and twenty times abandoned, remaining a problem.[8]

To solve this problem, Proudhon declared himself ready to carry out the work of Lucifer without demanding any reward from him. A contemporary symbol of Proudhon's radical resolve to adopt the fallen angel as godfather is the famous line of Baudelaire: "Race du Cain, au ciel monte et sur la terre jette Dieu."

And yet, like Baudelaire, Proudhon was deeply marked by Christianity in his blasphemies. There is certainly much rhetoric, pose, and exaggeration in his "anti-theism"; but there is also much of the passion and earnestness of a religious soul which needs a violent effort to assert its freedom and independence. He was one of the very few great men of letters of the nineteenth century who had studied Hebrew to read the Bible and had annotated the Scriptures.[9] His language, imagination, and turn of mind were decidedly theological. He needed, indeed, as he says in the Prologue to the *System of Economic Contradictions,* the "hypothesis of God," "more unrelenting than ever," to justify his "style" and his unusual treatment of economic problems.[10] He was not entirely unjustified in saying: "It is now up to us to instruct the theologians, for we alone continue the tradition of the church, we alone possess the sense of the Scriptures, of the Councils, and of the Fathers."[11] Thus an austere believer like Donoso Cortés could see in Proudhon an archenemy whose revolutionary thesis had to be refuted on theological grounds. Granted that it is, indeed, indicative of the modern situation that the flame of eschatology was kept alive in the nineteenth century not by liberal theologians but by "atheists" like Proudhon, Marx, and Nietzsche,[12] much can be said in defense of Proudhon's paradoxical comparison of himself with the early Christians who were accused by pagans of being atheists;[13] for Proudhon, too, in all his passion of destruction, wanted to prepare *la foi nouvelle,* asking for a "token of salvation" when he searched in the spectacle of modern revolutions "as in the entrails of a victim" for the secret of its destiny.[14] Deeper than Marx, who believed that humanity does not pose any questions which it is not able to solve, Proudhon eventually confessed that the antinomy between God and man does not find a final solution, for *on n'a jamais fini de se débattre contre Dieu.*[15] Hence his profound insight and sincere sadness with regard to the disintegration of the Christian Occident.

In 1843, describing the decline of old Europe, Proudhon, in "this last hour of Christianity," gratefully remembers its blessings and inspirations; for it is Christianity, he says, which has laid the foundations of our society, sanctioned its laws, unified the nations, and inspired generous minds with the passion for justice. And when, twenty years later, he analyzed once more the social dissolution, he understood the crisis of the nineteenth century again as one which is bound up with the decay of the Christian foundations of our Western civilization:

> Today civilization is indeed in a critical stage which has only one historical analogy: the crisis caused by the rise of Christianity. All traditions are used up, all beliefs abolished; on the other hand, the new program is not ready, that is, it has not yet entered the consciousness of the masses. This is what I call "dissolution." It is the most atrocious moment in the existence of societies. Everything contributes to sadden people of good will: prostitution of conscience, triumph of mediocrity, confusion of truth and falsehood, betrayal of principles, baseness of passions, cowardice of morals. . . . I have no illusion and I do not expect to see . . . reborn tomorrow in our country liberty, respect for law, public decency . . . , reason among the bourgeois, and common sense among the plebeians. No, no, I cannot see the end of decadence: it will not decrease within one or two generations. That is our lot. . . . I shall see the evil only and die in utter darkness, marked by the past with the seal of rejection. . . . Mass killings are going to come, and the prostration following the blood bath will be terrifying. We shall not see the work of the new age. We shall struggle in the night, and we must do our best to endure this life without too much sadness. Let us stand by each other, call out to each other in the dark, and do justice as often as an opportunity is given.[16]

There sounds a note of such hopeless despair as only a believer in progress could feel, but not a Christian. And yet it is the faith in a coming Kingdom of God which inspired Proudhon's fight against God and providence for the sake of human progress.

2. COMTE

HIS VIEW OF HISTORY

The only great counterpart to Hegel's philosophy of history[17] in comprehensiveness, though not in depth, is Comte's (1798–1857) *Cours de philosophie positive*.[18] Both works are, first of all, not only philosophies *of* history but intrinsically historical philosophies, permeated in their very method by the historical sense, whatever the special subject of their studies may be. Like Hegel, Comte is convinced that no phenomenon can be understood philosophically unless it is understood historically, through a demonstration of its temporal derivation and destination, its function, significance, and relative right in the whole course of history. This historical viewpoint became predominant only in the nineteenth century, but its roots stretch back into the Christian understanding of the universe as a creation, that is, as a universe created *once* for a *final* purpose and end. Only within such a supra-historical and yet temporal scheme can and must all events be related to their beginning and end, apart from which historical continuity does not make sense.

In consequence of this historical pattern, both works are also a theodicy, explaining and justifying every epoch as a "necessary" and "salutary" phase in the whole course of history. "Tout concilier sans concession," to reconcile the world to God in and by history, is the common maxim of Comte and Hegel. They convert the disturbing spectacle of apparently contradictory systems of thought and action into "a source of the firmest and most exclusive agreement," under the general viewpoint of a continuous "evolution" directed toward an end. This evolution is so far from being a merely biological category that it indicates rather the kind of teleology which is inherent in the Christian concept of a purposeful process of unified history.

With Comte, as well as with Hegel, the historical evolution of mankind is not vaguely universal but originates and is concentrated in the white race and the Christian Occident. Western civilization alone is specifically dynamic, progressive, and universal in its missionary zeal. But, while Hegel still understood the prerogative of the Occident as a consequence of its Christian qualification, Comte tries to explain it in a "truly positive way," by physical, chemical, and biological conditions of the white race.[19]

Both are postrevolutionary, i.e., inspired by the liberating impact of the French Revolution, and, at the same time, attempting to reintroduce an element of stability into the revolutionary dynamic of the modern progressive trend: Hegel by means of the absolute character of the "spirit," reflecting the finality of the Christian Logos; Comte by means of the relative power of "order," reflecting Catholic hierarchy. With Comte, history is no longer the temporal unfolding of an absolute truth and the providential fulfilment of an eternal design but a secular history of civilization, the truth of which is "relative" by being related to changing conditions and situations.

Positive philosophy is basically distinguished from theologico-metaphysical philosophy by rendering relative all the notions which were at first absolute.[20] While a theology or metaphysics of history is "absolute in its conception and arbitrary in its application," the positive philosophy of history is relative in its conceptions and necessary in its application, like the natural law of evolution and progressive development. In spite of this fundamental rejection of any absolute claim, Comte's systematic account of our intellectual and moral, social and political, history is still dependent on what it denounces; for, in order to substitute relativism for absolutism, he had to conceive relativity itself as an absolute principle, connecting all phenomena by the one and supreme law of progressive evolution. The leading idea of a temporal progression toward a final goal in the future reflects the derivation of positive philosophy from the theological interpretation of history as a history of fulfilment and salvation.

The general aim of the *Cours de philosophie positive* (1830–42) is to present "la marche fondamentale du développement humain" and to elucidate the progressive course of the human mind in its wholeness, through its whole historic continuity, leading up to final maturity in the scientific stage of our Western civilization. Comte purposely replaces the term *perfectionnement* by "development" and "progression" as more scientific terms excluding moral appreciation, but without denying that this continuous development is necessarily followed by improvements and ameliorations.[21] He refuses, however, to be involved in the sterile controversy over the increase of absolute happiness in the succession of different ages, for each age establishes a relative equilibrium between man's faculties, aspirations, and circumstances.

From the study of the general development, Comte deduces "the great fundamental law" (anticipated by Saint-Simon and Turgot) that each branch of our civilization and of our knowledge passes successively through three different stages: the theological or fictitious (childhood), the metaphysical or abstract (youth), and the scientific or positive (manhood). As the Christian epoch was conceived as the last one, so the scientific era is also an ultimate issue, concluding the story of man's historical progression. It began with Bacon, Galileo, and Descartes,[22] whose *Discourse on Method* has now to be extended and completed by an elaboration of the historicosociological method, which makes philosophy of history scientific.[23] The hierarchy of sciences from mathematics to sociology, as presented by Comte, is determined by one homogeneous method, and it culminates in "social physics," completing the system of natural sciences.[24]

In this progressive evolution, the theological system of conceptions is the point of departure, the metaphysical a state of transition, the scientific the final term. In the first stage the human mind is searching for the very nature of all things, their first and final causes, their origin and purpose—in short, for absolute knowledge. It represents all phenomena as if produced by the direct and continuous action of many (polytheism) or one (monotheism) supernatural agent. In the metaphysical stage, these supernatural agents are replaced by abstract entities. The questions asked by metaphysics are still the theological ones;

only the way to answer them is somewhat different. In the positive stage, the mind has finally understood the impossibility of grasping absolute notions; it renounces the vain search for the origin and destination of the universe and confines research, by the mutual support of empirical observation and logical reasoning, to the invariable relations of phenomenal successions and resemblances which constitute natural laws. Comte's new philosophy is relativism in the literal sense, being concerned exclusively with relations. While all investigation into the nature of things must be absolute, the study of the laws of phenomena must be relative. "It supposes a continuous progress of speculation subject to the gradual improvement of observation, without the precise reality being ever fully disclosed: so that the relative character of scientific conceptions is inseparable from the true idea of natural laws, just as the chimerical inclination for absolute knowledge accompanies every use of theological fictions and metaphysical entities."[25] There is no knowledge, unless by revelation, which is not conditioned by the medium acting upon us and by the organism reacting upon the first. Only within this interrelation or reciprocity can we know anything. Dark stars are not perceptible, and blind men cannot perceive. Thus all our speculations are deeply affected by the external constitution which regulates the mode of action and the internal constitution which determines its personal result; and in neither case are we able to assign its respective influence to each class of conditions generating our impressions and ideas.[26] This relativism is most evident in biology and sociology but is fundamental to all positive sciences. To "explain" a phenomenon means to the positive mind no more and no less than to establish a connection between single phenomena and some general facts, the number of which continually diminishes with the progress of science.[27] The unattainable ideal would be to explain all facts by one single law, like gravitation. Positive philosophy, which is the special study of scientific generalities, is concerned only with questions to which the answers are within our reach, while to the primitive man only those questions are of interest which are inaccessible, like the absolute quest for the origin, the purpose, and the nature of things.

And yet Comte insists on the historical necessity of the theological way of thinking. His argument is rather ingenuous: the mature mind soberly observes facts in order to form a theory, while, on the other hand, a guiding theory is required to retain and even to perceive facts.[28] To move freely back and forth within this circle of theory and facts, or of reasoning and observation, would have been too much for a scientifically uneducated mind. Such a mind has to begin its investigations with a more simple method, presupposing supernatural agents as the ultimate and direct cause of observable effects. If man had not begun with such an exaggerated estimate of his possible knowledge and of his own importance in the universe, he would never have known and done all that he is actually capable of knowing and doing. Thus the theological philosophy "administered exactly the stimulus necessary to incite the human mind to the irksome labor without which it could make no progress."[29] We can scarcely conceive of such a primitive state of things, now that our reason has become sufficiently mature to enter upon laborious researches without any such stimulus and finds motive enough in the hope of discovering the laws of phenomena. To advance, however, from the supernatural to natural philosophy, an intermediate system was necessary. In this the metaphysical conceptions had their utility and necessity. By the substitution of a corresponding entity for supernatural direction of nature and social history, attention became freer to deal with the facts themselves, until, at length, metaphysical agents had ceased to be anything more than abstract labels. Now (in the nineteenth century) the best minds of Europe are agreed that theological, metaphysical, and literary education must be superseded by a "positive" training which is advancing in the same degree as the older forms of higher education are inevitably declining.[30]

Thus the general outlook of Comte's universal history is determined by the open future of a linear progression from primitive to advanced stages. This progress is more conspicuous in the intellectual than in the moral field and is more firmly established in the natural than in the social sciences. But the ultimate aim and task is the application of the achievements of natural sciences to social physics or sociology[31] for the sake of social reorganization.

The great political and moral crisis that the most civilized nations[32] are undergoing arises out of an anarchy, primarily intellectual; for the sociohistorical world rests on the ideas and opinions by which men direct their affairs. The lack of stability in fundamental maxims and social order is accounted for by the confusing coexistence of three divergent philosophies—the theological, the metaphysical, and the positive. Any one of them alone might secure some sort of social order, but their coexistence neutralizes each and makes order impossible. The task, therefore, is to promote the triumph of positive philosophy in its bearing upon social life and to consolidate the whole into one body of homogeneous doctrine. "It is time to complete the vast operation begun by Bacon, Descartes, and Galileo, by reconstructing the system of general ideas which must henceforth prevail amongst the human race. This is the way to put an end to the revolutionary crisis which is tormenting the civilized nations of the world."[33]

To counterbalance the anarchical trend of mere progression toward individual rights (instead of common duties), abstract liberty (instead of voluntary subordination), and equality (instead of hierarchy)[34] and to terminate the revolutionary period of the last centuries, the stabilizing force of order has to be reorganized; for only a system which unites order with progress can direct the revolutionary state, which has been characteristic of Europe's history since the dissolution of the order of the Middle Ages, toward its final and positive term. Order and progress, which the ancients considered to be mutually exclusive, constitute in modern civilization two conditions which must prevail simultaneously. "Their combination is at once the fundamental difficulty and the principal source of every genuine political system. In our era no order can be established, and still less can it last, if it is not fully compatible with progress; no great progress can be accomplished if it does not tend to the consolidation of order.... Therefore the main feature in positive social philosophy must be the union of these two conditions which will be two aspects, constant and inseparable, of the same principle."[35] Only by a doctrine as progressive as it is hierarchical can we escape the vicious circle of anarchical revolutions and reactionary restorations, the one claiming progress, the other order. While historically the Catholic church has been the main protagonist of tradition, hierarchy, and order and the critical and negative spirit of Protestantism the main protagonist of progress, the new progressive order will be neither Catholic nor Protestant but simply "positive" and "natural," like the natural laws of social history.

Comte explains the relative lack of social progress before the advent of positivism by the undeveloped state of the positive sciences and by the narrow range of available facts wide enough to disclose the natural laws of social phenomena. Only with the modern political revolutions could the idea of progress acquire sufficient firmness, distinctness, and generality to serve a scientific purpose. To classical antiquity the course of history appeared not at all as a "course" but as a cyclic succession of identical phases, never experiencing a new transformation directed toward a definite goal in the future. Thus every idea of progress was inaccessible to the philosophers of antiquity. Even the most sagacious of them rather shared the popular belief that the contemporary state of things was far inferior to that of former times. Aristotle's *Politics,* which comes nearer to a positive view than do his other works, does not disclose "any sense of a progressive tendency nor the slightest glimpse of the natural laws of civilization,"[36] i.e., the law of evolution.

The first dawning sense of human progress was inspired by Christianity. By proclaiming the superiority of the law of Jesus over that of Moses, it gave rise to the idea of a fundamental historical progression toward fulfilment, from a less to a more perfect state. Christianity could not, however, suggest any scientific view of social progress; for any such view was at once barred by Christianity's claim to be the final stage at which the human mind must stop.

The first satisfactory view of general progress was proposed by a great Christian believer who was, at the same time, a great scientist—Pascal. He viewed the entire succession of man through the whole course of ages as *"one* man always subsisting and incessantly learning."[37] But, even so, the idea of continuous progress had no consistency until after the memorable controversy, at the beginning of the eighteenth century, over the "ancients and moderns." The greatest advances toward an adequate understanding of social history were made by Montesquieu and Condorcet. In particular, the latter's Introduction to his work on *The Progress of the Human Mind* anticipated clearly the continuous progression of the race. "These few immortal pages," Comte states, "leave really nothing to be desired in regard to the position of the sociological question at large, which will, in my opinion, rest through all future time, on this admirable statement."[38] Still, even Condorcet's project was imperfect and premature because of his exclusion of moral phenomena from treatment by the positive method. He lost himself in chimerical anticipations and wanderings after an indefinite perfectibility.

HIS APPRAISAL OF CATHOLICISM AND PROTESTANTISM

In a revealing footnote[39] Comte states that his "systematic preference" for the Catholic "system" as a social organization does not depend on the accidental fact of his having been reared a Catholic. The affinity of the Catholic and the positive systems rests rather on their common aim and on their ability to create a veritable social organism, though on different bases. They are also united by their common opposition to the social sterility of the Protestant philosophy, which is "radically contrary to any sound political conception." Protestantism's pretense of being able to reform Christianity actually destroyed the most indispensable conditions of its political existence. Thus we find throughout Comte's work not only many remarks of appreciation of the political and social wisdom of men like Bossuet and De Maistre[40] but also a general veneration for the Roman "Catholic system," as he calls it in preference to "Christianity," because it disciplined "evangelical anarchy." It is socially more distinctive than the message of Jesus, since it does not involve any special reference to a historical founder and since it comprehends the monotheistic principle without sectarian limitations. Not Jesus but St. Paul is the "great man" who ranks with Caesar and Charlemagne in Comte's positive cult of humanity. The settlement achieved in the Middle Ages seemed so satisfactory to Comte "that we have only to follow its lead in reconstructing the same system on a better foundation." It is positive philosophy which will first render justice to the Catholic system as the greatest achievement of human wisdom.[41] Positive philosophy has to complete what Catholicism has happily organized during ten centuries but what had remained at the head of the European system for only two centuries, from Gregory VII to Boniface VIII. Under Boniface its decline commenced, and the following five centuries exhibited only a kind of chronic agony. A solution to this problem of the power and degeneracy of Catholicism lies, for Comte, in the discrimination between Catholic doctrine and Catholic organization. The first was destined to expire, the second to be developed. Reconstructed upon a sounder and broader basis, the same constitution must superintend the spiritual reorganization of modern society. "We must either assent to this, or suppose (what seems to contradict the laws of our nature) that the vast efforts of so many great men, seconded by the persevering earnestness of civilized nations, in the secular establishment of this masterpiece of human wisdom, must be irrevocably lost to the most advanced portion of humanity."[42]

What Comte appreciates, first of all, in the Catholic system is the consequential division of spiritual and temporal power, a division by which the universal morality of Christianity was established outside and above secular standards and the sphere of political action. This division, unknown to classical paganism, where morality and religion were absorbed into the life of the polis,[43] established a spiritual authority equally respected by lord and serf, and it authorized the meanest Christian to invoke against the most powerful noble the inflexible prescriptions of the church. In the midst of a feudal order founded upon birth, fortune, and military valor, the church constituted an immense and powerful ecclesiastical class, in which intellectual and moral superiority was openly entitled to ascendancy and often led to the most eminent positions in the hierarchy of the church, which directed all education. By admitting all classes to office in the hierarchical organization of the church and causing the chief office, that of the pope, to be elective by inferiors, the Catholic system was more democratic and progressive than the hereditary principle ever could be. Being independent of the temporal power, the spiritual organization of the church could extend almost indefinitely across national boundaries and thus constitute the main bond among the European nations. If anywhere, it was among the leaders of the medieval church and her monastic institutions that a truly universal viewpoint prevailed with regard to human affairs. This social independence and freedom of mind was further fostered by the sacerdotal discipline, particularly by ecclesiastical celibacy, the favorable influence of which can be measured by its incompatibility with the hereditary principle which was still prevalent everywhere but in the ecclesiastical organization. Undeniable also is the progress in education brought about by the Catholic system, while in the pagan regime not only slaves but the majority of free men were deprived of all regular instruction, unless we may call "instruction" the popular interest in the observance of religious festivals, scenic sports, and military training. "Vast, then, was the elementary progress when Catholicism imposed on every disciple the strict duty of receiving, and as far as possible, of procuring that religious instruction which, taking possession of the individual from his earliest days, and preparing him for his social duties, followed him through life, keeping him up to his principles by an admirable combination of exhortations, exercises, and material signs, all converging towards unity of impression."[44] The military and national morality of antiquity, subordinated to polity, had given way to a more pacific and universal morality, predominant over politics, in proportion as the system of conquest became transformed by the progressive spirit of Catholicism, which lifted man above the narrow circle of his earthly pursuits and purified his habitual feelings. In order to show that the Catholic system was not hostile to moral and intellectual progress but, instead, favored it and was thus preparing under the theological regime the elements of the positive regime, Comte sketches the most important instances of Catholic advancement under the three heads of personal, domestic, and social morality.[45]

The personal virtues, which in ancient times were conceived mainly as a matter of magnanimity and prudence, were now, for the first time, understood as a principle of humility over against pride and vanity. Suicide, honorable among the ancients, now was condemned—though not as "antisocial" as with Comte but because of its incompatibility with the belief in man's being God's creature. Domestic morality was freed from the subjection to polity in which the ancients had placed it. Family life became greatly improved when Catholic influence penetrated every human relation and developed the sense of reciprocal duty without tyranny, sanctioning paternal authority while abolishing ancient patriarchal despotism. The social condition of woman also improved considerably, since Catholicism held women's lives essentially domestic and sanctified the indissolubility of marriage. In regard to social morality, Catholicism modified the savage patriotism of the ancients by the higher sentiment of universal brotherhood and charity. Thanks to uniform subordination to one spiritual authority, members of different positions and nationalities became fellow-citizens of Christendom. The advancement of international law and the more humane conditions imposed on warfare were also due to Catholic influence. The imperfect distribution of wealth was checked by the many admirable foundations devoted to the relief of suffering—institutions unknown in ancient times and growing out of private munificence. Expanding the universal sentiment of social union, Catholicism connected all times, places, and classes of society, thus creating the most durable system in the midst of and above the temporal powers of the state. And all that has happened in our history, from the Christian period up to now, is an unbroken chain which links modern society to the early days of Western civilization. It is no surprise, therefore, that universal historical speculation, as inaugurated by Augustine, should also be due to the genius of Catholicism, which preserved the inheritance of Athens, Rome, and Jerusalem when it made the history of the church the fundamental history of humanity.[46] "We shall see that the entire spiritual movement of modern times is referable to that memorable season in human history which Protestantism is pleased to call the Dark Ages." It is therefore with profound regret that Comte states the present barrenness of this great and noble organization, that has become static and retrograde, has lost its intellectual basis, and leaves us now only the memory of the vast services of every kind which connect it with human progress.[47]

While Christianity from its very beginnings was in harmony with the idea of progress by proclaiming the superiority of the law of Jesus to that of Moses, this great idea of a fundamental progression from the Old to the New Testament belongs less to Protestantism than to Catholicism; for the Reformation, in its "vulgar and irrational" recourse to the period of the primitive church, offered to modern peoples for guidance not the mature social system of Catholic Christianity but "the most backward and dangerous part of the Scriptures,"[48] that which relates to Hebrew antiquity. Like Bossuet and the many critics of Protestantism, including Protestants like Burckhardt, Lagarde, and Nietzsche, Comte saw in the Reformation an essentially negative movement, dissolving critically the declining Catholic system without replacing its educational and social achievements on a positive level. According to Comte, the Reformation simply put the seal on the state of modern society, such as it was after the changes of the two preceding centuries.

The change as such was universal, for the revolutionary condition of the modern age was as marked among the nations which remained Catholic as among those which professed Protestantism. The revolutionary change consisted mainly in the emancipation of the temporal and in the national subjection of the spiritual power. It affected all western Europe and all orders and persons: priests, popes, kings, nobles, and the common people. Charles V and Francis I were almost as fully emancipated as Henry VIII became by his separation from Rome. And the achievement of Luther, "with all its stormy grandeur," was, in fact, the simple realization of the first stage of Catholic decline. In attacking the Catholic discipline, the Reformation not only propitiated human passions but confirmed the destruction of sacerdotal independence by the abolition of clerical celibacy and general confession. When the Lutheran movement had reached the Calvinistic phase, it converted the clergy to a political subjection which had been repugnant to them before but in which they now saw the only security for their social existence. It was then, and in reaction to Protestantism, that the unfortunate coalition of interests between Catholicism and royal power began; in its best days the Catholic system had been glorious for its antagonism to all temporal power. The central organ of Catholic resistance against the dissolving power of Protestantism was the Society of Jesus. However, it shared fully all the vices of the decaying system, no less than Protestantism did after it had emerged from mere opposition. The only real promise of Christian reform, by Franciscans and Dominicans, had failed three centuries earlier. "Catholicism became retrograde against its nature, in consequence of its subjection to temporal power; and Protestantism, erecting that subjection into principle, could not but be retrograde to at least an equal degree."[49]

Protestantism served as the organ of universal spiritual emancipation, creating an intermediate situation which finally matured in Descartes, Hobbes, Voltaire, and Rousseau, if one considers the whole critical doctrine as reducible to the absolute dogma of free individual inquiry. This dogma of unlimited freedom of conscience and expression became the chief rallying-point of the revolutionary movement. Necessary as it was in its negative function, it could not become the positive principle of a new order; for social order is incompatible with the perpetual discussion of the foundations of society by a majority of minds who are incompetent to make the most delicate decisions. Unlimited freedom, like unlimited equality, condemns the superior to dependence upon the vast majority of inferiors. Protestantism laid the foundations of modern revolutionary philosophy by proclaiming the right of every individual to free inquiry on all subjects whatsoever, notwithstanding illogical restrictions in behalf of itself. After having audaciously discussed the most sacred powers, human reason was not likely to recoil before any social maxim or institution. On the other hand, Protestantism only extended to the Christian public the spirit of criticism which had been abundantly used long before by kings and scholars of the fourteenth and fifteenth centuries in discussions about the power of the popes and the independence of the national churches. The success of Luther, after the failure of various premature reformers, was mainly due to the ripeness of the time. Within the Catholic system, Jansenism was a heresy almost as injurious to the old spirit and constitution as was Luther himself. Both were necessary, though provisional, stages in the progressive development of Western civilization. Catholicism had virtually abdicated its direction of social life, now controlling only the weak, on whom it imposed obedience while it extolled the rights of rulers. The critical doctrine insisted upon the rights of those to whom Catholicism preached only duties, and so it inherited the moral prerogatives that Catholicism had abdicated. The insurrectionary tendency of Protestantism was necessary to avoid the moral abasement and political degradation to which modern society was exposed while awaiting the reorganization of a social order in harmony with progress, a reorganization which neither the revolutionary nor the theological doctrine was able to achieve.

The dissolution as inaugurated by the Reformation developed

in three stages: Luther overthrew ecclesiastical discipline, Calvin introduced more extensive modifications into the dogma and added to Luther's destruction that of the hierarchy, and the Socinian outbreak completed the destruction by attacking the chief articles of faith which distinguish Christianity from every other form of monotheism. Only the third stage doomed Catholicism beyond recall and, at the same time, led Protestantism, via theism, "which by a monstrous conjunction of terms metaphysicians have entitled 'natural religion' as if all religion were not necessarily supernatural,"[50] to mere deism.[51] "After this there remains really nothing to distinguish among the multiplicity of sects, in regard to social progress, except the general testimony borne by the Quakers against the military spirit."[52]

More important are the indirect consequences of Protestantism in all major political revolutions of the seventeenth and eighteenth centuries, in Holland, England, and America. All are "Protestant revolutions." The American Revolution, according to Comte, was simply an extension of the other two, though with a prosperous development under favorable circumstances. Yet this "new world" seemed to Comte in all important respects more remote from true social reorganization than were the nations of the old world—"whatever may be the existing illusions about the political superiority of a society in which the elements of modern civilization, with the exception of industrial activity, are most imperfectly developed."[53]

In principle, the whole degeneracy of the European system stems from one great cause: the political degradation of the spiritual power. But, considering that with the advent of the negative philosophy of Protestantism every immature mind was entrusted to his own decision on the most important subjects, the miracle is that moral dissolution has not been complete. A most general and mischievous error of the revolutionary doctrine of Protestantism was that it annulled the political existence of any spiritual power which was distinct and independent of the temporal power. Although historically inevitable, the Protestant revolution could not destroy the permanent value of the principle of the separation of the two powers, the theory of which is to Comte the most important legacy left to us by Catholicism and "the only one on which, when united with a true positive doctrine, the reorganization of society can proceed."[54] Unfortunately, the wholesomeness of this principle of separation has been lost from sight throughout Europe; and to the prevalence of this great error we may attribute modern man's irrational disdain of the Middle Ages and Protestantism's exclusive predilection for the primitive church and its injurious enthusiasm for the Hebrew theocracy. "The great concept of social progress has thus been overlaid, and well nigh lost." The reverse of the abandonment of the two-power principle is that, in modern times, political as well as philosophical ambition has tended toward absolute union of the two kinds of power. Rulers dreamed of absolute imperial power, while philosophers renewed the Greek dream of a metaphysical theocracy which they called the reign of mind. In the one case we may think of Napoleon, in the other of Hegel.

FINAL CONSIDERATION

In defense of his positive and historical method, Comte once remarked[55] that even such an eminent thinker of the Catholic school as De Maistre bore involuntary testimony to the necessity of the new era when he endeavored (in his work on the pope) to re-establish the papal supremacy "on simple historical and political reasonings," instead of ordaining it theologically by divine right; for this was the only appropriate ground for papal supremacy, and De Maistre, too, would have proposed it in any other age before the advent of modern historical positivism. Reading the splendid chapters in Comte's work on the many and lasting merits and services of the Catholic system, one may ask the question whether, conversely, Comte does not involuntarily bear testimony to the opposite necessity of preserving or reviving the theological foundations of Christianity, in order to establish a Catholic order on a contemporary basis. This problem did not arise in Comte's one-dimensional modern mind.[56]

He sincerely believed—and most beliefs are sincere, though not, for all that, necessarily true and intelligent—that one can improve the Catholic "system," i.e., its social organization, by eliminating the Christian faith from which the system derives and the Christian doctrine on which it rests. He believed in the Catholic system without faith in Christ, and in human brotherhood without a common father. He criticized the vague and arbitrary character of theological beliefs, without realizing the much greater arbitrariness and vagueness of his own belief in evolution and humanity. He blames Christianity for having barred its own progressive tendency by its claim to being the final stage of man's progression; and yet he attributes the self-same ultimacy to the scientific stage, "which alone indicates the final term of human history" that human nature will be "for-ever approaching," though never attaining, in accordance with the indefinite character of the secular progress toward a definite aim. In spite of his intelligent and sympathetic analysis of the contributions of Christianity to modern society, Comte, like all his predecessors and successors, did not realize the depth to which his leading idea of progress is still theological. Nor did he apprehend that it is positive only if one exempts the third stage from the general process of secularization which deter-mines the positive stage no less than it does the metaphysical one.[57]

The law of progressive evolution replaces the function of providential government, perverting the secret provision by providence into a scientific provision by a *prévision rationelle*,[58] which, according to Comte, is the ultimate scientific test not only in natural science but everywhere, as the fulfilment of prophecies was the ultimate test in the traditional biblical inter-pretation of the historical progress from the Old to the New Testament. Resolved to "organize" providence, Comte under-stood only the obvious antagonism between progress and provi-dence[59] but not the hidden dependence of the secular religion of progress on the Christian faith, hope, and expectation of progressing toward a final fulfilment of history by judgment and salvation. Involved in and fascinated by the social and political crisis which had agitated Europe since the French Revolution, Comte did not see that his expectation of a "fundamental modification of human existence"[60] after the full establishment of the positive philosophy is but a pale shadow of that eschatological expectation which constituted the core of early Christianity. Yet his confidence that "the future is full of promise" is hardly intelligible without reference to the Christian faith, which created the future as the decisive horizon of our post-Christian existence. "The future of Christianity" is, as Rosenstock-Huessy recently pointed out,[61] no casual combination of two words, like the future of motoring. The living toward a future *eschaton* and back from it to a new beginning is characteristic only for those who live essentially by hope and expectation—for Jews and Christians. To this extent future and Christianity are indeed synonymous. A basic difference between Christianity and secular futurism is, however, that the pilgrim's progress is not an indefinite advance toward an unattainable ideal but a definite choice in the face of an eternal reality and that the Christian hope in the Kingdom of God is bound up with the fear of the Lord, while the secular hope for a "better world" looks forward without fear and trembling. They have in common, nonetheless, the eschatological viewpoint and outlook into the future as such. The idea of progress could become the leading principle for the understanding of history only within this primary horizon of the future as established by Jewish and Christian faith, against the "hopeless," because cyclic, world view of classical paganism. All modern striving for improvements and progresses, in the plural, is rooted in that singular Christian progress from which the modern consciousness has emancipated itself because it cannot be known and demonstrated by reason as a natural law but only by hope and faith as a gift of grace.

Comte's dependence on the Christian tradition is more obvious in his insistence on a spiritual order independent of the temporal than it is with regard to the leading idea of progress.

Comte is, of course, aware of the theological derivation of this basic distinction, since it is already indicated by the terms "spiritual" and "temporal." But he believes that what has been established on the ground of a mystical opposition between heavenly and earthly powers could be re-established scientifically, on "sound intelligent and social appreciation" and on "evidence afforded by the whole human evolution."[62] Positive philosophy feels "the growing pressure of necessity for a spiritual power entirely independent of the temporal" and, consequently, for a supreme "spiritual authority" as the basis of the final system of human society. This authority is to be patterned on the spiritual government and education which the Christian church has established in the Middle Ages, but as a "positive" authority it is to be a-religious and relative, like all positive concepts. "Catholicism established a universal education, imperfect and variable, but essentially homogeneous and common to the loftiest and the humblest Christians: and it would be strange to propose a less general institution for a more advanced civilization."[63] But it seems that Comte felt the strange inconsistency which is implied in a supreme authority founded on a merely positive and thereby relative basis; for he frankly confesses: "as for the kind of persons who are to constitute the new spiritual authority, it is easy to say who they will not be, and impossible to say who they will be."[64] They will be neither priests nor *sàvants* nor any other class now existing, but "a wholly new class," constituting a "philosophical priesthood" and composed of members issuing from all orders of existing society, the scientific order having no sort of predominance over the rest. One may wonder how Comte would feel if he were confronted with the new powers, orders, and authorities of the twentieth century and with their attempts at a radical reorganization of human society on a merely positive basis, with the help of a secular religion.[65]

Comte himself and his many disciples and followers firmly believed that they had found the only sound and immovable basis on which the future of western Europe could be built. But if we assume with him that rational prevision and prediction are the ultimate test of positive philosophy, as they are, indeed, the test of science, then Comte has refuted himself more completely than any criticism could do. While Burckhardt, in his freedom from the modern illusion of progress, acutely predicted the convergence of modern industrial power with military might and authority, Comte predicted that modern industry would "necessarily" lead to the abolition of wars. In the fifty-first lecture[66] he gives a summary of his view: like everything else, the military way of life, too, was a necessary and salutary, though primitive, stage in the general course of social progress toward the industrial stage of modern times, which is scientific and thereby peace-loving. The general direction of the development is thus characterized by a gradual decline of the military spirit and the ascendency of the industrial spirit. The military enterprise of Napoleon was an exception, necessitated by "abnormal" circumstances, and it will be the last of this kind. And even Napoleon, "the hero of retrogression," set himself up as a protector of industry, art, and science—which seems to Comte a strange inconsistency,[67] which it is not at all. In future the conflicts between the modern national states will still require the intervention of a moderating spiritual power, but "the great wars are no doubt over," since the military spirit is doomed "to inevitable extinction."[68] For the scientific era will "inevitably" (a word which Comte repeats time and again to emphasize the "law" of evolution) destroy the military spirit and system together with the theological one. Both belong together by having an analogous function in disciplining the human race in its first stages, while in the modern age science and industry support each other. The occasional rivalry between the theological and the military power should not deceive us about their fundamental affinity, most clearly expressed in the religious consecration of the military power of the feudal system. "Without this intimate correlation . . . it is evident that the military spirit could never have fulfilled its high social destiny in the whole of human evolution."[69] Their correlation was most fully realized in antiquity, when both powers were concentrated in the same leader. It is true that science, too, renders great services to the military art; but, resting on rational discussion, it is in principle incompatible with military discipline and authority. Modern scientific industry is basically hostile to the theological, as well as to the military, spirit. Even the maintenance of a vast military apparatus of standing armies through conscription cannot prevent the decline of the military system; for modern conscription destroys the specific character and honor of the military profession by making of the army a multitude of antimilitary citizens, who assume their duty as a temporary burden, and by reducing the military system to a subaltern office in the mechanism of modern society. "Thus the time has come when we may congratulate ourselves on the final passing away of serious and durable warfare among the most advanced nations."[70] Blinded by his evolutionary optimism, Comte foresaw neither the rise of "industrial armies" (Marx) nor that of a militarized industry (Burckhardt). Moreover, he believed that "the scrupulous respect for life" would necessarily increase with our social progression, in proportion as the chimerical hope in immortality faded away, a hope which cannot but disparage the value of the present life.[71] The finality of individual death, far from obstructing the course of general evolution or diminishing the rate of progress, is the condition of progress. Discussing "social dynamics,"[72] Comte says that the most important among the permanent influences which affect the rate of progress is the limited duration of human life. "There is no denying that all social progression rests essentially on death" because progress requires the steady renewal of its agents by the succession of generations. An indefinite duration of human life would presently put a stop to all progress whatever. Even if human life were lengthened tenfold only, progress would be slowed down because in the stimulating contest between the conservative instinct of age and the innovating instinct of youth, the conservative age would then be much more favored. If, on the other hand, life were reduced to a quarter of its normal duration, the effect would be as mischievous as in the case of a too protracted duration, since this would give too much power to the instinct of innovation.

Another complementary cause which affects the rate of progress is the increase in population, concentrating ever more people in a given space; for it is of little consequence whether the more frequent renewal of individuals is caused by the short life of some or by the speedier multiplication of others.[73]

Either of these considerations shows that Comte, like all philosophers of history, thinks in terms of generalities but not of individuals or persons. Since Comte has constantly in mind "the whole human evolution," where everything "must be referred not to man but to humanity,"[74] the universality of history and its continuity are overemphasized at the expense of the finite and personal character of human life. Moral laws, too, according to Comte, are much more appreciable in the collective than in the individual case; and though individual nature is the type of general nature, all human advancement is characterized much more completely in the general than in the individual case. "Thus morality will always be connected with polity."

This sociopolitical viewpoint is indeed inevitable for the historian because the primary subjects of secular history are not single individuals but communities, groups, and states. Hence the primacy of politics in history. Political history can never adopt the Christian scheme of the history of salvation, since salvation refers to the individual soul—to each of us—but not to mankind.[75] Humanity cannot be saved because it does not exist except in individual men and women. It is the crux of all philosophies of history of a secular and positive tenor that they adopt the universal element of the Christian understanding of history but eliminate the Christian concern about persons; for the recognition of the *universal* significance of a *unique* personality like Jesus Christ would indeed cut across the linear stream of a continuously progressive development. The whole scheme of Comte's philosophy of history is thus as much theological as it is positive, the first by its universal claim and indefinite eschatology, the second by disowning the individual, who is the ultimate concern of the gospel—however "social" it might be. In consequence of this neglect of individual destiny, death is to Comte a merely statistical phenomenon, just like the increase in population. Apart from this positive, but utterly inadequate, viewpoint, death is, however, not a stimulant to a continuous social progress but the veritable end which discontinues all personal human progression. It is a source of ultimate hope or relief in the face of man's disastrous evolution to such a degree of "scrupulous respect of human life" as we have witnessed recently in both the aggressive and the peace-loving nations. In our positive age it is one of the strangest, though most obvious, dialectical contradictions that we take care for the preservation of individual life as never before by all means of scientific devices and, at the same time, destroy it en masse by means of the same progressive inventions. Indoctrinated with the modern doctrine of man's natural goodness, Comte never realized that each advance in man's rule over the world brings with it new forms and levels of degradation and that all our means of progression are just so many means of regression as long as mortal man is involved in the historical process.

Comte's dogmatic belief in historical continuity and development, without creation and final end, made him blind to the perpetual possibility and actuality of historical losses, reversions, and catastrophes, which are not at all contradictory to the laws of human nature and even less to the Christian faith. While the Greek, as well as the Christian, view of history was open to the stern facts of *hybris* and *nemesis,* of pride and doom, the positive outlook on history cannot but falsify historical reality for the sake of an unattainable secular solution. Comte's one-dimensional way of thinking levels the substance of history down to the superficial wholeness of a linear and natural evolution, the counterpart, as he realized, of supernatural creation.[76] But the immense reality of history, which is as much human as it is inhuman, has more than one dimension. It is at least as rich in contradictions as Goethe's *Natur* or Nietzsche's "Dionysian world"; and the mighty river of history which breaks the dike and overflows a country is essentially the same as the peaceful stream which seems to enjoy its orderly banks. If our sensitiveness were not blunted by the desire for security, we would discern the depths and heights of history in our everyday life, instead of being shocked by its eruptions. Comte did not see history's depth but only its cultural surface, and therefore his last word about the "positive polity" of the future is as shallow as its formulation in a "religion of humanity," the motto of which is "Réorganiser, sans Dieu ni roi, par le culte systématique de l'humanité." This poor artifice or *Gemächte,* to use a Lutheran expression, of man's self-adoration is to replace the Christian love of God and afford a positive synthesis, "more real, comprehensive, stable and permanent" than the medieval system. Love, understood as "social feeling," is to complete order and progress, now defined as "the development of order under the influence of love";[77] and every aspect of progress is to converge toward the Supreme Being, "Humanity," by which the provisional conception of God is to be entirely superseded. To promote the establishment of this relative Kingdom of God on earth, Comte transposed theology into sociology, theocracy into sociocracy, and the worship of God into that of humanity, thus consecrating political science religiously. The new spiritual power is to be in the hands of the learned, while the temporal power will be administered by the captains of finance and industry as the new superintendents of all occidental affairs. He even took pains to elaborate all details for the future administration of the new Western society, including a new flag, a new calendar, festivals, worship of new positive saints, and new churches. For the time being, however, the religion of humanity will avail itself of the Christian churches as these gradually become vacant, in the same way as Christian worship was carried on at first in deserted pagan temples. In a letter of 1851 Comte went so far as to predict that, before 1860, he would preach the gospel of positivism, "the only real and complete religion," in Notre-Dame! Though having resented in his youth Saint-Simon's tendency toward a new Christianity, Comte, too, came to construct positivism into the "definite religion," repudiating atheism as too simple and provisional a negativism, as he explained in a letter of 1845 to John Stuart Mill. Like Feuerbach, whose *Essence of Christianity,* i.e., Christianity reduced to humanism, appeared in the same year as Comte's *System,* he was a "pious atheist," rejecting the divine subject but retaining its traditional human predicates, such as love and justice.[78] The positive doctrine is a faith in mankind which does not question the humanness of man. Again, like Feuerbach, Comte had a massive honesty and a genius for simplification, but he was neither deep nor subtle.[79]

It is a pathetic experience to read, in 1948, Comte's "general view of positivism" of 1848, which contains a popular summary of his ideas in regard to Europe's reconstruction, on the basis of positive science, now concentrated on "the study of humanity," into the leading "great Western republic," formed of the five advanced nations: the French, Italian, Spanish, British, and German, "which, since the time of Charlemagne have always constituted a political whole." It is pathetic reading not only because it demonstrates the futility of Comte's claim to prognosticate the inevitable evolution of Western society but also because the word "reconstruction" is now associated with doom and destruction.

If Comte had really reasoned on a purely positive basis, that is, with the neutrality of the scientist, discarding the "exaggerated estimate of the importance of man in the universe," he would neither have "discovered" the ideal law of progression nor have been concerned with the final reorganization of human society, the abolition of wars, and the religion of humanity. On the other hand, if he had penetrated to the core of the theological system, which is, after all, no system but an appeal and a message, he would not have stopped with the scientific method as the final solution and salvation.

3. CONDORCET AND TURGOT

Comte was a disciple of Condorcet who, among other studies, wrote a biography of Voltaire, the master and friend of Turgot. There is little in Comte's ideas that cannot be traced back to either Saint-Simon, Condorcet, or Turgot, for it is not by originality but by the completeness and persistency of his elaboration that Comte is superior to his predecessors. The principle of order and progress had already been formulated by Condorcet, and the law of the three stages by Saint-Simon and Turgot. All three were working out the decisive transformation of the theology of history into a philosophy of history as inaugurated by Voltaire.

The circumstances under which Condorcet in 1793 composed his *Outlines of an Historical View of the Progress of the Human Mind*[80] are extraordinary: he wrote this enthusiastic sketch down without the aid of a single book when he was an outlaw and a fugitive, shortly before he became a victim of the French Revolution which he had served so nobly. By his death he gave, to quote Comte, "one of the most decisive examples of a sublime and moving personal abnegation, combined with a quiet and unshakable firmness of character which the religious beliefs pretend that they alone can produce and sustain."

Condorcet's idea of progress is distinct from Comte's positive concept of development by what Comte himself called Condorcet's "chimerical and absurd expectations" concerning man's perfectibility; but it is the very extremeness of Condorcet's secular faith in progress and perfectibility which links him, more closely than Comte, to the Christian hope of becoming perfect; for the Christian faith, too, is by its very nature extreme and absolute. In men like Condorcet, Turgot, Saint-Simon, and Proudhon the eighteenth-century passion for reason and justice engendered a fervor which can indeed be called "religious," though it was irreligious.

The object of Condorcet's study is the development of the human faculties in the successive societies "to exhibit the order in which the changes have taken place." The natural goal of this orderly progress is the perfection of knowledge and, thereby, of happiness. Our contribution to the natural process of progression consists in securing and accelerating it. Reasoning and facts alike show that nature has fixed no limits to our improvement. "The perfectibility of man is absolutely indefinite" and "can never be retrogressive."[81] Its only limit is the duration of the earth and the constancy of the laws of the universe. Granted that the earth retains its position, permitting the human race to preserve and exercise therein the same faculties, we can formulate definite hopes as to our future progress in knowledge, virtue, and liberty. We can foresee how the blessings

must necessarily amalgamate and become inseparable, the moment knowledge shall have arrived at a certain pitch in a great number of nations at once, the moment it shall have penetrated the whole mass of a great people, whose language shall have become universal,[82] and whose commercial intercourse shall embrace the whole extent of the globe. This union having once taken place in the whole enlightened class of men, this class will be considered as the friends of human kind, exerting themselves in concert to advance the improvement and happiness of the species.[83]

By inference from the progress achieved in the past, one can now safely predict its future prospects by the art of foreseeing the future improvements of the human race.

If man can predict, almost with certainty, those appearances of which he understands the laws; if, even when the laws are unknown to him, experience of the past enables him to foresee, with considerable probability, future appearances; why should we suppose it a chimerical undertaking to delineate, with some degree of truth, the picture of the future destiny of mankind from the results of its history? The only foundation of faith in the natural sciences is the principle that the general laws, known or unknown, which regulate the phenomena of the universe, are regular and constant; and why should this principle, applicable to the other operations of nature, be less true when applied to the development of the intellectual and moral faculties of man? In short, as opinions formed from experience, relative to the same class of objects, are the only rule by which men of soundest understanding are governed in their conduct, why should the philosopher be proscribed from supporting his conjectures upon a similar basis, provided he attribute to them no greater certainty than the number, the consistency, and the accuracy of actual observations shall authorise?[84]

It is pure science, experiment, and calculation, "without a mixture of superstition, prejudice, and authority," which transform arbitrary prophecy into rational prognostication and which enable us to replace divine providence by human prevision. It is, in particular, the application of the arithmetic of combinations and probabilities to the social sciences which will enable us to determine with almost mathematical precision "the quantity of good and evil."[85] The improvement which we may expect will also affect our moral and physical faculties; and then will arrive "the moment in which the sun will observe in its course free nations only, acknowledging no other master than their reason; in which tyrants and slaves, priests and their ... instruments will no longer exist but in history and upon the stage."[86] Having definitely abolished religious superstition and political tyranny, the wants and faculties of men will continually become better proportioned amid the improvement of industry and happiness, of individual and general prosperity.

A smaller portion of ground will then be made to produce a portion of provisions of higher value or greater utility; a greater quantity of enjoyment will be procured at a smaller expense of consumption; the same manufactured or artificial commodity will be produced at a smaller expense of raw materials, or will be stronger and more durable; every soil will be appropriated to productions which will satisfy a greater number of wants with the least labour, and taken in the smallest quantities. Thus the means of health and frugality will be increased, together with the instruments in the arts of production, of procuring commodities and manufacturing their produce, without demanding the sacrifice of one enjoyment by the consumer.[87]

Eventually, the perfectibility of the human race may also affect man's natural constitution and postpone, if not eliminate, death; for Condorcet does not doubt that the progress of the sanitive art, the use of more wholesome food and more comfortable habitations, must necessarily prolong the ordinary duration of man's existence. Thus it is not absurd

to suppose that a period must one day arrive when death will be nothing more than the effect either of extraordinary accidents, or of the slow and gradual decay of the vital powers; and that the duration of the middle space, of the interval between the birth of man and this decay, will itself have no assignable limit? Certainly man will not become immortal; but may not the distance between the moment in which he draws his first breath, and the common term when, in the course of nature, without malady, without accident, he finds it impossible any longer to exist, be necessarily protracted?[88]

This indefinite prolongation of human life is, to Condorcet, progress par excellence. It is an indefinite one in two senses: by being illimitable either in itself or for our experience. Knowing only that this progress can never stop, we are ignorant in which of the two senses the term "indefinite" is applicable, and this is precisely the state of the knowledge that we have so far acquired relative to the perfectibility of the species.

Lastly, man's moral and intellectual constitution, too, might progress in a natural way by cumulative inheritance; for why should not our parents, who transmit to us their advantages, defects, and propensities, transmit to us also that part of human organization upon which understanding, energy of soul, and moral sensibility depend? It is therefore probably that education, "by improving these qualities, will at the same time modify and improve this organization itself." And "one happy day" every nation, even Orientals (who, according to Condorcet, still live in a state of infancy), will arrive at the state of civilization now attained by the most enlightened and free nations: the French and the Anglo-Americans, who will restore freedom to Africa and Asia.[89] It is true that even those most enlightened nations have not yet arrived at the highest point of improvement and that "the accurate solution of the first principles of metaphysics, morals, and politics" is still recent, so that many questions remain to be solved before we can ascertain "the precise catalogue of the individual rights of man"; but great wars of conquest and revolutions have already become "almost impossible" and the use of firearms makes warfare much less murderous.[90]

Condorcet frankly admits the disconcerting fact that a period of most important advances through scientific inventions, e.g., of compass and firearms, was also a period of atrocious massacres. But he does not draw from it any conclusion which could have disturbed his rational optimism concerning the natural goodness of man, "the necessary consequence of his organization."[91] He only states that the discovery of the new world was tainted by a degrading "prejudice" against non-Christian natives, leading to the extinction of five million human beings by Christian nations and to the enslavement of other millions by treason and robbery, first dragging them from one hemisphere to another, then purchasing and selling them like commodities. The only inference which he draws from this coincidence of progress and crime is that the latter, committed by Christians, disproves the popular doctrine of the political utility of religions.[92]

Condorcet's hopes for the future perfection of men were not the result of scientific inference and evidence but a conjecture, the root of which was hope and faith. Even such a sympathetic study of Condorcet as that of John Morley[93] cannot but admit that there is nothing scientific, precise, and quantified in Condorcet's speculations about man's future progress. It took, however, only a few generations among the most enlightened nations to realize the hopelessness of all scientific progress toward a civilized barbarism.[94] In the midst of frantic progress by means of scientific inventions in the middle of the nineteenth century, a mood of aimlessness and despair cast its first shadow upon Europe's most advanced minds; for the very progress seemed to proceed toward nothingness. In France this nihilism found its most sophisticated expression in the writings of Flaubert and Baudelaire. Having exposed, in the *Temptation of St. Anthony,* all sorts of current beliefs and superstitions, Flaubert set about to disentangle and analyze the chaos of our modern, scientific culture. He made a list of human follies, intended as an ironical glorification of all that had passed for truth. The result of these absurd studies was the novel *Bouvard et Pécuchet*—the story of two Philistines, sincerely striving for their higher education; good-natured men of sense, who had been office clerks. In their happily acquired country seat they ramble through the entire maze of piled-up knowledge, from horticulture, chemistry, and medicine to history, archeology, politics, pedagogy, and philosophy—only to return to their copying, now making extracts from the books which they had perused in vain. The whole work leads to the conclusion that our entire scientific education is inane. Doctrines of age-long standing are expounded and developed in a few lines, then they are disposed of by other doctrines which are arraigned against them and then destroyed in turn with equal precision and passion. Page after page, line after line, some new kind of knowledge turns up; but at once another appears to knock the first one down, and then it, too, topples over, hit by a third. At the end of the unfinished sketch, Pécuchet draws a gloomy picture, Bouvard a rosy one, of the future of European mankind. According to the one, the end of the debased human race, sunk into general depravity, approaches. There are three alternative possibilities: (1) radicalism severs every tie with the past, entailing inhuman despotism; (2) if theistic absolutism is victorious, liberalism, with which mankind has been imbued since the French Revolution, will perish, and a revolutionary change will take place; (3) if the convulsions of 1789 continue, their waves will carry us away, and there will no longer be ideals or religion or morality: "America will conquer the world." According to the second picture, Europe will be rejuvenated with the aid of Asia, and there will develop undreamed-of techniques of communication, U-boats, and balloons; new sciences will be born, enabling man to place the powers of the universe at the service of civilization and, when the earth is exhausted, to emigrate to other stars. Together with human wants, evil will cease, and philosophy will become religion.

Baudelaire's intention to compose "The End of the World" dates from the same period. Some fragments of it, entitled *Fusées,* appeared in 1851:

The world is drawing to a close. Only for one reason can it last longer: just because it happens to exist. But how weak a reason is this compared with all that forebodes the contrary, particularly with the question: What is left to the world of man in the future? Supposing it should continue materially, would that be an existence worthy of its name and of the historical dictionary? I do not say the world would fall back into a spectral condition and the odd disorder of South American republics; nor do I say that we should return to primitive savagery and, with a rifle in our arms, hunt for food through the grass-covered ruins of our civilization. No, such adventures would still call for a certain vital energy, an echo from primordial times. We shall furnish a new example of the inexorability of the spiritual and moral laws and shall be their new victims: *we shall perish by the very thing by which we fancy that we live.* Technocracy will Americanize us, progress will starve our spirituality so far that nothing of the bloodthirsty, frivolous or unnatural dreams of the utopist will be comparable to those positive facts. I invite any thinking person to show me what is left of life. Religion! It is useless to talk about it, or to look for its remnants; it is a scandal that one takes the trouble even of denying God. Private property! It was—strictly speaking—abolished with the suppression of the right of primogeniture; yet the time will come when mankind like a revengeful cannibal will snatch the last piece from those who rightfully deemed themselves the heirs of revolutions. And even this will not be the worst. . . . Universal ruin will manifest itself not solely or particularly in political institutions or general progress or whatever else might be a proper name for it; it will be seen, above all, in the baseness of hearts. Shall I add that that little left-over of sociability will hardly resist the sweeping brutality, and that the rulers, in order to hold their own and to produce a sham order, will ruthlessly resort to measures which will make us, who already are callous, shudder?

Again, a few decades later, Burckhardt in Switzerland, Nietzsche in Germany, Dostoevski and Tolstoy in Russia, prophesied, instead of future progress, the decline of Western civilization. Arguing in his *Diary of a Writer* against the Russian enthusiasts for Western achievements, Dostoevski says that it is absurd to advise the Russians to catch up with Western progress in view of the imminent and terrible collapse of Western civilization. "The European ant-hill built up without a church and without Christianity—for everywhere in Europe the church has lost her ideal— this ant-hill on a rotten foundation, lacking every universal and absolute, is completely undermined."[95] What good will it do to take over from Europe institutions which will break down there tomorrow, institutions in which the most intelligent Europeans themselves no longer believe, while they are being slavishly copied by Russians as though the comedy of the bourgeois order were the normal form of human society?

Tolstoy, instead of believing that the Western nations would redeem the non-European peoples, judged that Europe not only is going to destroy herself but is also going to corrupt India, Africa, China, and Japan by spreading and enforcing her progressive civilization.

> The medieval theology, or the Roman corruption of morals, poisoned only their own people, a small part of mankind; today, electricity, railways and telegraphs spoil the whole world. Everyone makes these things his own. He simply cannot help making them his own. Everyone suffers in the same way, is forced to the same extent to change his way of life. All are under the necessity of betraying what is most important for their lives, the understanding of life itself, religion. Machines—to produce what? The telegraph—to despatch what? Books, papers—to spread what kind of news? Railways—to go to whom and to what place? Millions of people herded together and subject to a supreme power—to accomplish what? Hospitals, physicians, dispensaries in order to prolong life—for what? How easily do individuals as well as whole nations take their own so-called civilization as the true civilization: finishing one's studies, keeping one's nails clean, using the tailor's and the barber's services, travelling abroad, and the most civilized man is complete. And with regard to nations: as many railways as possible, academies, industrial works, battleships, forts, newspapers, books, parties, parliaments. Thus the most civilized nation is complete. Enough individuals, therefore, as well as nations can be interested in civilization but not in true enlightenment. The former is easy and meets with approval; the latter requires rigorous efforts and therefore, from the great majority, always meets with nothing but contempt and hatred, for it exposes the lie of civilization.[96]

Instead of the irreligion of progress Tolstoy resolved to restore the religion of Christ, which, in its early days, was no less confronted with spiritual disintegration and material progress than it is nowadays.

The chasm which separates us from the rational optimism, or at least meliorism, of Comte and Condorcet could hardly be deeper. But the radical change which occurred during the last hundred years does not consist in a cessation of progressive inventions but in the fact that our material progress fulfils and even surpasses all former expectations, without warranting any longer the hopes which were originally based on it. For Comte even death was an element of progress; we are now scared to death at the prospect that our latest progress in mastering nature might become used by us.

To return to the eighteenth-century from this excursion into the nineteenth, in accordance with our regressive scheme, we have now to consider a man who at the age of twenty-three years, composed a fragmentary view of history of which Toynbee[97] says that it has made a greater permanent contribution to the understanding of history than Acton succeeded in making by devoting a long and laborious life to historical industry.

Turgot's general view of history is found in what remained a brilliant sketch based on two discourses of 1750 on universal history. The leading theme of both lectures is the advancement of the human race and mind, with particular reference to the contribution which Christianity has made to progress.[98] The course of history is directed by the simple and single principle of a one-dimensional progression, though interrupted by periods of temporary decay. At first, man lived in a natural state until Christianity and then philosophy taught him universal brotherhood. Seen from this broad viewpoint, the progress of history toward perfection is "the most glorious spectacle," revealing a presiding wisdom.

We see the establishment of societies and the formation of nations which one after the other dominate other nations or obey them. Empires rise and fall; the laws and forms of government succeed one another; the arts and sciences are discovered and made more perfect. Sometimes arrested, sometimes accelerated in their progress, they pass through different climates. Interest, ambition, and vain glory perpetually change the scene of the world, inundating the earth with blood. But in the midst of these ravages man's mores become sweeter, the human mind becomes enlightened, and the isolated nations come closer to each other. Commerce and politics reunite finally all the parts of the globe and the whole mass of the humankind, alternating between calm and agitation, good and bad, marches constantly, though slowly, toward greater perfection.[99]

In initiating this process toward perfection, Christianity has had an important function. To prove its superiority, Turgot compares it with pagan irreligion or idolatry, which deified animals, human passions, and even vices, whereas Christianity is the "natural religion," spreading charity and gentleness. That those principles have been increasingly effective in the midst of man's tumultuous passions; that they have mitigated his rages, tempered his actions, and moderated the fall of states by having made man better and happier; that Christianity has brought about all these "advantages" (i.e., to secular culture) seems to Turgot a well-established and indisputable fact. It is, however, obvious that these "facts" are interpretations, or rather misinterpretations, determined by an ideal terminal "at which one has to arrive."[100] This secular terminal or *eschaton* is a religious respect for personal liberty and labor; inviolability of the right of property; equal justice for everyone; multiplication of the means of subsistence; increase of riches; and augmentation of enjoyments, enlightenment, and all means to happiness. Who does not recognize in these once so novel standards of Turgot, Condorcet, and Comte the traditional values of the American citizen, at least up to the depression of the thirties? It took two hundred years for the faith in increase, augmentation, and multiplication to become as doubtful as the popular identification of bigger with better.

Unlike Burckhardt's laconic statement that history deals with man "as he is, was, and ever shall be," Turgot, projecting his hopes into the facts and his wishes into his thoughts, sees everywhere a change for the better. He says:

In the ancient republics liberty was founded less on the sentiment of man's natural nobility of heart than on an equilibrium between ambition and power among particular individuals. The love of one's country was less the love of one's fellow citizens than the common hatred of strangers. Hence, the barbarities which the ancients committed against their slaves, and those horrible cruelties in the wars of Greek and Romans, and that barbaric inequality between the sexes. . . . Finally: everywhere the strongest have made the laws, and oppressed the weak ones.[101]

101

To recall the natural rights of man, a principle was needed which could elevate man to a viewpoint from which all nations appear equal as if seen through the eyes of God; and this is what the Christian religion has achieved by a general revolution of the minds. Christianity has assuaged even the horrors of war. "Thanks to it the terrible consequences of victory have ceased; cities reduced to ashes, whole nations handed over to the glaive of the victors, the prisoners and wounded massacred coldbloodedly or preserved for the shame of triumph, without regard even to royalty: all these barbarities of the public law of the ancients are unknown among us; the victors and the vanquished now receive the same aid in the same hospitals."[102] Superseding pagan antiquity, Christianity alone has also salvaged and preserved the achievements of classical education.

Though Turgot has never asked himself whether the Christian religion or, rather, the faith in Christ can be defended at all by pointing out its worldly "advantages" for secular happiness, he had a better understanding of it than did Condorcet, to whom religion generally (with the exception of Mohammedanism) was nothing but an irrational superstition. Turgot understood that historical movements are not a simple one-dimensional progression but an intricate system of passionate intentions and unexpected results. True, he did not explain them by a hidden working of providence; and, when he uses this word, it no longer conveys what it meant to Bossuet, but only "the leading-strings" by which "nature and its author" are guiding the human race.[103] But, even while replacing the supernatural will of providence with the natural law of progress, he still could see the ways of history more adequately than did his successors. Instead of subjecting the actions of men and their unpredictable outcome to a natural law of a gradual and constant development, Turgot's general view of history starts with man's ambitions, which, in creating and shaping historical movements, contribute willy-nilly to "the vistas of providence and the progress of enlightenment."

Man's passions, even their furies, have led them, without their knowing where they were going. I think I see an immense army whose movements are all directed by a mighty genius. At the sight of the military signals, at the tumultuous noise of trumpets and drums, whole squadrons deploy, even the horses are full of a fire which has no purpose, each group marches on across the obstacles without knowing the issue, only the chief perceives the effect of so many combined movements: the same way the blind passions have multiplied ideas, enlarged knowledge, and made minds more perfect, owing to the lack of a reason whose day had not yet arrived and which would have been less powerful if it had governed earlier.[104]

This distinction between the visible agencies and the hidden designs of the historical process goes back to the theological discrimination between the will of God and the will of man; and this discrimination is the basis of the two-dimensional structure of sacred and profane history on which all theological understanding of history depends. The philosophy of history of the Enlightenment, far from having enlarged the theological pattern, has narrowed it down by secularizing divine providence into human prevision and progress. But, as Turgot shows, even if history is understood merely on the human level and on the pattern of Voltaire, through a rational analysis of the general and particular causes which demonstrates "the sources and the mechanism of the moral causes and their effects,"[105] the theological scheme still remains visible as long as history is not completely simplified to a plain and intelligible progression of successive stages and events.

V

VOLTAIRE

THE crisis in the history of European consciousness,[1] when providence was replaced by progress, occurred at the end of the seventeenth and the beginning of the eighteenth centuries. It is marked by the transition from Bossuet's *Discourse on Universal History* (1681), which is the last theology of history on the pattern of Augustine, to Voltaire's *Essay on the Manners and Mind of Nations* (1756), which is the first "philosophy of history," a term invented by Voltaire. The inauguration of the philosophy of history was an emancipation from the theological interpretation and antireligious in principle.

Immediately after the death of Charles VI of Austria in 1740, Frederick the Great wrote to Voltaire: "The emperor is dead. His death alters all my pacific ideas, and I think that in June it will be rather a matter of cannon powder, soldiers and trenches than of actresses, of balls and stages.... Now is the moment for a complete change in the old political system; it is that falling rock striking the idol of four metals seen by Nebuchadnezzar which destroyed them all."[2] In Nebuchadnezzar's dream, as interpreted by Daniel, the falling rock that destroys the four empires is the Kingdom of God, which grows into a mountain covering the whole earth. To Frederick, who thought of the Christian doctrine as mere "fables, canonized by antiquity and the credulity of absurd people,"[3] the falling rock was he himself, destroying the Holy Roman Empire, that is, the Hapsburg monarchy of his time. On the intellectual plane he was assisted by his friend Voltaire, who attempted to destroy the old religious system and, in particular, the Christian interpretation of history. Both were conscious of promoting a great revolution by undermining the political edifice and "the ancient palace of imposture" ("founded one thousand seven hundred and seventy five years ago") at their very foundations.[4] "The axe is laid to the root of the tree ... and the nations will write in their annals that Voltaire was the promoter of that revolution in the human mind which took place in the nineteenth century."[5] Already "the magician's conjuring book is joked about; the author of the sect is bespattered; tolerance is preached; all is lost. It will take a miracle to restore the church. ... The Englishman Woolstone calculated that the *infamous* would last two hundred years; he could not calculate what has happened quite recently; the question is to destroy the prejudice which serves as foundation to this edifice. It is crumbling of itself, and its fall will be but the more rapid."[6]

When Voltaire wrote his *Essay on the Manners and Mind of Nations, and on the Principal Facts of History from Charlemagne to Louis XIII,* Bossuet's *Discourse on Universal History* was constantly in his mind. This work is a restatement of Augustine's theology of history brought up to date. It begins with the creation of the world, and it ends with Charlemagne. Voltaire took it up at that point and continued it to Louis XIII, having already published a book on the age of Louis XIV. Though at first intended as a continuation of Bossuet's work, it actually became a refutation of the traditional view of history, in principle as well as in method and content.

Voltaire began his essay with China, and Hegel followed him in this. China had just risen upon the horizon of the Christian Occident through the reports of French missionaries, who were deeply impressed by the antiquity and excellence of Chinese culture and of Confucian morals. The question arose of whether Christianity should accommodate itself to the Chinese religion. Many of the learned Jesuits who had been in China were in favor of it, but the church decided against it. Voltaire, from a secular viewpoint, supported the conviction of his Jesuit friends against the church. With this discovery of China, the old *orbis terrarum* of classical antiquity and Christianity became the object of an incisive comparison. For the first time the standards of Europe were measured by the achievements of a non-Christian civilization, and Europe had to learn to see herself from the outside. Hence the problem arose of how to reconcile the traditional unity and the focus of Christian history in the history of the chosen people with the new knowledge of the Far East. A particular difficulty was to harmonize the historical chronology of the Bible with the nonbiblical, astronomical chronology as elaborated by the Chinese. It reminds one of the difficulty which the early Christian writers experienced in harmonizing Jewish and Roman chronologies. But now it was exactly the mathematical preciseness of the Cartesian Jesuits which brought about uncertainty—even for Bossuet, who could not help spoiling his chronological edifice by supplementing each date with a second one in parentheses which differed from the first by no less than 959 years.[7]

Voltaire's first chapter on China was of fundamental significance, since he wished to challenge the biblical tradition as recorded in the Old Testament. His own justification for this unusual beginning was his concern with "civilization" as against barbarism. Chinese history, in his view, is not only older but also much more civilized than the histories related in the Old Testament. He underlines the superiority of Chinese history over the much less significant, but immensely presumptuous and "abominable," history of the Jews.

In following the historical fate of the petty Jewish nation, it is seen that no other end was possible for it. It prided itself on having issued from Egypt like a horde of robbers, carrying off all that it had borrowed from the Egyptians; it was its glory never to have spared age or sex in the towns which it had captured. It dared to manifest an irreconcilable hatred for all other nations; it revolted against all its masters; always superstitious, always barbarous, abject in misfortune, and insolent in prosperity. Such were the Jews in the eyes of the Greeks and Romans, who could read their books; but in the eyes of Christians enlightened by faith, they have been our precursors, they have prepared the way for us, they have acted as the heralds of Providence.[8]

"With the Jews," he sums up, "almost all events of purely human character are horrible to the utmost; everything which is divine in their history is beyond our poor comprehension. The one, like the other, reduces us to silence."[9] The history of the Chinese, on the other hand, is free from absurd fables, miracles, and prophecies. Confucius, whose picture Voltaire had in his bedroom ("Sancte Confuci ora pro nobis"), was to him far superior to a prophet, being a veritable sage.

After having dealt with the civilized humanity of the Chinese, Voltaire proceeds to deal with India, Persia, and Arabia and, in due time, with Rome and the rise of Christianity. In all these interesting and amusing, but also well-documented, descriptions, he speaks expressly as "philosopher" and "historian,"[10] that is, not as a believer in things divine but as a man who knows what is human. Consequently, he separates, time and again, sacred from secular history,[11] which were, for Bossuet, correlated by the unity of a divine purpose. And not only does Voltaire discriminate what we can know by reason from the belief in revelation; but he also attacks the biblical accounts with historical criticism.[12]

His method is rather simple; he collects as many significant cultural facts as possible and interprets them by the standard of common human reason. Civilization means to him the progressive development of sciences and skills, morals and laws, commerce and industry. The two great obstacles to this progress are dogmatic religions and wars—the main topics in Bossuet's theology of political history. The enormous success of Voltaire's essay is due mainly to the fact that it provided the rising bourgeoisie with a historical justification of its own ideals by suggesting that all history was leading up to the eighteenth century. In Voltaire's essay God has retired from the rule of history; he may still reign, but he does not govern by intervention.[13] The purpose and meaning of history are to improve by our own reason the condition of man, to make him less ignorant, "better and happier."[14]

No less than by the discovery of China is Voltaire's outlook conditioned by the revolution in the physical sciences, in which he took a great interest.[15] In its moral consequences the effect of this revolution was as if a man who dreamed that he lived in civilized Paris awoke to discover that Paris was a small and obscure island in the Pacific Ocean. The earth became small and, at the same time, the only real dwelling place of our race. The central importance of the human race was shown to be an illusion. The Christian scheme of creation consequently became less plausible. As J. Bury says, man had to invent a more modest theory of his meaning, confined to his little earth, and the eighteenth century answered his question by the theory of a laborious but gradual progress.

The classic essay on this radical change of perspective is Voltaire's *Le Micromégas,* i.e., literally, "The Little Great-One," a philosophical tale of the journey of an inhabitant of another star to the planet Saturn, where, incidentally, he picks up strange small animals. They call themselves "men" and are capable of speaking and curiously intelligent. They insist that they have a "soul." One of them, a Thomist, even maintains that the whole creation was made solely for man's benefit. At this speech the heavenly traveler chokes with inexstinguishable laughter.

In the philosophical tale *Candide* it is in particular the Christian view of a providential design and the teleological interpretation of history as presented by Leibniz (represented in the tale by Mr. Pangloss) which Voltaire subjects to his satirical criticism. Pangloss has proved that in this world everything is made for a certain purpose of man, and ultimately to the best purpose. "Observe how noses were made to carry spectacles, and spectacles we have accordingly. Our legs are clearly intended for shoes and stockings, so we have them. Stone has been formed to be hewn and dressed for building castles, so my lord has a very fine one. . . . Pigs were made to be eaten, and we eat pork all the year round." Upon the question as to whether he believes in original sin, Pangloss answers that the Fall of man and the consequent curse necessarily entered into the scheme of the best of all possible worlds. "Then, sir, you do not believe in free will?" "Excuse me," said Pangloss (and he could have referred to Augustine), "free will is compatible with absolute necessity for it was necessary that we should be free. . . ." To another co-traveler, however, who has seen so many extraordinary things that nothing seemed extraordinary to him, the purpose for which the world was created is "to drive us wild." Toward the end of his adventures Pangloss happens to meet six foreigners at a supper in Venice during a carnival masquerade. They are well-known kings, now dethroned, who, by relating their personal destinies, demonstrate the aimlessness and wretchedness of human history. After having gone through many disasters, Candide and his philosophical friends settle down on a little farm near Constantinople, sometimes still continuing their disputes on moral and metaphysical philosophy. Once they consult a celebrated dervish, the best philosopher in Turkey. "Master, we are come to beg that you will tell us why such a strange animal as man has been created." "Why should you meddle with the matter?" the dervish asked; "what business is it of yours?" "But, reverend father," said Candide, "there is a dreadful amount of evil in the world." "What does it signify," replied the dervish, "whether there be evil or good? When His Highness sends a ship to Egypt, does he concern himself whether the mice on board are comfortable or not?" Yet eventually Candide discovers the purpose of his existence. It is civilization or culture in the most primitive and literal sense: he has simply to cultivate his garden as Adam and Eve did in the Garden of Eden. "That is the only way of rendering life tolerable." All the little company enters into his praiseworthy resolution, each busily exerting his or her peculiar talents in their small houses and orchards. In his last conversation with Candide, Pangloss still holds to his theodicy: "For, look you, if you had not been driven out of a magnificent castle by hearty kicks upon your hinder parts for presuming to make love to Miss Cunegund, if you had not been put into the Inquisition, if you had not roamed over America on foot, if you had never run your sword through the Baron, or lost all your sheep from the fine country of El Dorado, you would not be here now eating candied citrons and pistachio-nuts." "Well said!" answered Candide; "but we must attend to our garden."

In the background of this brilliant tale, which so forcefully opposes the justification of God in this world's history,[16] was the experience of the great earthquake of Lisbon in 1755. This visitation produced a profound impression throughout Europe[17] and stimulated the revision of the contemporary rationalistic interpretation of providence. We are now used to much more comprehensive destructions, brought about not by nature but by our own will. One may wonder if the purposeful extinction of some hundred great cities has produced any similar impulse to reconsider the traditional phrase of God's working out his purpose in history with the "co-operation" of man. It seems that nowadays even professional theologians get along without any theodicy[18]— unless they venture to assert that providence has managed to give the atomic bomb, and the bigger industries, into the hands of the peace-loving nations.

Two points were in Voltaire's mind when he wrote his essay against Bossuet: first, that Bossuet's universal history is not universal[19] and, second, that providence is not evident in the empirical course of history.

He pointed out that Bossuet's history relates only to four empires of antiquity, representing them primarily in their relation to the Jews, as if the destiny of the Jews were the center of interest and meaning.

What I admire the most in the work of our modern compilers is the wisdom of good faith with which they prove that all that happened once in the greatest empires of the world happened only for the instruction of the inhabitants of Palestine. If the kings of Babylon in their conquests fall incidentally upon the Hebrews, it is only to chastise these people for their sins. If a king named Cyrus becomes the master of Babylon, it is in order to allow a few Jews to go home. If Alexander is victorious over Darius, it is in order to establish some Jewish secondhand dealers in Alexandria. When the Romans annex Syria and the small district of Judea to their vast empire, it is again for the instruction of the Jews. Arabs and Turks come in only to correct these likable people. We must admit that they have had an excellent education: nobody has ever had so many teachers. This shows how purposeful history is.[20]

"We," says Voltaire, "will speak of the Jews as we would speak of Scythians or Greeks."

Persuasive as this reduction of sacred history to its profane aspect may be, it does not result in a more complete universality; for history does not become universal by surveying, instead of the four civilizations of Bossuet, a score or twenty-one. It only becomes general. A glance at the Table of Contents in Voltaire's *Essay* shows that its universal aspect rests on material comprehensiveness without a center of meaning and organization. What unites his interesting observations is only chronological succession and the idea of progress as a hypothetical principle. A universal history directed toward one single end and unifying, at least potentially, the whole course of events was not created by Voltaire but by Jewish messianism and Christian eschatology, on the basis of an exclusive monotheism. Once this belief had been adopted generally and had prevailed for centuries, man could discard the doctrine of providence, along with that of creation, judgment, and salvation, but he would not return to such views as had satisfied the ancients. Man will seek to replace providence, but within the established horizon, by secularizing the Christian hope of salvation into an indefinite hope of improvement and faith in God's providence into the belief in man's capacity to provide for his own earthly happiness.

Voltaire was much too intelligent to overwork the idea of progress. He believed in a moderate progress, interrupted by periods of regression and subject to chance inasmuch as reason does not prevail. This sobriety of judgment distinguishes him from Condorcet's enthusiastic expectations, and it separates him from the Christian hope in a final perfection. Nevertheless, it is not by chance that the religion of progress did not emerge and develop in antiquity, with its veneration for the past and the ever present.[21] It is Jewish-Christian futurism which opened the future as the dynamic horizon of all modern striving and thinking. Within a cyclic Weltanschauung and order of the universe, where every movement of advance is, at the same time, a movement of return, there is no place for progress. But even the modern unbeliever still lives, like Christian in *Pilgrim's Progress,* by hope and expectation. And even those who attack the idea of progress as a bourgeois illusion hold that they are more progressive than their opponents. Both believe in a better world in the future. The whole significance of progress depends on "looking forward." If some astronomer were to convince us that our planet would become uninhabitable in 2048, our progressiveness would lose its meaning; for why should we busy ourselves with producing better cars and better homes and better food and better health if time is running out and all betterment comes to the worst? But, even granted that the idea of progress is ultimately derived from Christian hope and expectation, one still has to ask: How could Christianity produce such anti-Christian consequences? Is it progressive in itself and therefore capable of producing secular progress as its natural child?

The question of whether Christianity is or is not "progressive" can be answered only if we distinguish between the modern *religion of progress,* the *progress of religion,* and *religious progress.*[22] To begin with the last, there can be no doubt that the Gospels live by the confidence in personal religious advance toward judgment and salvation but not by a belief in secular progress, though progress must have been quite impressive under Augustus and his successors. What the Gospels proclaim is never future improvements in our earthly condition but the sudden coming of the Kingdom of God in contradistinction to the existing kingdom of man. The inward preparation, not the least through repentance, for judgment and salvation is the only true "religious education," the progressiveness of which is to be measured by the earnestness and single-mindedness of this spiritual preparation. Salvation is not to be reached by a gradual development of our natural faculties but through a decisive conversion, converting the sinful nature of man. Hence, St. Paul's admonition to "press forward" has nothing to do with modern activism and futurism; he is concerned with a transcendent transformation and consummation which will happen in a future, still distant but at any time imminent. Christianity, far from having opened the horizon of an *indefinite* future like the religion of progress, has made the future paramount by making it *definite,* and it has thereby immensely accentuated and deepened the earnestness of the present instant. In this faithful expectation of a definite future glory and judgment is implied the assumption, not that history is indefinitely progressing, either by natural law or by man's continuous efforts, but that history has virtually reached its end. Christian progress from the old Adam to a new creature is certainly a momentous progress, yet it is entirely independent of historical changes in man's social and political, cultural and economic, conditions. The "pilgrim's progress" is essentially the same for St. Paul, St. Francis, and Bunyan. Christianity has made no progress for the very reason that a Christian's progress consists in a progressive imitation of Christ, who did not care for worldly improvements. His divine perfection cannot be surpassed by human imitators.[23]

Another thing is the progress of religion in general. There is no historical religion which does not necessarily share in the process of history—a process both progressive and retrograde when measured by certain standards. But it would be very naïve to think, for example, of the Christian religion as having continually advanced from "primitive" Christianity through the church of the Middle Ages to the Reformation, to find its perfection in the most recent forms of liberal Protestantism and neo-orthodoxy. The changes of a historical world religion cannot but conform to the changes of general world conditions, but all religious reformations try to re-form the original, primitive message under new conditions. This is possible because the religious progress of an individual soul is incommensurate with the general progress and decay of religions.

Again another thing is the modern religion of progress which is an irreligion; for it is a belief in man's perfectibility, apart from the religious faith in Him who alone is perfect. The standards by which secular progress is measured may be as variable and different as man's secular aims, but they are decidedly worldly and immanent. The crux of the modern religion of progress is not, as has been suggested, that it forgot the spiritual "center" of its secular "applications" but that it applied an idea of progress which is antireligious and anti-Christian both by implication and by consequence. It is the weakness of modern Christianity that it is so very modern and so little Christian that it fully accepts the language, the methods, and the results of our worldly improvements in the illusion that all these inventions are but neutral means which can easily be christened by moral, if not religious, ends. In reality, they are the result of extreme worldliness and self-confidence. And yet the irreligion of progress is still a sort of religion, derived from the Christian faith in a future goal, though substituting an indefinite and immanent *eschaton* for a definite and transcendent one.

VI

VICO

THE great crisis in the history of our understanding of history which occurred between Voltaire and Bossuet has no greater and more significant representative than the Italian, Giambattista Vico (1668–1744), a man as poor and modest in his private life as he was rich and proud as the author of a New Science.[1] It is a system in fragments, an immense project of comparative universal history in which each part begins anew with the principles of the whole. It is, therefore, often repetitious and obscure, but it has that kind of obscurity which derives from the passionate search and re-search of a genius.

The *New Science* appeared in its first edition in 1725 and in its complete form in 1730 and was again revised in 1744, four years before Montesquieu's *L'Esprit des lois,* ten years before Voltaire's *Essay,* a hundred years before Schelling's *Philosophy of Mythology and Revelation,* and almost two centuries before it was rediscovered and recognized as the most original advance toward a philosophy of history. It is the fruit of a lifelong search into the depth of historic humanity. It anticipates not only fundamental ideas of Herder and Hegel, Dilthey and Spengler, but also the more particular discoveries of Roman history by Niebuhr and Mommsen, the theory of Homer by Wolf, the interpretation of mythology by Bachofen, the reconstruction of ancient life through etymology by Grimm, the historical understanding of laws by Savigny, of the ancient city and of feudalism by Fustel de Coulanges, and of the class struggles by Marx and Sorel.[2]

In his own day Vico was scarcely known. He was too far ahead of his time to have immediate influence. The intelligent verdict of a royal censor was that the *New Science* is a work "marking a most unfortunate crisis in European history."[3] Vico, a loyal

Catholic, was himself hardly aware of the revolutionary character of his *New Science;* and the final statement of his work—
that one cannot have science or wisdom without piety—was certainly no concession to the church (as modern interpreters want
to have it) but pure sincerity. When he published his work in
Naples, it was anything but a best seller. In a letter to a friend he
wrote: "In publishing my work in this city I seem to have
launched it upon a desert. I avoid all public places, so as not to
meet the persons to whom I have sent it, and if by chance I do
meet them, I greet them without stopping; for when this happens, these people give me not the faintest sign that they have received my book, and so confirm my impression of having
published it in a wilderness." And yet he knew that he had
accomplished something lasting and new when he had wrestled
with the riddle of history, like Jacob with God, and strained his
thigh. The result of this struggle was the first empirical construction of universal history—of religion, society, governments, legal
institutions, and languages—on the philosophical principle of an
eternal law of providential development which is neither progressive and redemptive nor simply cyclic and natural.

THE PRINCIPLES AND THE METHOD OF THE "NEW SCIENCE"

Toward the end of his book,[4] Vico makes the bold statement
that he could not refrain from giving his work the "invidious"
title of a *New Science,* "for it was too much to defraud it unjustly
of the rightful claim it had over an argument so universal as that
concerning the common nature of nations," which is the subtitle
of his "Principles of a New Science." What are these principles
and what is the new method of his science?

Discussing its "principal aspects,"[5] Vico gives the following
definitions: It is (1) "a rational civil theology of divine providence," that is, a demonstration of divine providence in social
history, including such civil matters as marriage, burial, laws,
forms of government, class struggles, etc. It is (2) "a philosophy
of authority," in particular of the origin of property, since the
original founders (*auctores*) of human society were also the

116

founders of property, laws, and traditions. It is (3) "a history of human ideas," in particular of man's oldest religious ideas about the heavens. It is (4) "a philosophical criticism" of the most ancient religious traditions, in particular of theogonies. It is (5) "an ideal eternal history traversed in time by the histories of all nations," that is, expounding the ever recurrent typical pattern of the process of civilization. It is (6) "a system of the natural law of nations," the naturalness of which is based on primitive necessity and utility. It is (7) a science of the most ancient and obscure beginnings or "principles" of "profane universal history" of the gentile world, interpreting the hidden truth of mythological fables. Altogether, the *New Science* is in all its aspects a rational theology of the *mondo civile,* the historic human world, emphasizing, throughout, the primitive, heroic, and imaginatively religious mentality which Vico regarded as the creative foundation of the more domesticated and sophisticated humanity of later ages.

To the reader of the twentieth century who is familiar with Hegel's philosophy of objective mind and with the more recent attempts at a "history of ideas" and "philosophy of culture," Vico's discovery of the *mondo civile* as the subject matter of a particular science may, like so many of his discoveries, seem rather trivial. It was not so at the beginning of the eighteenth century, when the only true "science" was the new science of nature, of mathematical physics. To measure the effort which it had cost him to establish history, in particular socioreligious history, as a science, one has only to remember that even a hundred years after him Comte still labored to found his "social physics" on the pattern of natural science and mathematics. The newness of Vico's science has to be judged by the established science of the Cartesians, the revolutionary newness of which was less than a hundred years old when Vico ventured to challenge and to reverse the *Principles* and the *Discourse on Method* of Descartes.[6]

In the first part of the *Discourse on Method* and again in the first *Meditation on the First Philosophy* Descartes narrates the story of his radical resolve to doubt everything which is not "certain," in order to find, by methodical doubt, absolute certainty and thereby scientific truth. No such truth can be found in common sense, jurisprudence, medicine, eloquence, the study of languages, the histories and fables of ancient writers and moralists, or revealed theology and philosophic opinions. All rest on traditional authority, on "example" and "custom," instead of on certain knowledge. Thus Descartes decided to pull down the whole edifice of splendid "superstructures" in order to commence anew the work of building from a firm foundation, though he realized that such a radical design was impracticable in the field of "public affairs," e.g., the reform of a state or of an established religion, where man has to rely on authority, custom, example, and tradition and, theoretically, on probability instead of certain truth. Historical sciences are, for Descartes, no sciences at all. The historian who pretends to know ancient Roman history knows less of it than did a cook at Rome, and to know Latin is to know no more than did Cicero's servant girl. All knowledge based on sensual experience has, therefore, to go overboard, for no absolute certainty can be found in the senses, which deceive us so often. The one tiny, but all-important, certainty which Descartes found by way of elimination is the formal certainty of the *cogito ergo sum,* with its innate ideas. From there the physical world can be reconstructed scientifically by means of mathematical ideas, the true "language" of nature.

Upon the model and by the standard of mathematical science and certainty, Descartes endeavored to reform philosophy and all the sciences. Vico, who came from jurisprudence to history and philosophy, questioned the very criterion of the Cartesian "truth," on the principle that real knowledge is a knowledge by causes, that is, we know intimately and thoroughly only that which we have caused or made. The true or *verum* is identical with the created or *factum.*[7] But has man ever made the natural world of the physical cosmos? Only God can have perfect knowledge of it because he created it. To us creatures, nature necessarily remains opaque. Descartes's certainty is related only to consciousness, not to knowledge, to a mere *cogitare* instead of a true *intelligere* or penetrating insight. For man, perfect, demonstrable knowledge is attainable only within the realm of mathematical fictions, where we, like God, are creating our objects. They are, however, abstractions that cannot provide a foundation for a concrete science of nature. But what about the "common nature of the nations," which is the main concern of Vico's science? Is it also opaque like physical nature, or is it transparent to our insight?

In answering this question, Vico adopts and at the same time reverses the methodical doubt of Descartes, by asserting that amid the "immense ocean of doubt" there is a "single tiny piece of earth" on which we can gain a firm footing.[8] This single piece of certain truth from which the *New Science* can and must proceed is that the conversion of *verum* and *factum* becomes a real possibility by the indubitable fact that the historical world has been created by man. We can know something about history, even the most obscure beginnings of history, because "in the night of thick darkness enveloping the earliest antiquity ... there shines the eternal and never-failing light of a truth beyond question: *that this world of civil society has certainly been made by men,* and that its principles can and must therefore be found *within the modifications of our own human mind.*"[9] The principles are not immediately given, but they can be found by an effort of constructive interpretation. Vico confesses that it had cost him twenty-five years of arduous meditation to break through the prejudices of modern intellectualism and recapture the precivilized mentality of Homeric and pre-Homeric humanity in its laws, customs, languages, and religions. Whoever reflects, he says, on this possibility of investigating ancient history through the modifications of our own human mind "cannot but marvel that the philosophers should have bent all their energies to the study of the world of nature which, since God made it, he alone knows; and that they should have neglected the study of the world of nations or civil world, which, since men had made it, men could hope to know."[10] The *New Science,* which is at

once a philosophy and a history of humanity, is possible because
the "nature" of man and nations is in itself a historical human
nature, not fixed by physical properties but becoming (by
natura = nascendo)[11] what it is by a historic law and development.

Our Science therefore comes to describe at the same time an ideal
eternal history traversed in time by the history of every nation in its rise,
progress, maturity, decline and fall. Indeed, we go so far as to assert that
whoever meditates this Science tells himself this ideal eternal history only
so far as he makes it by that proof "it had, has, and will have to be." For
the first indubitable principle above posited is that this world of nations
has certainly been made by men, and its guise must therefore be found
within the modifications of our own human mind. And history cannot
be more certain than when he who creates the things also describes them.
Thus our Science proceeds exactly as does geometry, which, while it con-
structs out of its elements or contemplates the world of quantity, itself
creates it; but with a reality greater in proportion to that of the orders
having to do with human affairs, in which there are neither points, lines,
surfaces, nor figures. And this very fact is an argument, O reader, that
these proofs are of a kind divine, and should give thee a divine pleasure;
since in God knowledge and creation are one and the same thing.[12]

It is this "conversion" of the true and the created, realized in
the understanding of history, which liberated Vico from the
starting-point of Descartes and led him toward the philosophical
truth of all those "philological" certainties which appear in the
human world of languages, customs, laws, and institutions. Ultimately, Vico neither restates the Cartesian ideal of geometric
certainty on the level of the knowledge of history nor renounces
scientific truth for the sake of *verosimilitas* or probable truth of
experience. What he is really striving for is to overcome the
whole Cartesian distinction between theoretical truth and sen-
suous practical probability by a dialectic of the true and the
certain which anticipates Hegel's "truth of certainty" (*Wahrheit
der Gewissheit*) in the first paragraphs of the *Phenomenology*.
He thereby elevates "philology," that is, external historic infor-
mation, treated by Descartes with such contempt, to the rank of a

philosophical science.[13] He established the primacy of the "philosophy of mind," as we have called it since Hegel, through the critical refutation of the primacy of modern natural science. Physical nature is only one half of reality, and the less significant half. Hence, the strange position of the globe on the allegorical picture with which Vico introduces the idea of his work. The picture shows in the upper left-hand corner the eye of God, allegorizing providence; on the right side a woman (metaphysics) contemplating God, while standing upon the celestial globe (the physical world), which is supported by an altar (symbol of the oldest sacrifices to heaven) on one side only; on the left side stands a statue of Homer (the theological poet), representing the oldest wisdom of the world. A ray of divine providence connects the eye of God with the heart of the lady metaphysics, and a second ray connects her with Homer. The Christian ray of providence is thus connected, through metaphysics, with Homer, i.e., with the civil world of the Gentiles, by-passing the physical world of nature. Vico's explanation points out that metaphysics contemplates God "above the order of natural things" through which hitherto the philosophers have contemplated him. She contemplates "in God the world of human minds" in order to show his providence in the world of human spirits, which is the civil world or the world of nations. The globe is supported on one side only by the altar, "for, until now, the philosophers, contemplating divine providence only through the natural order, have shown only a part of it.... The philosophers have not yet contemplated His providence in respect of that part of it which is most proper to men whose nature has the principal property: that of being social."[14]

The eminent place of providence in the allegorical picture, as well as in the whole of Vico's work, shows that the principle of *verum = factum* would be completely misunderstood if interpreted in the modern secular way, that is, as though Vico had intended to say that the civil world of man is nothing else than the product of his spontaneous creativity.[15] In the first, as well as in the second, *New Science,* after having established his principle, Vico hastens to add that the rediscovery of the origins of history, through our own mind and its power of consorting with its own past, establishes a philosophy of the human mind "in order to lead us to God as eternal providence."

The last section of the first book then deals explicitly with providence as the completion of the principles of the *New Science*. Providence is characteristically introduced as the "method" of the *New Science,* as the orderly, lawful way by which the historical world takes its form and course. There is, according to Vico, no civil world which has ever been established on atheism.[16] All civilizations, laws, and institutions, in particular the most primitive institutions of marriage, burial,[17] and agriculture, are founded on sacrifices and rituals, on some form of religion, whether it be the true or a false one, Christianity or heathenism. "Since all nations began with the cult of some divinity, in the family state the fathers must have been the sages in auspicial divinity, the priests who sacrificed to take the auspices or to make sure of their meaning, and the kings who brought the divine laws to their families."[18] Even the most savage and monstrous men do not lack religious sense and institutions, and the wildest superstition is morally superior to, and more creative than, barren atheism. Philosophy, too, cannot replace religion; and, if Polybius says that if the world had philosophers there would be no need of religion, he is badly mistaken, for there would be no philosophers without an established commonwealth which, in turn, cannot arise without religion.[19] The more man is overwhelmed by the power of nature, the more he desires something superior to "save him."[20] But something superior to man and nature is God, whose power is at first apprehended in and by fear,[21] which prompts man to seek protection by sacrifice and divination.

The chief attribute of all gods, however, is providence. "Divinity," according to Vico's etymology, is derived from "divination," the endeavor to provide and secure foresight of that which divine power has provided for man. The questioning of oracles and augury with respect to man's social and political undertakings is, therefore, one of the most ancient and important features of all primitive religions. Left to himself, man is under the tyranny of self-love, desiring only his selfish utility, which would destroy any social and historical existence and thereby human existence as such. It is only by divine providence that man can be held within the orders of family, society, state, and mankind. Out of the passions of men, each bent on his own advantage, out of ferocity, avarice, and ambition, providence or divine legislation creates the military, merchant, and governing classes; the strength, riches, and wisdom of commonwealths; and the natural law of nations. Providence turns man's natural vices, which would wipe all mankind from the face of the earth, into civil happiness, "for things do not settle or endure out of their natural order."[22] The so-called "natural" law is, from the outset, a civil law based on civil theology.

In spite of its supernatural origin, providence as conceived by Vico works, however, in such a "natural," "simple," and "easy" way[23] that it almost coincides with the social laws of the historic development itself. It works directly and exclusively by secondary causes, in the "economy of civil things," as it works, less transparently, in the physical order. "It develops its order as easily as the natural customs of men."[24] The *New Science* is, therefore, "a demonstration, so to speak, of the *historical fact of providence,* for it must be a history of the forms of order which, without human discernment or intent . . . , providence has given to this great city of the human race."[25] Once these orders were established by divine providence, the course of the affairs of the nations *"had to be, must now be, and will have to be"* such as the *New Science* demonstrates.[26]

In view of this statement, modern critics of Vico's notion of providence are indeed justified in saying that, with Vico, providence has become as natural, secular, and historical as if it did not exist at all.[27] For in Vico's "demonstration" of providence nothing remains of the transcendent and miraculous operation which characterizes the faith in providence from Augustine to Bossuet. With Vico it is reduced to an ultimate frame of reference, the content and substance of which are nothing else than the universal and permanent order of the historical course itself. Vico's God is so omnipotent that he can refrain from special interventions. He works completely in the natural course of history by its natural means: occasions, necessities, utilities. And for those who can read this natural language of factual historic providence in man's social history, history is, from its first to its last page, an open book of admirable design.

Established on the principle of civil theology, the *New Science* is therefore able to describe the "ideal eternal history" traversed in time by the history of every nation. Contemplating this typical pattern of history in all the extent of its places, times, and varieties, man experiences a "divine pleasure" and satisfaction, viz., the satisfaction of a divinely willed and provided necessity; for man's selfish will alone, without such help, is too weak and corrupted to turn anarchy into order and vices into blessings.

The emphasis on providence goes along with a polemic against the belief in fate and chance of Stoics and Epicureans,[28] both ancient (Zeno and Epicurus) and modern (Spinoza and Hobbes, as well as Machiavelli). Both Stoics and Epicureans deny providence because they are "monastic" or solitary thinkers, unaware of the providential economy of civil things. What distinguishes the belief in providence from that in fate or chance is that divine providence uses for the attainment of its universal ends the free, though corrupted, will of man. The doctrine of fate ignores the dialectic between providential necessity and the freedom of will, while the Epicurean doctrine of chance reduces freedom to mere capriciousness. The principles of providence and freedom are, however, equally true and important.[29] Yet it is obvious that in Vico's presentation they are not equally balanced. The mere fact that providence seems to him demonstrable implies that it directs with perfect necessity what seems to be occasioned by chance.[30]

THE DIALECTIC OF HISTORY

Decisive as Vico's theory of knowledge is for the foundation of the *New Science,* it must not be taken literally; for in its purely theoretical consequences the conversion of the true and the created would necessarily lead to the absolutely un-Vician conclusion that man is the god of history, creating his world by his free activity and therefore spontaneously knowing what he has made, now makes, and will make. Croce, for whom history is a "story of liberty" but not of providence, interprets Vico in this sense and is therefore compelled to eliminate Vico's thought of providence as much as possible from his allegedly "real tendencies." According to Croce's interpretation, human knowledge of human affairs is, indeed, qualitatively identical with divine knowledge; for man creates the historical world by his free actions, and, by thinking it, he re-creates his own creation and thus knows it fully. "Here is a real world; and of this world man is truly the god."[31] Croce understands the coincidence between the *verum* and the *factum* not on the basis of Vico's belief in providence but on the basis of the Hegelian dialectic of subject and object and of that of the particular and the universal subject. The particular individual who freely makes history is supposed to be a rational and universal individual, i.e., a "concrete universal." On this presupposition, providence is as superfluous and disturbing as are chance and fate, for all separate the creative individual from his product by working behind his back. Instead of eliminating the capricious element in history, says Croce, fate, chance, and providence alike reinforce it. But, since the Christian view that history is the work of God has this superiority over the ancient doctrine of chance and fate that it assumes a free creative activity as the ultimate source of the historical process, it is natural that "out of gratitude to this higher view ... we should be led to give to the rationality of history the name of God ... and to call it the divine providence."[32] Understood in this way, providence has the double value as a "criticism of individual illusions" (as if individual interests were the entire reality of history) and as a "criticism of divine transcendence." All minds gifted with the historic sense must adopt this viewpoint, Croce thinks, and must answer the problem of history in and by history itself, without recourse to fate and chance or God and providence. But it is obvious that this was not the viewpoint of Vico, who saw the course of history much more adequately, namely, as a world made by men and, at the same time, everywhere surpassed by something which is closer to fate than to free choice and action. History is not only deed and action but also and even primarily event and happening. It is not single minded but double minded.

Vico's description of this dialectic of history is most impressive and agrees much better than does Croce's philosophical liberalism with mankind's common experience and an unprejudiced sense of historical happenings. Vico makes his point clear from the outset, when he explains the allegorical picture and distinguishes between nature and history. Metaphysics contemplates the civil world of human minds "in God," that is, in the light of providence; and an altar for worship and sacrifices stands in the center of the picture because "He has given us existence through our social nature and preserves us through it." "In providing for this property [our social nature] God has so ordained and disposed human affairs that man, having fallen from complete justice by original sin, and *while intending almost always to do something quite different and contrary*—so that for private utility they would live alone like wild beasts—*have been led by this same utility and along the aforesaid different and contrary paths* to live like men in justice and to keep themselves in society and thus to observe their social nature."[33] Through such divine legislation providence creates, out of ferocity, avarice, and ambition, the strength, riches, and wisdom of commonwealths.[34] And again, toward the end of his work, when Vico restates the first incontestable principle of the *New Science* that men have themselves made this world of nations, he goes on to say—and this, too, is to him incontestable—that this same civil world has issued from a mind *"often diverse, at times quite contrary and always superior* to the particular ends that men have proposed to themselves; which narrow ends, made means to serve wider ends, it has always employed to preserve the human race upon the earth."[35]

In history men do not know what they will, for something different from their selfish will is willed with them.

Men mean to gratify their bestial lust and abandon their offspring, and they inaugurate the chastity of marriage from which the families arise. The fathers mean to exercise without restraint their paternal power over their clients, and they subject them to the civil powers from which the cities arise. The reigning orders of nobles mean to abuse their lordly freedom over the plebeians, and they are obliged to submit to the laws which establish popular liberty. The free peoples mean to shake off the yoke of their laws, and they become subject to monarchs. The monarchs mean to strengthen their own positions by debasing their subjects with all the vices of dissoluteness, and they dispose them to endure slavery at the hands of stronger nations. The nations mean to dissolve themselves, and their remnants flee for safety to the wilderness, whence, like the phoenix, they rise again. That which did all this was mind, for man did it with intelligence; it was not fate, for they did it by choice; not chance, for the results of their always so acting are perpetually the same.[36]

This dialectic between particular aims and universal ends, between man's actions and their results, is not, as Croce puts it, a human comedy of errors but a divine comedy of truth, comparable to the working of providence in Hegel's philosophy of history, i.e., to the "cunning of reason." The same dialectic which the foregoing paragraph described in terms of social institutions operates in the temporal order of ages, in the succession of divine or theocratic, heroic, and human epochs. In all these historical developments divine providence is to be supremely admired, "for, when men's intentions were quite otherwise, it brought them in the first place to the fear of divinity, the cult of which is the first fundamental basis of commonwealths."[37]

THE TRUE RELIGION AND THE FALSE RELIGIONS

It has rightly been observed that Vico's sharp distinction between the true religion and the false religions, between Christianity and heathenism, has little bearing upon his concrete philosophy of history and that the original and interesting point of his work is not the conventional distinction between biblical and profane history but rather the ingenuity with which he treats the religions of the Gentiles on the same footing with the true religion, thus minimizing the difference between credulity and faith, between poetic imagination and revealed truth. What links them together is the all-embracing providence of historic developments. But how can providence establish a continuity between the primitive belief in Jupiter (*deus optimus maximus*)—the god of heavens, of thunder and lightning, to whom the gentile nations, "truly though in a false sense,"[38] attributed the direction of their affairs—and the true faith in the true Christian God, who is, however, also a *deus optimus maximus?* The answer is that true providence, operating in history for the preservation of mankind, deceived the first generations of men into the truth through a false religion, for they were by nature incapable of conceiving the true religion in spirit and in truth. Historical providence, before revealing itself in the self-sacrificial love of Christ, in his apostles, and in the church, had to appear for the Gentiles in thunder and lightning to make man, through fear, religious and civilized. In their corporeal imagination these first generations of men could not create their gods but by inventing them, like poets, literally, "makers."[39]

This point was to Vico of such importance for the genesis of the civil world that he chose as the motto of the first edition the words from Virgil: *A Jove principium musae.*[40] Jove, the supreme god of heavens, appears to the first generations of men in terrifying thunder and lightning. From him comes all "vulgar" wisdom, that is, wisdom which is neither revealed nor rational but is originally a science of divination, of divining by auspices—the vulgar but religious wisdom of all gentile nations. Frightened by the great effect of lightning, the first race of men—the giants— became aware of the sky (*uranos*), which they pictured, in analogy to themselves, as a great animated body, which they called "Jove," who was attempting to tell them something. "Thus they began to exercise that natural curiosity which is the daughter of ignorance and the mother of knowledge (*musae*)."[41] To these men all things were "full of Jove" (*Jovis omnia plena*). He is the strongest and the best (*optimus*) and the greatest (*maximus*) *numen,* the king of gods and men. And, since he did not destroy mankind by his thunderbolts, he also received the title of "savior" (*soter*). These rough and savage men apprehended divinity and providence by such human sense as they possessed and, in despair of nature's succor, desired something superior to nature to save them. Providence itself *"permitted them to be deceived into fearing the false divinity of Jove."*[42] Thus, through the thick clouds of those first tempests, intermittently lit by flashes, they made out the great truth that divine providence watches over the welfare of all mankind.

Nothing is said in the *New Science* about Jesus Christ as the turning-point in the world's history and almost nothing about the rise and expansion of the Christian church when Vico describes the rise of the "modern" times, i.e., the Middle Ages. Much more important for Vico than the unique appearance of Christ within the gentile world is the parallelism and the ideal contemporaneity of ancient Roman and early Christian institutions. The early Christian times are to him primarily a recurrence, a second heroic barbarism of personal heroism (martyrs), of "pious wars" (crusades), of "heroic slavery" (e.g., in the relations between Christians and Turks), of king-priests and feudal institutions.[43] The new development after the disintegration of Rome again begins with religion, this time, however, not with Jove but with the true, revealed religion. In Vico no trace is left of the apologetic tendency which inspired the work of Augustine. He neither defends the Christian faith nor attacks or criticizes the pagan superstitions. Personally, he was much too firmly rooted in the Catholic Christian tradition to reflect upon the possible consequences of his comparative interest and scholarly preference for the non-Christian ancient authorities and traditions. Christianity he took for granted, the "vulgar" wisdom of gentile humanity and the hidden truth of mythology he had to discover. Likewise, he took for granted the Christian virtues of hope, faith, and charity, while vindicating—not morally but

historically—the heroic virtues of strength, prudence, and magnanimity of the Gentiles.[44] Fascinated by the ancient traditions
of the gentile world, he took the "vain science" and the "empty
wisdom" of the Gentiles much more seriously than had Augustine and his followers, who saw in Roman and Greek mythology
only nonsense, while Vico discovered its sense. In principle,
Vico interprets religion as a "civil" phenomenon, profane and
historical. Each profane nation has its Jove, as it has its Heracles,
its agricultural rites, its marriage and burial cults. But, since
it is divine providence which works by such simple and natural
means as customs and traditions, the continuity between the pre-
Christian and the Christian tradition seemed to him well established. Rousseau's alternative that the political religions of antiquity were useful but false, while Christianity is true but socially useless, did not occur to him. Hence he could also be unconcerned about Rousseau's attempt at a synthesis between the
universal (Christian) religion of "man" and that of the "citizen"
in a new kind of Christian "civil religion."[45] For Vico, Christian
theology is a mixture of the "civil theology" of the theological
poets of antiquity and the "natural theology" of the metaphysicians with the "loftiest revealed theology."[46]

Only occasionally Vico asserts what was to him self-evident,
namely, the exceptional origin and character of the Christian
religion and of the Hebrew people.[47] The Hebrews are exempted
from the common nature and development of all the other nations that had to pass from a brutish condition through a divine
and heroic age in order to attain rational humanity. Thanks to
God's special revelation, the Jews were human from the beginning, and even physically of normal stature from the outset,
while the race of giants, stemming from Ham, Japheth, and
Shem (who had repudiated the religion of their father Noah),
had to undergo a long and laborious process of domestication.
Over against all profane or gentile religions, the Hebrew religion
was founded on the explicit prohibition of divination, for Israel's
God is Spirit, not to be apprehended by the senses.

Nevertheless, the difference is striking between Vico's civil theology and the traditional theology of history from Augustine to Bossuet, where the explanation of the history of the gentile nations centers around the destiny of the Jews. In a certain way Vico's divergence is even greater than that of Voltaire from Bossuet, since Voltaire simply discarded sacred history altogether and spoke of the Jews as if they were "Scythians or Greeks." The only link in Vico which connects biblical history with the first beginnings of profane mankind after the great Flood is the idea that these wild and savage beginnings are the punishment for original sin and a retrogression from the preceding sacred history of the chosen people. Actually, however, Vico eliminates the Bible as a historical source in spite of his many endeavors to prove its truth from profane sources. He asserts the separate origin of the chosen people, but just for this reason the *New Science* does not comprise the principles of their history. The emphasis is everywhere on the rise and decay of ancient Rome as the pattern of universal history and the typical model of the second *corso* in the history of the Middle Ages.[48]

THE HISTORICAL COURSE AND ITS RECURRENCE

According to an ancient Egyptian tradition, Vico throughout his work distinguishes three ages, following the prehistoric time of the giants. These three ages are:

1) The age of the gods, in which the gentiles believed they lived under divine government, and everything was commanded them by auspices and oracles, which are the oldest things in profane history. 2) The age of the heroes, in which they reigned everywhere in aristocratic commonwealths, on account of a certain superiority of nature which they held themselves to have over the plebs. 3) The age of men, in which all men recognized themselves as equal in human nature, and therefore there were established first the popular commonwealths and then the monarchies.[49]

The divine age is strictly theocratic, the heroic age one of true mythology, and the human age rational. The first and the second are "poetical" epochs in the literal sense of the word, i.e., imaginatively creative. Corresponding with these three kinds of human nature and government, Vico distinguishes and analyzes in detail three kinds of languages and characters (sacred, symbolic, and vulgar), of natural laws, of civil states and jurisprudence— all unified in their succession and informed by divine providence. This regular, typical course of humanity is a progress in so far as it leads from anarchy to order and from savage and heroic customs to more rationalized and civilized ones. It is, however, a progression without end and fulfilment. The real end of it is decadence and fall, after which the whole course (*corso*) begins anew from a new barbarism in a recurrence (*ricorso*) which is, at the same time, a resurgence. Such a recurrence has already occurred once, after the fall of Rome, in the creative return of barbaric times in the Middle Ages. Whether a similar *ricorso* will occur at the end of the present *corso*, which is already a *ricorso*, is to Vico an unsettled question, but it must definitely be affirmed in accordance with his emphatic thesis that what has happened in the past will, in a similar way, also happen in the future, in conformity with the permanent pattern of historic development.[50] Croce is right, therefore, when he says that Vico had "missed the idea of progress," though he is wrong in attributing Vico's failure to "elevate his providential deity into a progressive deity" to the limitation of his thought by the idea of transcendence.[51] It is rather the very immanence of Vico's view which prevented him from transcending the historiconatural cycle of flux and reflux toward a *telos* by a "perpetual enrichment."[52] This is proved indirectly by the fact that Vico becomes inconsistent when considering, toward the end of his work, the possibility of a final *telos* and settlement of the historical process. Reviewing the contemporary scene of Europe, Russia, and Asia, he ventures to say that today a "complete" humanity "seems" to be spread through all nations because a few Christian monarchs rule over this world of peoples, though there are still some barbarous peoples surviving.[53] Thanks to the Christian religion, the world seems to have become most human in its customs. Sovereign powers have united in leagues, comparable to the ancient form of government under sovereign family kings.

Incompatible with this tentative outlook toward a "Christian world" as the fulfilment of history is the consistent theme of his work, which stresses that history has no fulfilment and solution but is ruled by recurrences. The normal course is simple enough: "Men first feel necessity, then look for utility, next attend to comfort, still later amuse themselves with pleasure, thence grow dissolute in luxury, and finally go mad and waste their substance."[54] Sometimes providence finds a remedy from within the nation, by a ruler like Augustus, or from without, by allowing the nation to be conquered and subjected to a foreign people if it cannot govern itself. "But if the peoples are rotting in this last civil illness and cannot agree upon a monarch from within, and are not conquered and preserved by better nations from without, then providence for their extreme ill has its extreme remedy at hand."[55] This last remedy is the *ricorso* to the simplicity and religious awe of primitive barbarism.

The *ricorso* is not a cosmic recurrence but a historical structure with the juridical connotation of "appeal."[56] Since the historical *corso* has failed to attain its end, it must, as it were, appeal to a higher court to have its case rehearsed. The highest court of justice is, however, providential history as a whole, which requires an age of disintegration and oversophistication, the "barbarism of reflection," to return to the creative barbarism of sense in order to begin anew.

For such peoples, like so many beasts, have fallen into the custom of each man thinking only of his own private interests and have reached the extreme of delicacy, or better of pride, in which like wild animals they bristle and lash out at the slightest displeasure. Thus in the midst of their greatest festivities, though physically thronging together, they live like wild beasts in a deep solitude of spirit and will, scarcely any two being able to agree since each follows his own pleasure and caprice. By reason of all this, providence decrees that, through obstinate factions and desperate civil wars, they shall turn their cities into forests and the forests into dens and lairs of men. In this way, through long centuries of barbarism, rust will consume the misbegotten subtleties of malicious wits, that have turned them into beasts made more inhuman by the barbarism of reflection than the first men had been made by the barbarism of sense. For the latter displayed a generous savagery, against which one could defend oneself or take flight or be on one's guard; but the former, with a base savagery, under soft words and embraces, plots against the life and fortune of friends and intimates. Hence peoples who have reached this point of premeditated malice, when they receive this last remedy of providence and are thereby stunned and brutalized, are sensible no longer of comforts, delicacies, pleasures and pomp, but only of the sheer necessities of life. And the few survivors in the midst of an abundance of the things necessary for life naturally become sociable and, returning to the primitive simplicity of the first world of peoples, are again religious, truthful and faithful. Thus providence brings back among them the piety, faith and truth which are the natural foundations of justice as well as the graces and beauties of the eternal order of God.[57]

When describing this radical remedy for a radical illness, Vico had in mind the end of the Roman cycle; but he expresses his thought in such a general language that it can be referred as well to the year 500 as to the year 2000. This conclusion contains the last and final wisdom of Vico and of providence itself. What he reviews in the one thousand one hundred and twelve paragraphs of the *New Science* is the semicreative city of fallen man. It has no substantial relation to the City of God, except by calling the historiconatural law of the nations "providence." Vico's outlook is therefore, in principle, rather classic than Christian. Like the ancients, he is deeply concerned with "origins" and "foundations" but not with hope and faith in a future fulfilment. History repeats itself, though on different levels and with modifications, and the cycle of *corso,* fall, and *ricorso,* if judged on its own merits, is not "hopeless," as Augustine felt, but the most natural and rational form of historical development. Compared with Polybius' theory of cycles, Vico's *ricorso* is, however, much more historicized in conformity with his historicized notion of nature. The cyclic recurrence provides for the education and even "salvation" of mankind by the rebirth of its social nature. It saves man by preserving him.[58] This alone, but not redemption, is the "primary end" and providential meaning of history. The recurrence of barbarism saves mankind from civilized self-destruction.

CONCLUSION

Within the limited scope of this study we have had to refrain from giving a concrete description of the sociological wealth of Vico's scheme of universal history. But, even so, one can safely say that he is more penetrating and comprehensive than Voltaire, far profounder than Comte and Condorcet, and more inspired by original intuition than Hegel. He freed himself from Cartesian rationalism and from the theological rigidity of Bossuet's history without sacrificing his keen intellect and Machiavellian realism to the progressive illusions of the Enlightenment.

He neither replaced providence by progress, like Voltaire, nor introduced, like Bossuet, orthodoxy into history. When he investigated history as a philosophical historian, he never intended to discard revelation; and when he asserted, from the first to the last page, that providence is the first principle for the understanding of history, he did not distort the sociopolitical history by an eschatological viewpoint. His leading idea is neither the progression toward fulfilment nor the cosmic cycle of a merely natural growth and decay, but a historicocyclic progression from *corso* to *ricorso* in which the cycle itself has providential significance by being an ultimate remedy for man's corrupted nature. The return to a new barbarism does not redeem earthly history but cures man from the overcivilized barbarism of reflection. Vico's perspective is still a theological one, but the means of providence and salvation are in themselves historiconatural ones. History as seen by Vico has a prehistoric beginning but no end and fulfilment, and yet it is ruled by providence for the sake of mankind.

Thus his whole work is neither an Augustinian theology of history nor a philosophy of history in the polemical sense of Voltaire, for whom the separation of sacred and secular history served to the degradation of the first. Vico's philosophy of history is a "rational civil theology," halfway between Voltaire and Bossuet, vindicating God's providence directly as history. It is precisely on the border line of the critical transition from the theology to the philosophy of history and, therefore, deeply ambiguous. The ambiguity of his work appeared at once in the different ways in which it was received. A review in the *Journal* of the Leipzig Academy held that the author was a "Jesuit" and his work a reactionary attempt at apologetic for the Roman Catholic church. The conservative Italian Catholics[59] attacked the *New Science* because they saw that a providence which is inherent in history as its natural law undermines the biblical conception of God's transcendent working and that Vico's sharp distinction between sacred and secular history might actually lead to a purely human understanding of the origin and course of civilization, including religion. The Italian anticlerical Socialists, however, reprinted the *New Science* and propagated it as a weapon in the imminent revolution at the end of the eighteenth century. Vico himself did not realize that his doctrine contained implicitly a criticism of the biblical view of history no less radical than was the "new art of criticism" which he had applied to the interpretation of Homer.[60]

VII

BOSSUET

BOSSUET'S understanding of history stands and falls with the thesis that the whole course of human history is guided by providence—a thesis which was denied by the freethinkers of his day. "The freethinkers declare war on divine providence and they find no better argument against it than the distribution of good and evil which seems unjust and irrational since it does not discriminate between the good and the wicked. It is there that the godless ones entrench themselves as in an impregnable fortress from which they throw bold missiles at the divine wisdom which rules the world, falsely convinced as they are that the apparent disorder of human affairs is an evidence against this very wisdom."[1] He was further convinced that the doctrine of providence is the most powerful check of immorality. "They have wished to shake off the yoke of this providence, in order to maintain, in independence, an unteachable liberty which moves them to live at their own fancy, without fear, discipline, or restraint."[2] Like Hegel, Bossuet did not deny that the first glance at history shows neither reason nor justice, for actual history makes no difference between pious and impious men. It is a field of passions and interests, where evil succeeds and justice fails. But, in refuting the arguments of the freethinkers, Bossuet goes on to say that this immediate impression of apparent confusion is due to a viewpoint which is too close to its subject. If we detach ourselves and look at history from a greater distance, from an eternal point of view, that is, with the eyes of faith (or, as Hegel would say, with the eyes of reason), the whole picture changes, and the apparent meaninglessness reveals a hidden justice. "If you know how to fix the point from which things have to be viewed, all iniquities will be corrected, and you will see only wisdom where before you saw disorder."[3]

The only sound inference from the fact that at present a just order in history is not yet established is, according to Bossuet, that man still has to expect something from the future or, more properly, from eternity. Facing the Last Judgment, we have to live in a constant suspense, in fear and hope, until all things are disentangled by a final and irrevocable decision. God has infinite time to work out his purpose, and so we should not be impatient in regard to the confusion of all temporal affairs. Faith in providence inspires two sentiments in regard to all temporal things: not to admire anything of terrestrial grandeur and not to fear anything of terrestrial misery. Christ, the Lord of history, who alone will distribute the final rewards and punishments, does not mind abandoning temporarily even a whole Christian empire to unbelievers like the Moslems, just as he permitted the children of Abraham to be enslaved. While all particular designs of the political powers of the world are bound to be opposed and upset by the designs of other powers, the all-embracing design of God cannot be upset by any means. Involuntarily and unconsciously, all temporal events co-operate eventually in the fulfilment of his eternal purpose. Thus the believer in providence will never despair. Whatever may happen in actual history will frighten as well as comfort him, for the hidden secret of history is that it reveals as many *coups de grâce* as *coups de rigueur et de justice*. On the summit of historical fortune, Christian people will remember that things might suddenly and completely change and that in the extremities of misfortune they are in the hands of God.

On this presupposition of providence, Bossuet worked out his universal history from the creation of the world up to the establishment of the new Christian empire of the Occident by Charlemagne, holding that the French monarchy is heir to the Roman and Holy Roman empires. His work served for the instruction of his royal pupil, the son of Louis XIV. Compared with Augustine's *City of God,* the *Discourse* of Bossuet shows a greater historical sense for the grandeur of political history and a greater interest in the pragmatic concatenations of causes and effects.[4]

On the other hand, Bossuet is more of a churchman than Augustine is. His work is not so much a city of God as a history of the triumphant church on the pattern of Eusebius, adviser of Constantine.

The first part of Bossuet's *Discourse* gives the general outline of the succession of the twelve epochs and seven ages of the world, without discriminating between sacred and profane events. He introduces, for example, the chapter on the sixth epoch by saying: "About the 3000th year of the world, the 488th from the departure out of Egypt, and to adjust the times of sacred history with those of profane, 180 years after the taking of Troy, 250 before the foundation of Rome, and 1000 years before Jesus Christ, did Solomon finish that stupendous edifice." The ages are divided by Jesus Christ, whose birthday was fixed by providence and exactly prophesied by Daniel (9:24).[5] The three outstanding dates are 4004 (or 4963, for Bossuet was not quite sure which of these two dates was the correct one), the date of creation; 754, the foundation of Rome; and the year 1. It goes without saying that the seventh age, beginning with the birth of Jesus Christ, is also the last one, for empires may rise and perish but the church of Christ is everlasting. The Christian religion not only is founded on the most ancient and thereby most authoritative scriptures but also has the most continuous tradition.

The second part explains the history of religion as centered in the destiny of the Jews; the third part deals with the history of the empires. The *Civitas Dei* extends from Abraham to the victorious church, the *Civitas Terrena* from Egypt to the Roman Empire. This distinction between sacred and secular history is necessary to understand what is proper to each of them, but it does not exclude their actual correlation. "These two important objects run on together in that great movement of ages, where they have, if I may say so, one and the same course."[6] Ultimately, not only sacred history but also the rise and fall of empires must be explained by secret ordering; they cannot be understood by mere historical, i.e., particular, causes. The whole possibility of demonstrating an ultimate "meaning" in the whole course of history depends on this relation of sacred to secular history.

The most obvious manifestation of divine providence in the events of a nation's history is to Bossuet the history of the chosen people,[7] chosen by God as a particular people and therefore demonstrating, like no other nation, the religious meaning of political history. The other terrestrial empires are related to a divine purpose mainly indirectly, through some kind of relationship to the history of Israel. But, according to Bossuet, there are also many other instances of divine guidance in political history, manifested by miraculous coincidences, that is, by coincidences which are what they are not by chance but by the fulfilment of a hidden design. An illustration is the providential coincidence between the *Pax Romana* under Augustus and the birth of Jesus Christ, the *Pax Romana* being the prerequisite for the expansion of the gospel and the church. In sacred history, nothing happens which is not preordained by the purpose of God. Jerusalem, for example, had to be destroyed in spite of Titus' attempt to prevent the destruction and in spite of Julian's attempt to restore the city and temple. Divine providence used the Assyrians and Babylonians to chastise the people of God, the Persians to restore them, Alexander to protect them, Antiochus to harden them, the Romans first to support their liberty against the kings of Syria and then to exterminate them after they had rejected the Savior. But when Rome persecuted the Christian church, Rome again served God's purpose by testing and fortifying the church, which eventually succeeded in converting Constantine to the true religion, thereby transforming the eternal Rome of the pagans into the truly eternal Rome of Christianity.

Thus it is that the empires of the world have ministered to religion, and to the preservation of the people of God: wherefore that same God, who caused the different states of his people to be foretold by his prophets, caused the succession of empires to be also predicted by them. You have seen the places where Nebuchadnezzar was pointed out as the person that was to come and punish the haughty nations, and especially the Jewish people for their ingratitude to their Maker. You have heard Cyrus named two hundred years before. his birth, as him who was to restore God's people, and to punish Babylon's pride. The destruction of Niniveh hath been no less clearly foretold. Daniel, in his admirable visions, hath made the empire of Babylon, that of the Medes and Persians, that of Alexander and the Grecians, pass away in a moment before you. The blasphemies and cruelties of Antiochus Illustris have been there prophesied, as well as the miraculous victories of God's people over that violent persecutor. We there see those famous empires fall one after another, and the new empire which Jesus Christ was to establish, is there described so expressly by its proper characters, that it is impossible to mistake it. It is the empire of the Son of Man, the empire that is to stand amidst the ruin of all others, and to which alone eternity is promised.[8]

Who would still dare to demonstrate the meaning of history by the fulfilment of prophecy "at the precise hour"? To Bossuet, as to Augustine, it was the most convincing of all possible proofs, as convincing as are natural sciences to us because they are able to predict future occurences exactly. To Bossuet the fulfilment of prophetic predictions proved that the history of the empires ultimately serves the Christian church. True, "God does not every day declare his will by his prophets, concerning the kings and monarchies, which He sets up or pulls down. But having done it so many times in those great empires we have been speaking of, He shows us by those famous instances, how He acts in all others, and teaches kings these two great fundamental truths; first, that it is He who forms kingdoms, in order to give them to whomsoever He will; and secondly, that He knows how to make them subservient, in his own good time and order, to the designs He has upon his people."[9] And, even if we consider this progression of empires "in a more human light," there is much to be learned from this spectacle. Empires die as well as emperors—a "beautiful lesson" of the vanity of human grandeur—for what else should the dreadful wreck of all human efforts teach us if not the basic inconstancy and agitation of all human things, their inherent mortality and irreparable frailty.

After discussing the particular causes of Rome's grandeur and decline, Bossuet, in the last chapter, once more takes up the question of providence. Only to our ignorance, shortsightedly involved in particulars, do the ups and downs of historical events seem to be mere chance and fortune. In the proper perspective this mixture of chance and fate is an orderly design, where the final outcome is prepared in its remotest causes. This outcome, however, is unknown to the agents of history.

Therefore it is that all who govern, find themselves subject to a greater power. They do more or less than they intend, and their counsels have never failed to have unforeseen effects. Neither are they masters of the dispositions which past ages have given affairs, nor can they foresee what course futurity will take; far less are they able to force it. . . . Little did Alexander think that he was labouring for his captains, or to ruin his house by his conquests. When Brutus inspired the Roman people with a boundless love of liberty, he never dreamt that he was sowing in their minds the seeds of that immoderate licence, whereby the tyranny he meant to destroy was to be one day restored more grievous than under the Tarquins. When the Caesars were flattering the soldiers, they had no intention of giving masters to their successors, and to the empire. In a word, there is no human power that does not minister, whether it will or no, to other designs than its own. God only knows how to bring every thing about to his will: and therefore every thing is surprising, to consider only particular causes; and yet every thing goes on with a regular progression.[10]

This descriptive analysis of the process of history agrees not only with Hegel's "cunning of reason" but, what is more, with the truth—and this quite apart from its explanation by reason or providence. "Ye have built houses of hewn stone, but ye shall not dwell in them; ye have planted pleasant vineyards, but ye shall not drink the wine thereof" (Amos 5:11). Unfortunately, Bossuet and Hegel both proved too much. What has been said concerning contemporary Christendom could also be said concerning the elaborate application of the belief in providence to the understanding of history: "the less the better": A more modest use of providence would be less questionable and more Christian.[11]

If Bossuet had kept the cross as "the proper law of the Gospels,"[12] only *one* inference as to the meaning of history would have been adequate: that history is a discipline of suffering, an opportunity for the creature to return to its creator—no more and no less. Nothing else than the life and death of Jesus Christ, the "Suffering Servant," who was deserted and crucified, can be the standard of a Christian understanding of the world's history.

Thus was given to the world in the person of Jesus Christ, the lively image of an accomplished virtue, which has nothing, and expects nothing upon earth; which men reward only by continual persecutions; which does not cease to do them good; and on which its own good offices draw the most ignominious punishment. Jesus Christ dies, without finding either gratitude in those he obliges, fidelity in his friends, or equity in his judges. His innocence, though acknowledged, does not save Him; his Father Himself, in Whom alone He had placed his hope, withdraws all marks of his protection; the just One is delivered up to His enemies, and dies forsaken both by God and man.[13]

The lesson which Bossuet draws from the fact that the Son of Man and of God died without any visible mark of divine protection is that ordinary man in his extremity should not claim what has not been granted to Christ. "Let him but love and trust, resting assured that God is mindful of him though He give him no token of it."

It is this very absence of any visible mark of providence in the history of the world which proves the need of faith in things unseen and which evokes it. Faith does not rest on objective certainty or fifty per cent probability but rather on the absence of them. It implies commitment and risk, courage and suspense. It is a belief in what is otherwise unbelievable. To make providence *post festum* intelligible and transparent in the political history of the world is the attempt of unbelievers, who say, like the devil to Jesus: "If you are God's son, throw yourself down" (Matt. 4:6).

For a follower of Christ there is only one mark of election: the cross.

When judges want to make somebody infamous and unworthy of human honors, they often brand his body with a shameful mark of disgrace which bears evidence of his infamy to everyone. . . . God has printed on our forehead . . . a mark, glorious before him, ignominious before men, in order to keep us from receiving any honor on this earth. This does not mean that, because of being good Christians, we are unworthy of worldly honors, but rather that worldly honors are unworthy of us. According to the world we are infamous because, by the standards of the world, the cross which is our glory is the epitome of all sorts of infamy. . . . Our forefathers believed emperors were hardly worthy of being Christians. Things now have changed. We believe that Christian piety is hardly worthy of persons in high places: we are horrified by the baseness of the cross, we want to be applauded and respected.[14]

If, however, the cross is the outstanding mark of an imitation of Christ, one cannot expect that the world will ever follow him. A *World* which calls itself *Christian* is a contradiction in terms, and a Christian understanding of history can be based only on the fundamental antagonism between the Kingdom of God and the kingdoms of man. And yet it is one of the great paradoxes in the history of Christianity that the most authentic imitation of Christ, that of St. Francis, merged into a revolutionary interpretation of the "Eternal Gospel" which led, by many detours and perversions, to a progressive interpretation of history which expected the *eschaton* not only in history but eventually also from it.

VIII

JOACHIM

THERE have always occurred and recurred apocalyptic speculations and expectations of an imminent consummation, but never until Joachim of Floris (1131–1202)[1] have they been elaborated into a consistent system of historico-allegorical interpretation. On account of its revolutionary implications, this interpretation caused violent conflicts within the Catholic church. Far remote and dead as this quarrel of the thirteenth and fourteenth centuries seems to be today, there can be little doubt that it re-enacts the spiritual fervor of early Christianity and also conditions the modern irreligions of progress.

What matters for the understanding of history is Joachim's revolutionary attempt to delineate a new scheme of epochs and dispensations by which the traditional scheme of religious progress from the Old to the New Testament became extended and superseded. The immediate subject and vehicle of this new interpretation of history as a history of salvation was the Revelation of St. John, with its symbolic figures and events. It is here that the expression "Eternal Gospel" occurs,[2] the title under which Joachim's doctrine later came to be known. According to the traditional commentaries on the Apocalypse, e.g., that of Bossuet, the explanation of this passage is simply that after the victory over pagan idolatry there remained only one task: to spread the gospel of Jesus Christ as the supreme rule which was to endure until the end of the world, while the old dispensation, the Law of Moses, could last only until the appearance of Christ. The implication of this traditional interpretation is that the existing, that is, the Roman Catholic, church is also to continue to the end of the world as the only legitimate representation of God's will on earth. Joachim, however, uses the term "Eternal Gospel" in a much wider and, at the same time, more specific

145

sense, applying it critically to a "spiritual" interpretation of the Old and New Testaments; and the implication is that in the last epoch of history the church will no longer be a clerical hierarchy grown worldly but a monastic community of saints in the succession of St. Benedict, destined to cure, by an ultimate effort, a disintegrating world. After Joachim's death, both Franciscans and Dominicans claimed to be the true church by following their Lord and Master unconditionally, in poverty and humility, in truth and in spirit. To quote from Rufus Jones:

Joachim's discoveries and visions and prophecies of a "new age" fell on tinder and worked like magic on his disciples and followers who produced in his name a large stock of kindling books which circulated widely and which exercised a propagating effect on the prepared minds of that period. The climax of the movement was reached in 1254 in the appearance in Paris of a book entitled *Introduction to the Eternal Gospel*. It was written by a young lector of theology in the University of Paris, named Gerard of Borgo San Donnino. He boldly announced that the era of the Eternal Gospel, the dispensation of the Holy Spirit, would begin in six years, that is to say, in 1260. He declared that Joachim had already introduced a new stage of contemplative life and that the "spiritual" followers of St. Francis, of whom Gerard was one, were to be the organs and interpreters of the new age. The storm which burst on the world with the discovery of this book ... swept the saintly John of Parma out of his office as Minister General of the Franciscan Order and it carried St. Bonaventura into place and power. It had the effect of ending abruptly, within the membership of the official Church, the surging dreams of a new epoch of the Spirit, while it carried over into the camps of heresy a swelling flood of dreams and hopes and expectations.[3]

Gerard of Borgo San Donnino was condemned to imprisonment for life.

THE PROVIDENTIAL PROGRESS TOWARD A HISTORICAL *eschaton*

It was a decisive moment in the history of the Christian church when an Italian abbot, a renowned prophet and saint and a man trained in the most austere discipline of the Cistercian order, after arduous study and meditations in the wilderness of his

146

Calabrian mountains, received an inspiration at Pentecost (between 1190 and 1195) revealing to him the signs of the times in the light of St. John's Revelation. Joachim describes his experience in the following words: "When I awoke at dawn, I took to the Revelation of St. John. There, suddenly, the eyes of my spirit were struck with the lucidity of insight, and it was revealed to me the fulfilment of this book and the concordance of the Old and New Testaments." This revelation, like Nietzsche's inspiration which revealed to him the truth of the Eternal Recurrence, was the sudden result of a long struggle for a systematic understanding of the hidden destiny of man. What was revealed to Joachim was both the historical and the mystical significance of the symbols and figures of the Old and New Testaments, converging in a total picture of the history of salvation from beginning to end and the historical fulfilment of the Apocalypse. Developing the historical logic of the New Testament both into the past and into the future, he finally understood the secret meaning of all its personages, figures, and animals as strictly significant, that is, as signifying definite persons and events of the actual history which to his religious understanding was nothing else than sacred history in terms of secular history. Once the key was found which, through typological and allegorical interpretation,[4] opened the enigmatic meaning of all successive pictures and events, a final and comprehensive understanding of history was made available. Demonstrating in his exposition of the Apocalypse those of its figures which had already come to fulfilment and those which had not, he was able to construct prophetically the future stages of the providential evolution in the whole process of history. The critical time which served Joachim as a criterion of such discrimination between past and future events was his own century, as one of radical deformation. "The signs as described in the gospel show clearly the dismay and ruin of the century which is now running down and must perish. Hence I believe that it will not be in vain to submit to the vigilance of the believers, through this work, those matters which divine economy has made known to my unworthy person in order to awaken the torpid hearts from their slumber by a violent noise and to induce them, if possible, by a new kind of exegesis to the contempt of the world."[5]

The general scheme of Joachim's discriminating interpretation is based on the trinitarian doctrine. Three different dispensations come to pass in three different epochs in which the three persons of the Trinity are successively manifested. The first is the dispensation of the Father, the second that of the Son, the third that of the Holy Spirit. The latter is beginning just now (i.e., toward the end of the twelfth century) and is progressing toward the complete "freedom" of the "spirit."[6] The Jews were slaves under the law of the Father. The Christians of the second epoch were, though incompletely, spiritual and free, namely, in comparison with the moral legality of the first dispensation. In the third epoch, St. Paul's prophetic words will come true, that we know and prophesy now only in part, "but when that which is perfect is come, that which is in part shall be done away."[7] And "already we can apprehend the unveiling of the final liberation of the spirit in its plenitude." The first epoch was inaugurated by Adam in fear and under the sign of the law; since Abraham it had borne fruit to become fulfilled in Jesus Christ. The second was inaugurated by Uzziah in faith and humility under the sign of the gospel; since Zechariah, the father of John the Baptist, it had borne fruit to become fulfilled in future times. The third was inaugurated by St. Benedict in love and joy under the sign of the Spirit; it will come to pass with the reappearance of Elijah at the end of the world. The three stages are overlapping, since the second begins to appear within the first and the third within the second. At one and the same time, spiritual periods of different level and meaning are coexistent. Thus, since St. Benedict, the coming church of monks already exists within the church of clerics. The first dispensation is historically an order of the married, dependent on the Father; the second an order of clerics, dependent on the Son; the third an order of monks, dependent on the Spirit of Truth. The first age is ruled by labor and work, the second by learning and discipline, the third by contemplation and praise. The first stage possesses *scientia,* the second *sapientia ex parte,* the third *plenitudo intellectus.* The times which have passed before the law, under the law, and under grace were as necessary as the coming epoch which will fulfil those preparatory stages; for the fundamental law of the history of salvation is the continuous progress from the time of the Old and New Testament "letter" to that of the "spirit,"[8] in analogy to the miraculous transformation of water into wine.

Thus the coming times of the Holy Spirit are successively prefigured in the first and second epochs of the Father and Son, which are strictly concordant, for each figure and event of the Old Testament, if understood spiritually, is a promise and signification of a corresponding figure and event of the New Testament. This correspondence is one of meaning as well as of succession, i.e., certain events and figures of the Old Testament are spiritually contemporary with certain events and figures of the New Testament by having a concordant historical position and significance. Thus, for example, John's baptism by water reappears intensified in Elijah's baptism by the fire of the Holy Spirit, which swallows everything carnal and merely of the letter. This whole process of a progressive *consummatio* is, at the same time, a continuous process of *designatio,* invalidating the preceding promises and significations. The periods of each dispensation have to be reckoned, however, not by homogeneous years but by generations which are concordant not by their length but by their numbers, each of them extending over about thirty years. The number 30 has no natural, but a spiritual, foundation. It refers to the perfection of the Trinity of the one Godhead and to Jesus who was thirty years of age when he gained his first *filii spirituales.* According to Joachim's calculations (chiefly based on Rev. 11:3 and 12:6; Matt. 1:17) his own generation is the fortieth, and the assumption of his followers was that, after a period of two further generations, that is, in 1260, the climax would be reached, revealing Frederick II as the Antichrist and the Franciscan Spirituals as the providential leaders of the new and last dispensation, which would end with history's definite consummation by last judgment and resurrection. Within historical time, the goal and meaning of the history of salvation is the uncompromising realization of the evangelical precepts and exhortations, in particular of the Sermon on the Mount.

What is new and revolutionary in Joachim's conception of the history of salvation is due to his prophetic-historical method of allegorical interpretation. In so far as it is allegorical and typological, it is not new but only a coherent application of the traditional patristic exegesis.[9] But this exegesis served Joachim's amazingly fertile imagination not for static—i.e., moral and dogmatic—purposes but for a dynamic understanding of revelation through an essential correlation between Scripture and history and between their respective interpretations. The one must explain the other if history, on the one hand, is really sacred and full of religious meaning and if, on the other hand, the gospel is the *rotulus in rota* or the central axis of the world's happenings. Granted that history *is* a history of salvation and that the history of the church is its pattern, then the only fitting key to its religious understanding must be the Sacred Scriptures, the concordance of which proves to Joachim not an absolute doctrine but the meaningful structure of a historical process. On the basis of the simple belief in the inspired character of the Scripture, Joachim could extract from it a strictly religious understanding of history and, on the other hand, discover in actual history the hidden presence of purely religious categories. This attempt to explain history religiously and the Revelation of St. John historically is no more and no less than an intricate elaboration of the Christian presupposition that the church is the body of Christ and that therefore her history is intrinsically religious and not merely a department of the history of the world. And, since the history after Christ is still on its way and yet revealed as having an end, the fulness of time is not to be conceived traditionally as a unique event of the past but as something to be worked out in the future, in the perspective of which the church, from Christ until now, is not an everlasting foundation but an imperfect prefiguration. The interpretation of history thus necessarily becomes prophecy, and the right understanding of the past depends on the proper perspective for the future, in which the preceding significations come to their end. This consummation does not occur beyond historical time, at the end of the world, but in a last historical epoch. Joachim's eschatological scheme consists neither in a simple millennium nor in the mere expectation of the end of the world but in a twofold *eschaton:* an ultimate historical phase of the history of salvation, preceding the transcendent *eschaton* of the new aeon, ushered in by the second coming of Christ. The Kingdom of the Spirit is the last revelation of God's purpose on earth and in time. Consequently, the institution of the papacy and clerical hierarchy is limited to the second epoch. This implies a radical revision of the Catholic doctrine of succession from St. Peter to the end of the world. The existing church, though founded on Christ, will have to yield to the coming church of the Spirit, when the history of salvation has reached its plenitude. This ultimate transition also implies the liquidation of preaching and sacraments, the mediating power of which becomes obsolete when the spiritual order is realized which possesses knowledge of God by direct vision and contemplation. The real significance of the sacraments is not, as with Augustine, the signification of a transcendent reality but the indication of a potentiality which becomes realized within the framework of history.

Belonging himself to the second epoch, Joachim did not draw any revolutionary conclusions from the implications of his historico-eschatological visions. He did not criticize the contemporary church, nor did his interpretation of the angel of the Apocalypse (Rev. 7:2) as the *novus dux,* entitled to "renovate the Christian religion," mean that he intended a revolutionary reorganization of the existing institutions and sacraments. To him it only meant that a messianic leader was to appear, "whosoever it will be," bringing about a spiritual renovation for the sake of the Kingdom of Christ, revealing but not abolishing what hitherto has been veiled in significant figures and sacraments. The revolutionary conclusions were drawn later by men of the thirteenth and fourteenth centuries, by the Franciscan

Spirituals, who recognized in Joachim the new John the Baptist, heralding St. Francis as the *novus dux* of the last dispensation, even as the "new Christ." To them the clerical church was indeed at its end. Rejecting the alleviating distinction between strict precepts and flexible counsels, they made a radical attempt to live a Christian life in unconditional poverty and humility and to transform the church into a community of the Holy Spirit, without pope, clerical hierarchy, sacraments, Holy Scripture, and theology. The rule of St. Francis was to them the quintessence of the gospel. The driving impulse of their movement was, as with Joachim, the intensity of their eschatological expectancy with regard to the present epoch as a state of corruption. The criterion by which they judged the corruption of their times and the alienation from the gospel was the life of St. Francis. And, since Joachim had already expected that within two generations the final battle would be fought between the spiritual order and the powers of evil, his followers could even more definitely interpret the emperor as the Antichrist—eventually, however, as the providential instrument for the punishment of an anti-Christian church which obstructed its own renovation by persecuting the real followers of Christ.

These passionate men who, like the early Christians, were inspired by a fervent expectation of the new aeon and whose missionary zeal overcame obstacles which otherwise would have seemed insurmountable, attempted indeed the impossible: to realize the laws of the Kingdom of God without compromise in this *saeculum*. While the message of St. Francis still remained within the framework of the traditional eschatology, his followers became revolutionaries by interpreting St. Francis, themselves, and the events of their time as the fulfilment of Joachim's prophecy. They thus became involved in severe conflicts, first, with the rival aspirations of the Dominicans; second, with the imperial messianism of Frederick II;[10] and, third, with the Roman Catholic church. The church was astute and intransigent enough during her momentous struggle with the Joachites to achieve the mitigation, integration, and assimilation of the dangerous movement into her institution as an authorized sect among other sects. The collapse of the movement was as final as its aspirations had been. It is, however, remarkable that as late as the nineteenth century a positivist like Comte could venture to call the Franciscan movement "the only real promise of a Christian reform."

In the fourteenth century a pathetic caricature of the politico-religious eschatology excited for a short time the minds of Italy when the Roman tribune, Cola di Rienzo, styled himself the *novus dux,* if not of the *imperium mundi,* at least of Italy, re-enacting, as it were, the messianic claim of Frederick II. Convinced, like the Franciscan Spirituals, that the descent of the Holy Ghost is not a single event of the past but something which may happen again, Cola di Rienzo believed himself to be the political counterpart to St. Francis, destined to support and renew a falling empire as St. Francis had supported and renewed a crumbling church.[11] His ambition was to blend the messianic aspirations of the Ghibellines with those of the Franciscan Spirituals for the sake of the national regeneration of Rome and Italy. His attempt to play the role of the promised *dux* failed miserably, and from 1349 to 1350 he took refuge with Franciscan eremites who still believed in the forbidden teachings of Joachim. In his correspondence with Emperor Charles IV, who later kept him imprisoned for several years, and with the Archbishop of Prague, he tried to convince them of the truth of Joachim's prophetic predictions.

The tragic story of the Joachites shows once more that there cannot be any such thing as a Christian World, century, or history in the proper sense of these words; for to live in this world without being of it, to "weep as though they wept not," and "to rejoice as though they rejoiced not," and all the paradoxical tensions of a truly Christian existence mean more than a sound equilibrium between being comfortable and charitable, between self-assertion and self-surrender. It is true, of course, that "real" Christianity lives by a compromise and that the history of Christianity is inevitably involved in the history of the world. But it is equally true that for this very reason the authentic history of a Christian is, and always has been, a constant struggle of the spiritual man against the natural pride and appetites, the *superbia vitae* and *concupiscentia,* of the man of the world.[12] The price which Christianity had to pay to the world for its worldly existence is as high, though of a different kind, as the price which a Christian has to pay for renouncing the world. To "adjust" the Christian message to contemporary conditions is a superfluous endeavor because the world by itself takes care of such an adjustment. But to retrieve, time and again, the austerity of the Christian demands from a surrender to the apparent needs of the *saeculum* is a task as lasting as the worldly existence of the faith in God's revelation in Christ.

<h3 style="text-align:center">CONCLUSION</h3>

The political applications of Joachim's historical prophecies were neither foreseen nor intended by him. Nevertheless, they were plausible consequences of his general scheme; for, when Joachim opened the door to a fundamental revision of a thousand years of Christian history and theology by proclaiming a new and last dispensation, he questioned implicitly not only the traditional authority of the church but also the temporal order. His expectation of a last providential progress toward the fulfilment of the history of salvation within the framework of the history of the world is radically new in comparison with the pattern of Augustine. The latter never indulged in prophetic predictions of detailed and radical changes within the temporal order or *saeculum,* which is essentially subject to change.

Challenged by disruptive innovations, the church had to restate its fundamental propositions about the course of history as a history of salvation on the basis of Augustine's and Anselm's conceptions.[13] She had to insist on the traditional division into the two dispensations of the Old and the New Testaments, excluding a third one, and to stress the transcendent character of the ultimate consummation. Death and resurrection, deformation and reformation, corruption and renovation, have no place in the straight progression toward a supra-historical fulfilment and end.[14] Moreover, said the church, it is against the nature of the history of salvation to allow regresses from a perfect to a less perfect state. The first was reached when the time was fulfilled, and therefore it cannot follow the present state.[15] The *spiritualis intelligentia* was a prerogative of the apostolic age, from which the church developed in an uninterrupted succession. The history and the means of salvation are, once and for all, institutionalized in the church, which is founded on Christ. As such it will outlast all illegitimate innovations and last until the second coming of Christ. This single, unique, and transcendent *eschaton* alone defines and delimits the history of the church. While the Franciscan Spirituals expected everything from the future, the established church had to stress the unchangeableness of its state and tame the eschatological fervor of its opponent; for its own existence depended, then as now, on the ineffectiveness of this original core of the Christian hope and faith. The logic of self-preservation and justification cannot but be opposed to the existential and historical relevance of eschatological thinking. The viewpoint of the Franciscan Spirituals was fixed on the imminence of a thorough transformation; the viewpoint of the church was, and is, fixed on its everlasting foundation, with the effect of enervating the eschatological outlook of the teachings of Jesus.

The Christian doctrine from Augustine to Thomas had mastered history theologically by excluding the temporal relevance of the last things. This exclusion was achieved by the transposition of the original expectations into a realm beyond historical existence. Joachim viewed everything in a historical perspective. Christ himself means to him not only the fulfilment of the prophecies of the Old Testament but also the beginning of a new age; Christ remains central but as a center of significations, leading to him but also from him into future developments. His significance is truly historical not because it is unique but because it consummates and initiates significations within a historical continuity in which the generations after Christ are as important as were the generations before Christ. Joachim thinks strictly theologically and at the same time historically in terms of a continuous *cursus temporis* instead of an inarticulate interim. This course of history is marked by transitions toward higher stages, in which each stage supplants the preceding one in such a way that each has *in suo tempore* its own kind of truth and necessity—as with Comte and Hegel, but in the midst of the "unhistorical" thought of the Middle Ages. The Christian truth itself has, like the *logos* of Hegel, a temporal setting in its successive developments. With Augustine and Thomas, the Christian truth rests, once and for all, on certain historical facts; with Joachim the truth itself has an open horizon and a history which is essential to it.

In Augustine's thought, religious perfection is possible at every point of the course of history after Christ; in Joachim's thought only in a definite period at a definite juncture. To Augustine the Christian truth is revealed in one single event, to Joachim in a succession of dispensations. The one expects the end of the world, the other the age of the Holy Spirit before the ultimate end. Both agree that *nihil stabile super terram;* but to Augustine it means that everything is perishable, to Joachim that everything is subject to transformations, including the church and its doctrines. Compared with Augustine and Orosius, but also with Thomas and Otto of Freising, the thought of Joachim is theological historism.[16]

The reaction of the Catholic church against the followers of Joachim had, in principle, the same motivation as the reaction of Augustine against the surviving expectations of the early Christians. Once established in the historical world, the church had to secure her own position and practice the wisdom of this world in administering the means of salvation on a secure foundation. The triumphant church smoothed, stabilized, and neutralized the anarchical potentialities of the radical eschatology of the early Christians, who were heroically unconcerned with the continuous history and civilization of this world.[17] The church did not change the doctrine concerning the last events, yet she postponed indefinitely the expectation of their actual occurrence.

After a thousand years of historical existence, she was saturated with worldliness and her theology with philosophy, both Arabic and Aristotelian. The original elements of the Christian faith— the coming of the Kingdom of God, the second coming of Christ, repentance, rebirth, and resurrection—were overlaid by a vast mass of vested interests and secular concerns.

The Franciscan movement reminded the church that beginning or creation implies and also demands an end or *eschaton* and that history is an interim not because of the indefinite time of its possible duration but because of the decisive threat of a definite termination. Against, but also within, the established church, the Franciscan Spirituals revived the eschatological passion, together with the historical consciousness—as Luther had to revive the purity of faith against the doctrine of meritorious works and the scholastic system, and Kierkegaard the intensity of a Christian existence against the Hegelian philosophy of religion and the mediocrity of a complacent Protestantism. Hence the profound tension between their religious passion and their world-historical setting. Being bound up with a definite situation and even a definite date—the year 1260—the expectations of many a prominent Joachite collapsed with an unexpected turn in the actual happenings. A real historical event, the premature death in 1250 of Frederick II, who was supposed to play his role as the great confounder and Antichrist to its end, refuted their historico-eschatological interpretation.

Apart from this "mistake," which is the kind that seems to be inseparable from any historical calculation of supra-historical revelations and which is yet unable to uproot the profoundly Christian conviction that "the fashion of this world passeth away," there remains a permanent significance to this thirteenth-century struggle. It re-enacted the primitive ideals and expectations of a period when the Christian faith was still confronted with idolatry and the standards of the pagans—but now within a Christian setting, confronted with a Christian Rome as the new Babylon. One can hardly deny that Christianity has always been at its best when it was in such a critical, discriminating situation, when it was attacked and had to defend itself: first against Jews and pagans (St. Paul), then against heresies (Tertullian and Augustine), then against Averroism (St. Thomas), then against the clerical church (Joachim) and the scholastic Aristotelianism (Luther), then against Cartesian rationalism (Pascal), and eventually against its own historical "success" through secularization (Kierkegaard). One may wonder if contemporary American Protestantism knows when to resist and how to defend itself instead of capitulating to scientism and planetary divagations. The trouble with contemporary Christianity is precisely that there is no genuine paganism, neither in Europe nor in America, against which Christianity could once more become what it was. Since our world is nominally Christian and actually secular, one has to "introduce Christianity into Christendom," to use a phrase of Kierkegaard. This, however, is much more difficult than it was to introduce it into a paganism which was religious and not secular.

This perplexing situation of an apology *contra Christianos* did not yet exist at the time of Augustine. The world was then still worldly or rather pagan, without ambiguity and hypocrisy, while the church, though established, was strongly aware of her genuine task and constructive, though critical, function: of desecularization instead of secularization, in conformity with all biblical teaching. The biblical world is not a world in the sense of a "universe," i.e., everything combined into one whole, but a creation with beginning and end. This depreciation of the cosmos is implied in the story of Genesis,[18] for a world which is created has no substance in itself, and is explicit in the eschatological teachings of the New Testament.

Joachim, like Luther after him,[19] could not foresee that his religious intention—that of desecularizing the church and restoring its spiritual fervor—would, in the hands of others, turn into its opposite: the secularization of the world which became increasingly worldly by the very fact that eschatological thinking about last things was introduced into penultimate matters, a fact which intensified the power of the secular drive toward a final solution of problems which cannot be solved by their own means and on their own level.[20] And yet it was the attempt of Joachim and the influence of Joachism which opened the way to these future perversions; for Joachim's expectation of a new age of "plenitude" could have two opposite effects: it could strengthen the austerity of a spiritual life over against the worldliness of the church, and this was, of course, his intention; but it could also encourage the striving for new historical realizations, and this was the remote result of his prophecy of a new revelation. The revolution which had been proclaimed within the framework of an eschatological faith and with reference to a perfect monastic life was taken over, five centuries later, by a philosophical priesthood, which interpreted the process of secularization in terms of a "spiritual" realization of the Kingdom of God on earth. As an attempt at realization, the spiritual pattern of Lessing, Fichte, Schelling, and Hegel[21] could be transposed into the positivistic and materialistic schemes of Comte and Marx. The third dispensation of the Joachites reappeared as a third International and a third *Reich*, inaugurated by a *dux* or a *Führer* who was acclaimed as a savior and greeted by millions with *Heil!* The source of all these formidable attempts to fulfil history by and within itself is the passionate, but fearful and humble, expectation of the Franciscan Spirituals that a last conflict will bring history to its climax and end. It needed a sacrifice like that of Nietzsche to re-establish, in an "Antichrist," the Christian alternative between the Kingdom of God and the world, between creation with consummation and eternal recurrence without beginning and end.

IX

AUGUSTINE

HIS REFUTATION OF THE CLASSICAL VIEW OF THE WORLD

THE viewpoint of a Christian interpretation of history is fixed on the future as the temporal horizon of a definite purpose and goal; and all modern attempts to delineate history as a meaningful, though indefinite, progress toward fulfilment depend on this theological thought. Consequently, the supreme test of the latter can be found only in a conception of the temporal process, which is neither Christian nor modern. Christianity had to refute the classical notion of time as an eternal cycle, the visible pattern of which is the cyclic revolution of the heavenly bodies. It is not by chance that we find the most explicit Christian discussion of this classical *theory* of the *cosmos* in a *theology* of *history* concerned with man's happiness; for the logical place for a Christian treatment of cosmological problems is, indeed, not the universe but God and man because the existence of the world depends entirely on God and its significance on man as the purpose of God's creation. Conversely, the logical place for a classical treatment of God and man is the cosmos, because it is itself eternal and divine and controls man's nature and destiny. In view of this fundamental divergence between the Christian and the classical approach, one may expect in advance that Augustine's refutation of the theory of eternal recurrence in a *City of God*[1] could succeed only in so far as it concentrated on the moral deficiency of the pagan theory, refuting it practically but not theoretically. Augustine's question is not so much whether the universe is a creation of God or an eternal cosmos divine in itself as it is whether the moral implications of creation and consummation are more satisfactory than those of eternal recurrence without beginning and end.

The fourth chapter of the eleventh book of the *City of God*

160

begins with the statement: "Of all visible things, the world is the greatest: of all invisible, the greatest is God. But, that the world is, we see; that God is, we believe. That God made the world, we can believe from no one more safely than from God Himself. But where have we heard Him? Nowhere more distinctly than in the Holy Scriptures, where His prophet said, 'In the beginning God made the heavens and the earth.' " A truly classical statement of the Christian position, this passage shows at once why it is irreconcilable with the thesis of the ancients but also incapable of refuting the latter on theoretical grounds; for there is no transition from believing to seeing unless a direct vision of God is accomplished. Judged by the eyes of the senses, faith is indeed "blind." Greek *theoria* is literally a vision or contemplation of what is visible and thereby demonstrable or capable of being shown, while Christian faith or *pistis* is a firm trust in what is invisible and thereby undemonstrable, though capable of being professed by a commitment. The Christian God is inaccessible by natural theology. Since God is superior to his creation in power and being, there can be no genuine explanation of God by the world. The whole world can be, as well as not be, if it depends on God's creative word; the Christian world does not exist essentially. The only authentic witness of the visible world is the invisible God, who reveals his creatorship to man through his prophets.

Only secondarily and in answer to pagan objections which imply the eternity of the world without beginning and end, Augustine argues further that the world by itself already demonstrates the mark of creation, even when the voices of the prophets are silent. The world bears testimony to having been created by its own mutability, the well-ordered character of its changes, and the fair appearance of all visible things.[2] Far, however, from using this second argument as the decisive one and from inferring the existence of an ordering and immutable God from the world's teleological structure and mutability, Augustine emphasizes that all the greatness, order, and beauty of the universe are nothing and cannot even be said to "be" compared with the invisible greatness, wisdom, and beauty of the eternal God, who created heaven and earth out of nothing.[3] A world which is created out of nothing is a priori deprived of a proper being. This Christian depreciation of the world holds true not only for Genesis but also for the Psalms and the praises of St. Francis.[4] The biblical world is full of beauty and wonder and is like a brother and sister because it manifests the common creator of man and the world but not because it manifests simply itself as beautiful, orderly, and divine.[5] What the ancient universe loses of divine independence it gains in the Christian perspective through transcendent dependence.

Simultaneously with the world, time was created; for it is impossible to imagine a time "before" the creation of something which moves and changes,[6] while God is changeless and time-less. God creates the universe not in time but simultaneously with time, as a temporal world. "For that which is made in time is made both after and before some time, after that which is past, before that which is future. But none could then be past, for there was no creature by whose movements its duration could be measured. But simultaneously with time the world was made, if in the world's creation change and motion were created, as seems evident from the order of the first six or seven days."[7] If, therefore, pagan philosophers hold that the world with its ever recurrent motion is eternal, without beginning and end, they are strangely deceived, not so much by lack of intelligence as by "the madness of impiety." They attribute to the world what can be said only of a God who is infinitely distinct from the world. But, instead of refuting the pagan error on theoretical grounds, Augustine refers to the authority of the Scriptures, whose truth is proved to him by the fulfilment of their predictions. According to the sacred record, not only does the world have a beginning, but this beginning is a very definite one: not even six thousand years have passed since the creation.[8] But even if we calculate the duration of the world at six hundred thousand years, that would not matter, for any imaginable length of finite time is as nothing compared with the interminable eternity of an eternal creator. An extension of time which starts from some beginning and is limited by some termination, be it of whatever extent it may, is incomparably short or rather nothing in comparison with God, who has neither beginning nor end.[9]

As to the human race, which some ancient philosophers believe has also always existed, since experience shows that man cannot exist at all save as produced by man, Augustine answers that these philosophers "say what they think but not what they know." Augustine "knows" that man has a real beginning, independent of other men, because he knows by the eyes of faith that man is not the mere product of procreation but a unique and absolute creation. The primary fact of human existence is not generation and identity through generations, but the fact that each individual and generation is weak and ignorant, decaying and dying, and yet capable of being renewed by a spiritual regeneration. What is at stake in this short interval of human existence is the alternative between being eternally blessed or being condemned. It is true that pagan philosophers, too, speak of a renewal, but it is with reference to nature and by introducing fixed cycles of time. They assert that these cycles will ceaselessly recur, like sunrise and sunset, summer and winter, generation and corruption. This theory of eternal recurrence, which to the Greek mind quite naturally manifested an immutable and rational order regulating the temporal changes, assured them of the reliability of the cosmos.[10] To Augustine it is no more than a "vicissitude" which has to be rejected all the more since it does not even exempt the immortal soul and destiny of man.

His final argument against the classical concept of time is, therefore, a moral one: the pagan doctrine is hopeless, for hope and faith are essentially related to the future and a real future cannot exist if past and future times are equal phases within a cyclic recurrence without beginning and end. On the basis of an everlasting revolution of definite cycles, we could expect only a blind rotation of misery and happiness, that is, of deceitful bliss and real misery, but no eternal blessedness—only an endless repetition of the same but nothing new, redemptive, and final. The

Christian faith truthfully promises salvation and everlasting blessedness to those who love God, while the godless doctrine of futile cycles paralyzes hope and love itself. If everything were to happen again and again at fixed intervals, the Christian hope in a new life would be futile.

Who, I say, can listen to such things? Who can accept or suffer them to be spoken? Were they true, it were not only more prudent to keep silence regarding them but even ... it were the part of wisdom not to know them. For if in the future world we shall not remember these things, and by this oblivion be blessed, why should we now increase our misery, already burdensome enough, by the knowledge of them? If, on the other hand, the knowledge of them will be forced upon us hereafter, now at least let us remain in ignorance, that in the present expectation we may enjoy a blessedness which the future reality is not to bestow; since in this life we are expecting to obtain life everlasting, but in the world to come are to discover it to be blessed, but not everlasting.[11]

Thus it is, in the last analysis, the exclusion of true happiness which makes the theory of eternal cycles "abominable" and "hostile" to the Christian faith, which is a faith in the radical newness that came into the world and its history with the Savior.

For if the soul, once delivered, as it never was before, is never to return to misery, then there happens in its experience something which never happened before; and this, indeed, something of the greatest consequence, to wit, the secure entrance into eternal felicity. And if in an immortal nature there can occur a novelty, which never has been, nor ever shall be, reproduced by any cycle, why is it disputed that the same may occur in mortal natures?[12]

It is of secondary importance that Augustine further argues that the newness of certain happenings is not extraneous to the "order of nature"; for he conceives the latter not as a *physis* but as a providential order provided for by God, who created nature and man. "God can create new things—new to the world but not to him—which he never before created but yet foresaw from all eternity." To a renewed Christian soul misery and happiness are new happenings, the first by originating in sin, the second by aiming at the deliverance from it. And if Ecclesiastes, who says that there is nothing new under the sun, had meant the pagan repetition of the same (an assumption which Augustine rejects), then Ecclesiastes, too, would be an unbeliever instead of a sage.

Augustine does not make any attempt to refute theoretically the theory of cyclic recurrence and of the eternity of the world. Though using all the armory of his mind in tearing to pieces the cyclic theory of the ancients, Augustine says that faith would smile at their argumentation, "even though reason could not refute the godless who endeavor to turn our simple piety from the right [i.e., straight] way."[13] He abruptly concludes the discussion by saying: "Far be it from us to believe this! for once Christ died for our sins, and rising from the dead he dieth no more." It is not by accident that the discussion of the eternal recurrence, which is related to the sameness and constancy of cosmic events, thus ends with the supra-natural argument that Christ's appearance and his resurrection are both unique and yet universal events. For the power to raise the dead to eternal life is, indeed, the highest test of the power of God and, to a Christian believer, of infinitely greater concern than is the world's eternal existence. In the miracle of resurrection, the miracle of creation is once more restated and intensified.[14] The right doctrine leads to a future goal, while "the wicked walk in a circle."[15] The circle, in the view of the ancients the most perfect because self-contained figure, is a vicious one if the cross is the virtue of life and its meaning bound up with a purpose.

Modern man is still living on the capital of the cross *and* the circle, of Christianity and antiquity; and the intellectual history of Western man is a continuous attempt to reconcile the one with the other, revelation with reason. This attempt has never succeeded, and it cannot succeed unless by compromise. Both Nietzsche and Kierkegaard have shown that the initial decision between Christianity and paganism remains decisive; for how could one reconcile the classical theory that the world is eternal with the Christian faith in creation, the cycle with an *eschaton,* and the pagan acceptance of fate with the Christian duty of hope?[16] They are all the more irreconcilable because the classical view of the world is a view of things visible, while the Christian "view" of the world is, after all, not a view but a matter of hope and faith in things invisible. And invisible is necessarily also the principle of Augustine's *City of God* as a story of salvation.

AUGUSTINE'S THEOLOGY OF HISTORY

Augustine's *City of God* (412–26) is the pattern of every conceivable view of history that can rightly be called "Christian." It is not a philosophy of history but a dogmatic-historical interpretation of Christianity. Though he is demonstrating the truth of the Christian doctrine in the material of sacred and profane history, the history of the world has for him no intrinsic interest and meaning.[17] The City of God is not an ideal which could become real in history, like the third age of Joachim, and the church in its earthly existence is only a representative signification of the true, transhistorical city. For Augustine the historical task of the church is not to develop the Christian truth through successive stages but simply to spread it, for the truth as such is established. So far as the church is related to history, Augustine is satisfied with those facts which Eusebius had already presented. It is a long way from the mystical concept of the church as the body of Christ to the concept of the Middle Ages, where the church embodies in her turn, as an institution, the means of salvation, and further to the modern notion, where it is a part of the history of civilization and thereby subject to variation and changes. That everything in this *saeculum* is subject to change goes for Augustine without saying; for this very reason profane history has no immediate relevance for faith in things everlasting. Whatever may still happen between now and the end, as both *finis* and *telos,* is irrelevant in comparison with the religious alternatives of either accepting or rejecting Christ and our redemption through him. Augustine's faith does not need any historical elaboration because the historical process as such can never establish and absorb the central mystery of the Incarnation. The faith in it cuts across all linear developments. Apart from such foundation stones of the Christian faith as Abraham, Moses, and Christ, neither Augustine nor Thomas[18] knew, as Joachim did, of a "history" of the Christian religion in the sense of a successive articulation into meaningful stages of the interim between the first and the second coming of Christ. In comparison with the absolute newness of the single event of Christ, nothing really new can happen. What Augustine achieves in the *City of God* is, therefore, an integration not of theology into history but of the faith of the primitive church into the doctrine of the church established. Thus he defended the latter against the persistent chiliastic expectations (Christian, Jewish, and pagan) which were far more "historically" minded than was the doctrine of the church, which no longer expected the historical imminence of the last events.[19] On the other hand, it is due to the elimination of messianic, apocalyptic, and chiliastic end-expectations within the time of history that Augustine was able to construct universal history for the first time as *one* purposeful *procursus* from beginning to end, without an intermediate millennium. Profane events and transcendent goal are, in this view, separated in principle and yet related through the *peregrinatio* or "pilgrimage" *in hoc saeculo* of the faithful toward the ultimate *telos*.

The full title of Augustine's work, *De Civitate Dei contra paganos,* indicates its critical and apologetic purpose. It was occasioned by the sack of Rome by Alaric in 410, an event which made an immense impression upon the peoples of the Roman Empire, comparable to that made by the destruction of Jerusalem upon the Jews and by the fall of Constantinople in the fifteenth century upon the Christian Occident. In our time the occupation of Vienna and Berlin by the Russians may have produced a similar effect upon the peoples of central Europe. The Romans argued after the sack of Rome that the pagan gods had deserted Rome because of the intrusion of those "atheists" called "Christians" who had suppressed and abolished the cult of the Roman gods. Augustine's answer was that, long before the rise of Christianity, the Romans had suffered similar disasters and that Alaric (who was a Christian) had behaved comparatively well. Polytheistic worship, Augustine argued, does not assure worldly prosperity, and the Roman conquest was due, after all, not only to Roman virtue but also to an unscrupulous policy which did not balk at the wholesale extermination of inoffensive populations.

Augustine's estimate of the Roman Empire is distinguished by a remarkable frankness and sobriety. He judges the happenings of his time with as much sympathy as detachment. He rejects the traditional interpretation of Rome as the fourth empire of Daniel's prophecy, because he rejects in principle any *world*-historical, i.e., political, eschatology. Augustine personally believed in the survival of the Roman Empire, but he considered neither the survival nor the decline of an empire as a matter of final importance in the order of the last things. Instead of elevating, as Symmachus, Claudianus, and Prudentius did, the *urbs* to a sacred entity, identifying it with the *orbis Romanus,* Augustine points out that the barbaric invasions did not imperil Constantinople, the eastern capital of the Empire. The irony of the one hundred and fifth sermon is directed against pagan, as well as Christian, believers in the singular importance and sacredness of Rome. The first ten books of the *City of God* are likewise a purposeful depreciation of the traditional Roman pride of pagan and Christian Romans. Within the order of the genuine history of salvation, the real significance of imperial Rome is to preserve earthly peace as the condition for spreading the gospel (xviii. 46). Empires and states are neither the work of the devil, nor are they good and hence justified by natural law. Their origin is man's sin and their relative value the preservation of peace and justice.

What really matters in history, according to Augustine, is not the transitory greatness of empires, but salvation or damnation in a world to come. His fixed viewpoint for the understanding of present and past events is the final consummation in the future: last judgment and resurrection. This final goal is the counterpart of the first beginning of human history in creation and original sin. With reference to these supra-historical points of origin and destination, history itself is an interim between the past disclosure of its sacred meaning and its future fulfilment. Only within this perspective of a decisive *Heilsgeschehen* does profane history enter at all into the viewpoint of Augustine. Accordingly, only four books out of twenty-two deal in part with what we would call "history," the meaning of which depends on the prehistory and posthistory in heaven, on the transcendent beginning and end. Only by this reference to an absolute beginning and end has history as a whole a meaning. On the other hand, beginning and end are also not meaningful in themselves but with reference to the story which they begin and end, and the central happening of this history is Jesus Christ's advent, the eschatological event.

The substance of the history of man, which is universal because of being united and controlled by one single God to one single end, is a conflict between the *Civitas Dei* and the *Civitas Terrena*. These cities are not identical with the visible church and the state but are two mystical societies constituted by two opposite species of man. On earth the *Civitas Terrena* begins with Cain the fratricide, the *Civitas Dei* with his brother Abel. Like the two cities, their representatives, too, are to be understood allegorically. Cain is "the citizen of this *saeculum*" and, by his crime, the founder of the earthly city. Abel is in this *saeculum* *"peregrinans,"* on a pilgrimage toward a nonearthly goal. The spiritual descendents of Abel live *in hoc saeculo* in the city of Cain but without being its founders and settlers (Heb. 13:14). Hence the "history" of the City of God is not co-ordinate with the history of the City of Man but is the only true history of salvation, and the historical course (*procursus*) of the City of God consists in its *peregrinatio*. For Augustine and all genuine Christian thinking, "progress" is nothing else than a pilgrimage toward. As a *civitas peregrinans,* the church is related to the profane happenings according to their relative usefulness in serving the transcendent purpose of building the house of God. Judged by its own standards, however, the *Civitas Terrena* is governed by expediency, pride, and ambition, the *Civitas Dei* by self-sacrifice, obedience, and humility. The one is *vanitas,* the other *veritas*. The *Civitas Terrena* lives by natural generation, the *Civitas*

Dei by supernatural regeneration; the one is temporal and mortal, the other eternal and immortal. The one is determined by love of God, even to the contempt of self; the other by love of self, even to the contempt of God. The children of light consider their earthly existence as a means of enjoying God; the children of darkness consider their gods as a means of enjoying the world. Thus history is an age-long contest between faith and unbelief.[20]

The sacred history of salvation is not an empirical fact ready at hand but a succession of faith, while the history of the empires, that is, of sin and death, comes to a real and definite end, which is, at the same time, a consummation of history and a redemption from it. The historical process as such, the *saeculum,* shows only the hopeless succession and cessation of generations. If seen with the eyes of faith, however, the whole historical process of sacred and secular history appears as a preordained *ordinatio Dei.*

Hence the whole scheme of Augustine's work serves the purpose of vindicating God in history. Yet history remains definitely distinct from God, who is not a Hegelian god in history but the Lord of history. God's dealing in history is beyond our disposal, and his providence (like Hegel's "cunning of reason") overrules the intentions of men. It is, in particular, the historical destiny of the Jews which reveals to Augustine the history of the world as a court of justice and thereby the meaningfulness of purposeful history.[21] This does not mean that we are able by our own wisdom to judge the deserts of earthly kingdoms, which God gives to both pious and impious men. We can discern only some fragments of meaning—those that God pleases to manifest to us. History is a divinely appointed pedagogy, operating mainly through suffering.

On the basis of this theological framework Augustine distinguishes six epochs, according to the six days of creation. The first extends from Adam to the great Flood; the second from Noah to Abraham, and the third from Abraham to David, with Nimrod and Nimus as their wicked counterparts. The fourth epoch extends from David to the Babylonian Exile, the fifth from there to the birth of Jesus Christ. The sixth and last epoch, finally, extends from the first to the second coming of Christ at the end of the world.

In this traditional division, which was still accepted by Thomas, the duration of the Christian epoch remains, with Augustine, indefinite. Lactantius still computed that the world would end in about 500. Augustine refrains from any apocalyptic calculation of the duration of the last epoch. What matters from an eschatological viewpoint is not the negligible difference of a few hundred or a few thousand years but the fact that the world is created and transient. Besides the division into six epochs, and their analogy with six individual ages (infancy, childhood, youth, early manhood, later manhood, old age), there is also a division into three epochs according to the spiritual progress of history: first, before the law (childhood); second, under the law (manhood); and third, grace (old age or *mundus senescens,* corresponding to Hegel's *Greisenalter des Geistes*).

In consequence of this strictly religious viewpoint we cannot expect from Augustine a detailed interest in secular history as such. Only two empires represent terrestrial history in his work: that of the Assyrians in the East, and that of the Romans in the West, an anticipation of Hegel's thesis that all meaningful history moves progressively from the east to the west. Egypt, Greece, and Macedonia are scarcely mentioned. Alexander the Great figures only as a great robber who desecrated the temple of Jerusalem by *impia vanitas.* Jerusalem symbolizes the City of God, Babylon and Rome (the second Babylon) the City of Man.

As a Roman citizen, nurtured by Virgil and Cicero, Augustine was not insensible to the greatness and virtue of Rome, whose history was also a means to the purpose of God. But, in comparison with Origen and Eusebius, his view was considerably detached.[22] He refrains from the traditional harmonization of the Roman Empire with the rise of Christianity. "As far as this life of mortals is concerned, which is spent and ended in a few days, what does it matter under whose dominion a dying man lives if they who govern do not force him to impiety and iniquity."[23] His central theme and concern is the eschatological history of faith, which is, as it were, a secret history within secular history, subterranean and invisible to those who have not the eyes of faith. The whole course of history becomes progressive, meaningful, and intelligible only by the expectation of a final triumph, beyond historical time, of the City of God over the city of sinful men.

To a man like Augustine all our talk about progress, crisis, and world order would have seemed insignificant; for, from the Christian point of view, there is only one progress: the advance toward an ever sharper distinction between faith and unbelief, Christ and Antichrist; there are only two crises of real significance: Eden and Calvary; and there is only one world order: the divine dispensation, whereas the history of the empires "runs riot in an endless variety of sottish pleasures."

Modern philosophers and even theologians often complain that Augustine's sketch of the world's history is the weakest part of his work and that he did not do justice to the "intrinsic" problem of historical processes.[24] It is true that Augustine failed to relate the first cause, that is, God's providential plan, to the "secondary causes" operative in the process as such. But it is precisely the absence of a detailed correlation between secular and sacred events which distinguishes Augustine's Christian apology from Bossuet's more elaborate theology of political history and from Hegel's philosophy of history, both of which prove too much by deducing guaranties of salvation and success from historical events. What to us seems a lack in Augustine's understanding and appreciation of secular history is due to his unconditional recognition of God's sovereignty in promoting, frustrating, or perverting the purposes of man.

To expect from the author of the *Confessions* a historical criticism of empirical facts would be as much out of place as to expect from a modern historian an interest in the problem of bodily resurrection, a problem to which Augustine dedicated the entire last book of his *City of God*. It is indeed very hard for us to imagine the passion of faith, together with the belief in miracles and in the fulfilment of prophecies, which inspired his work. To understand a mind like that of Augustine, we have to forget the standards of history as a "science" and its supreme ambition to manage future events; and remember the authority of the Bible, in particular the authority of prophetic predictions and of God's unmanageable providence.

X

OROSIUS

THE *Seven Books of History against the Pagans*[1] were written by Orosius in about 418, upon the request of his master, Augustine. The principle of providential guidance, the theme, and the apologetic purpose are the same as those of Augustine's *City of God,* particularly of Book iii. But Orosius' work is more elaborate in historical material and places greater emphasis on the problem of the comparative happiness or unhappiness in pagan and Christian times. Though contemporary with Augustine's *City of God,* the work of Orosius shows an interesting change in the attitude toward the Roman Empire; for, in spite of Orosius' pride in being a "Roman and Christian" who can take refuge anywhere and yet find "his native land, law, and religion,"[2] it seems that the younger generation had reconciled itself to the new barbaric conditions. Orosius argues that the barbarians are not so bad after all, that they soon became civilized and treated the rest of the Romans as comrades and friends, "so that now among them there may be found some Romans who, living with the barbarians, prefer freedom with poverty to tribute-paying with anxiety among their own people."[3] True, the barbarians were a menace over a long period; but, instead of taking for themselves as much as they could have done when the whole world lay open to them, they asked only for an alliance with Rome and for enough land to establish a small settlement, offering their services to protect the Roman Empire.[4] Moreover, many of them (Huns, Suebi, Vandals, Burgundians) became loyal Christians; and it would seem that the mercy of God ought to be praised by which so many nations received a knowledge of the truth, which they would not have received "but for this opportunity [the barbarian invasions], even at the cost of our own weakening."[5] Whatever disasters

174

they may have brought upon a decaying world, the same disasters might well become the dawn of a new world, preserving the benefits of Roman civilization, its *Romania,* though not the Roman rule.[6]

History, to Orosius as to Augustine, is a history of salvation for the very reason that it is the story of a sinful race, which used its freedom against its creator. Since man is tainted by original sin, the history of his salvation cannot but be a story of discipline and chastisement, which is as just as it is merciful.

Everyone who sees mankind reflected through himself and in himself perceives that this world has been disciplined since the creation of man by alternating periods of good and bad times. Next we are taught that sin and its punishment began with the very first man. Furthermore, even our opponents, who begin with the middle period and make no mention of the ages preceding, have described nothing but wars and calamities. What else are these wars but evils which befall one side or the other? Those evils which existed then, as to a certain extent they exist now, were doubtless either palpable sins or the hidden punishments for sin.[7]

To set forth the passions and punishments of sinful man, who by the "torch of greed" has set on fire the world; to set forth the tribulations of the world and the judgments of God from the creation to the present day (i.e., through a period of 5,618 years), is the aim of Orosius' comprehensive presentation. It rests on the faith that one true God, revealed by one single event at one definite time, has established the historical process for one single purpose—to bring man back to his creator. Pagans, of course, may argue that if God had the power to create the world, to establish peace therein, and to make himself known, what need was there of extending this interim period of history, i.e., of disasters and sufferings, over thousands of years, instead of fulfilling his purpose in the very beginning? Orosius answers that only narrow-minded people resent the fact that great power is associated with great patience. Having misused God's gift of freedom, man has to be grateful for the patience of his creator who, instead of destroying man, permits him to suffer trials, thus giving him a chance of repentance and redemption.[8]

175

Seen in the perspective of the Fall of man, all human history, be it that of Babylon or of Rome, is essentially the same; for whatever has been built by the hand of man falls and comes to an end through the passage of time. "As we anxiously watch the structure of the once powerful Roman Republic," we can only debate "whether it is trembling more from the weakness of old age or from the blows struck by foreign invaders."[9] It is true that the disasters of the present time (the fifth century) seem to have boiled over and to exceed all usual limits; "but now I have discovered that the days of the past were not only as oppressive as those of the present but that they were the more terribly wretched the further they were removed from the consolation of true religion." The beginning of man's misery is the beginning of his sin, and the disasters that afflict the human race are therefore world wide. Only one exception has to be made with regard to the essential identity of past, present, and future events: in the last days of this world, when Antichrist shall appear and when judgment shall be pronounced, "there shall be distress such as there never was before."[10] The sufferings of mankind, far from refuting the rule of God, demonstrate it most clearly. Only pagans cannot understand why Christians delight in the chastisement and discipline which their loving Father justly sends as a necessary means to a blessed end. "If a man knows himself, his acts and thoughts, and the judgments of God, would he not admit that all his sufferings are just and even insignificant?" To suffer in this life for the sake of an eternal glory is more reasonable than to bear suffering, like the pagans, for the sake of worldly fame.

That God governs the course of human history through suffering follows simply from the fact that he is the Lord of creation and, in particular, the creator of man; for, if we are the creation of God, we are also the object of his concern, not the least by censure. And if all power derives ultimately from God, all the more so are the kingdoms from which all other powers proceed. If the kingdoms, however, are rivals, it is better that some one kingdom be supreme. Thus in the beginning there was the Babylonian kingdom, then the Macedonian, later the African, and finally the Roman. These four kingdoms, preordained by God's inscrutable plan, were pre-eminent in successive stages at the four cardinal points of the world: the Babylonian kingdom in the east, the Carthaginian in the south, the Macedonian in the north, and the Roman in the west. The second and third of these four providential kingdoms have, according to Orosius, only transitional significance, while the histories of Babylon and Rome show a distinct parallelism, in origin, power, size, and age. "It was as if the one fell and the other arose," so that the rule of the West succeeded that of the East.[11] This meaningful succession, culminating in Christian Rome, indicates that "one God has directed the course of history, in the beginnings for the Babylonians, and in the end for the Romans." But how different is their decline and fall! While Babylon lost her rule, Rome retains hers because in Babylon the punishment was visited upon the king, whereas in Rome the even temper of the Christian faith was preserved in the person of the king. For the sake of the Christians, mercy was shown to Rome. Unlike Augustine, Orosius stresses the meaningfulness of the coincidence between the rule of Caesar Augustus and the birth of Jesus Christ, elaborating what has aptly been called the "political monotheism"[12] of many apologists. When the Roman Empire had gained the mastery of Asia, Africa, and Europe, God conferred all things by his decree upon a single emperor, who was pre-eminent in power and mercy. The whole world became unified by Roman law and peace. This was the earthly condition by which the gospel could spread abroad without hindrance. "Men, though prompted to blasphemy by hatred, are unwillingly forced to recognize and to concede that this quiet, serenity, and peace throughout the entire world has come not from the greatness of Caesar but by the power of the Son of God who appeared in the time of Caesar" to illuminate the world through his disciples, who, passing through different nations, could speak as Roman citizens to Roman citizens. Thus the empire of Augustus might be proved to have been prepared for the future event of Christ, already announced by many signs and prodigies. Nothing is more evident than that Augustus had been predestined by some hidden order of events for the service of His preparation. "Neither is there any doubt ... that it was by the will of our Lord Jesus Christ ... that Rome was brought to such heights of power since to her, in preference to all others, He chose to belong when He came, thereby making it certain that He was entitled to be called a Roman citizen...."[13]

Answering the charge of the pagans that the present, that is, Christian times, in which the worship of the pagan gods became neglected and suppressed, are beset with calamities as never seen before, while Rome had prospered during the persecution of the Christians, Orosius argues, first, that the record of history shows that the ruin of war, the burning of cities, enslavement of whole provinces, plundering of wealth, pillage of flocks, robbery of the dead and slavery of the living, famines and diseases, floods and earthquakes—in short, all the miseries and calamities which constitute history—have subsisted ever since; and, second, that, if a fair comparison is to be made between the past and the present times, the Christian times are rather less afflicted with those evils. What must be compared are not our immediate feelings about present evils with our rosy records of past events, but events with events. In other words, we must overcome a natural tendency that refuses to attach the same importance to a story of past disasters as to a calamity suffered in the present by ourselves. "The more trying past events were in actual experience, the more pleasing, it is held, they are to relate. Future events, which become desirable because of our feeling of disgust for the present, we always believe will be better. But so far as present events are concerned, we can make no just comparison of miseries; for no matter how insignificant present evils may be, they cause much more trouble than either those which have taken place in the past or those which will come in the future."[14] The bitterest calamities of others become pleasant tales in the distorting perspective of memory, which recalls only the glorious deeds and achievements while forgetting the sufferings caused by them.

Let judgment be passed whether the days of Alexander should be praised on account of his valor in conquering the world or be accursed because of the ruin he brought upon mankind. Many people will be found today who think the present good because they themselves have overcome obstacles and because they consider the miseries of others their own good fortune. Yet someone may say: "the Goths are enemies of the Roman world." We shall reply: "The whole East in those days thought the same of Alexander, and so, too, have the Romans appeared to others when they attacked distant and harmless peoples." The destruction wrought by an enemy is one thing, the reputation of a conqueror another. The Romans and Alexander formerly harried with wars peoples whom they later received into their empires and ruled by their laws. The Goths as enemies are now throwing into disorder lands which, if they should ever succeed in mastering (which God forbid) they would attempt to govern by their own code. Posterity will call mighty kings those whom we now regard as our most savage enemies.[15]

People are always looking for better times, either expecting them from the future or projecting them into the past because they are afflicted with the evils of the present. But "what else can be deduced, when both berate their own times, but that the times either have always been good though unappreciated, or that they will never be better in the future."[16] The narrow interest which people take in their own well-being or misery makes them incapable of seeing things as they are in their true proportion. Thus when pagans say that Rome was happy in the times of her continuous triumphs, victories, imposing processions, and wealth, one has to point out to them that whenever Rome conquered and was happy the rest of the world was conquered and unhappy.

Should we therefore attach too much importance to this small measure of happiness when it has been obtained at so enormous an expenditure of effort? Granted that these times did bring about some happiness to a particular city, did they not also weigh down the rest of the world with misery and accomplish its ruin? If these times are to be considered happy because the wealth of a single city was increased, why should they not rather be judged as most unhappy in view of the wretched destruction and downfall of mighty realms, of numerous and civilized peoples?[17]

179

It is only in Burckhardt's *Reflections on History,* in particular in the essay "On Fortune and Misfortune in History," that we find a similar insight into the fallacy of our comparative judgments and into the correlation of action and suffering as the general pattern of all human history. The difference in their analyses is, however, that Burckhardt was confronted with modern optimism and the belief in progress, Orosius with ancient pessimism and the idea of decay. Consequently, Burckhardt had to emphasize the ultimate insignificance of our claims to happiness, while Orosius, as an apologist, had to insist on a relative betterment of Christian times, separating them on account of "the more present grace of Christ" from "the former confusion of unbelief"; for, by whatever names great deeds are known, "whether as sufferings or acts of bravery, when compared with former times, both are less numerous in our own age. In either case comparison with the times of Alexander and the Persians points to our advantage. If 'bravery' is the proper word, the valor of the enemy is less marked; if 'suffering' is the word to use, the distress of the Romans is less acute."[18] In spite of this attempt to distinguish Christian and pagan times even on the secular level and to establish therein a correlation between punishment and sin, Orosius would have agreed with Burckhardt's realistic statement that man is primarily a *Dulder* or patient and history a kind of pathology, reflecting the nature of man, and that nothing is more un-Christian than to promise earthly happiness in this *saeculum* as a divine reward for human virtue; for both understood, the one as a believer,[19] the other as a skeptic, that the power of evil is an essential element in the economy of the world, evoking and provoking, revealing and testing, the power of good, and that Christianity is a victorious religion of suffering, of the glory of the cross, but not a "better adjustment." Burckhardt withdrew himself into the serenity of pure contemplation, Orosius into the serenity of an absolute faith. As St. Paul when imprisoned did not think of escaping (or of improving the conditions of prison) but had but one concern: that the things which had happened unto him might serve "the progress of the gospel" among the whole praetorian guard (Phil. 1:12), so Orosius, when considering the possible effects of the barbarian invasions, had but one concern: that they might offer an opportunity for spreading the gospel among the pagans. "For how does it harm a Christian who is longing for eternal life to be withdrawn from this world at any time or by any means? On the other hand, what gain is it to a pagan who, though living among Christians, is hardened against faith, if he drag out his days a little longer, since he whose conversion is hopeless is destined at last to die?"[20] If these pagans knew anything of the Father, and of the hope that has now been given to the nations, "they would consider the chastisement lighter even if they suffered more."[21] To a Christian believer like Augustine or Orosius secular history is not meaningful in itself but is a fragmentary reflection of its supra-historical substance, the story of salvation, which is determined by a sacred beginning, center, and end.

XI

THE BIBLICAL VIEW OF HISTORY[1]

PRE-CHRISTIAN as well as post-Christian paganism reckons historical time from a *beginning*. Its histories usually begin with a decisive political event (e.g., the foundation of Rome or a new revolutionary beginning) as the lasting foundation of the following happenings. The Jews, too, reckon historical time from a beginning—the world's creation—though in view of an *eschaton*. What is particular to the Christian time-reckoning is that it counts from a *central* event, which occurred when the time had been fulfilled. For the Jews, the central event is still in the future, and the expectation of the Messiah divides for them all time into a present and a future aeon. For the Christian the dividing line in the history of salvation is no longer a mere *futurum* but a *perfectum praesens,* the accomplished advent of Jesus Christ. With regard to this central event the time is reckoned *forward as well as backward.* The years of the history B.C. continuously decrease while the years A.D. increase toward an end-time. In this linear, though double-faced, chronological scheme the biblical view of history is delineated as a history of salvation, progressing from promise to fulfilment and focused in Jesus Christ.

In this linear, but centered, movement a progressive condensation and reduction takes place, culminating in the single representative figure of Christ, to be followed by a progressive expansion of the central event into a world-wide community of believers, who live in and through Christ, constituting the church out of Jews and Gentiles.[2] Referring to St. Paul's outline of the history of salvation (Gal. 3:6 ff.; Romans, chaps. 9–11, and 5:12 ff.), O. Cullmann thus describes the *Heilsplan,* i.e., the historical economy of salvation:

Man was meant to rule over the rest of creation. He fell, and this fall into sin involved the whole creation under the curse of God (Gen. 3:17; Rom. 8:20). Out of sinful mankind God chose one group, the people of Israel, for the salvation of the world. Within this people, however, a further reduction takes place to a still smaller human community which is to fulfil the purpose of God—the "remnant of Israel," the *qehal Jahve.* This remnant once more is compressed and reduced to *one* man, who alone is able to take over Israel's function. He is the "servant of Jahve" in II Isaiah, the "Son of Man" in Daniel, who represents the "people of the saints" (Dan. 7:13 ff.). This single person must enter history in the Son of God, Christ, who through his vicarious death at last accomplishes the purpose for which God had chosen the people of Israel. Thus the history of salvation up to Christ develops as a progressive reduction: mankind (Adam)—the people of Israel—the remnant of Israel—the One, Christ (second Adam). Thus indeed has the history of salvation arrived at its center, but it has not yet run its complete course. Now it becomes necessary, in a manner of speaking, to reverse the process, namely, to proceed from the One to the Many, but in such a way that *the Many represent the One.* Now the way leads from Christ to those who believe in him, who know themselves to be saved in their faith in his vicarious death. Thus the way leads to the church, which is the body of the One; she is now to fulfil for mankind the task of the "remnant," of the "people of the saints." Therefore she also applies to herself the title of that "remnant" (*qehal Jahve*), which is the Hebrew equivalent of *ekklesia,* "church." Thus the history of salvation runs its course in two movements. The first runs from the Many to the One. This is the Old Covenant. The other runs from the One to the Many. This is the New Covenant. Precisely in the middle is the decisive *factum,* the death of Christ.[3]

In the process of this divine economy everything is from God and to God through Jesus Christ as the mediator. The theological principle which determines this formal scheme of the historical process as a history of salvation is man's sin against God's will and God's willingness to redeem his fallen creation. In this theological perspective the pattern of history is a movement progressing, and at the same time returning, from alienation to reconciliation, one great detour to reach in the end the beginning through ever repeated acts of rebellion and self-surrender. Man's sin and God's saving purpose—they alone require and justify history as such, and historical time. Without original sin and final redemption the historical interim would be unnecessary and unintelligible.

This "interim," i.e., the whole of history, is neither an empty period in which nothing happens nor a busy period in which everything may happen, but the decisive time of probation and final discrimination between the wheat and the tares. Its constant content are variations of one single theme: God's call and man's response to it. To experience history as an "interim" means to live in a supreme tension between conflicting wills, running a "race," the goal of which is neither an airy ideal nor a massive reality but the promise of salvation.

The Christian claim that the whole and only meaning of history before and after Christ rests on the historical appearance of Jesus Christ is a claim so strange, stupendous, and radical that it could not and cannot but contradict and upset the normal historical consciousness of ancient and modern times. To a classical mind like Celsus'[4] the Christian claim is ridiculously pretentious because it endows an insignificant group of Jews and Christians with cosmic relevance. To a modern mind like Voltaire it is equally ridiculous because it exempts a particular history of salvation and revelation from the profane and general history of civilization. Both Celsus and Voltaire realize the *scandalon* of a history of salvation. They had, therefore, a more correct understanding of it than do those liberal theologians who adorn the "stern facts" of social and economic history with "spiritual values" of questionable validity, calling this modern compound of facts and values a "Christian" interpretation.[5] The possibility of a Christian interpretation of history rests neither on the recognition of spiritual values nor on that of Jesus as a world-historical individual; for many such individuals have had a world-wide effect and more than one has claimed to be a savior. The Christian interpretation of history stands or falls with the acceptance of Jesus as Christ, i.e., with the doctrine of the Incarnation.

Seen in the light of the faith that God is revealed in the historical man, Jesus Christ, the profane events before and after Christ are not a solid chain of meaningful successions but spurious happenings whose significance or insignificance is to be judged in the perspective of their possible signification of judgment and salvation. The historical interest and outlook of the Old and New Testaments is definitely limited by being concentrated upon a few outstanding persons and events, which are related by providence to the dogmatic history of salvation as the only history of relevance and significance.[6]

In spite of this divergence between religious and profane history, theologians and secular historians alike have, time and again, tried to assimilate what is foreign to their viewpoints, explaining either the political history of the world religiously (Bossuet) or revealed religion in terms of profane history (Voltaire), without ever succeeding in reducing the one to the other. To integrate the one into the other is to abolish the difference between man and God, between creature and creator. The most that can be said from the standpoint of faith is that the history of salvation includes all the other stories, inasmuch as it is reflected in them.[7] Being relevant only through such relation, the profane events cease to be absolutely profane. They are then open to allegorical and typological interpretation. As a history of salvation, the history of the world is a "parable" (Mark 4:10–12) manifested in hiddenness.

Even the articulation of all historical time into past, present, and future reflects the temporal structure of the history of salvation. The past points to the first things, the future to the last things, and the present to a central presence which connects the past with the future through teleological succession. It is only because of our habit of thinking in terms of the Christian tradition that the formal division of all historical time into past, present, and future times seems so entirely natural and self-evident. But the theoretical observation of natural space-time and the distinction of an indifferent "now"-point from its "before" and "after"[8] do not explain the experience of a qualitative historical time. A historical now is not an indifferent instant but a *kairos,* which opens the horizon for past as well as for future. The significant now of the *kairos* qualifies the retrospect on the past and the prospect upon the future, uniting the past as preparation with the future as consummation. Historically, it was the appearance of Jesus Christ at the appointed time which opened for the Christian faith this perspective onto the past and onto the future as temporal phases in the history of salvation. Within this temporal scheme of salvation, the birth, death, and resurrection of Christ are not a particular now but a single once-for-all which happened once-upon-a-time.[9] Prefiguring and unfolding this outstanding time when the time was fulfilled are other *kairoi* in the past and the future which together delineate the historical *oikonomia* of the divine dispensation. A mere before and after of a neutral now could never have constituted historical past and historical future. True, modern historical consciousness has discarded the Christian faith in a central event of absolute relevance, yet it maintains its logical antecedents and consequences, viz., the past as preparation and the future as consummation, thus reducing the history of salvation to the impersonal teleology of a progressive evolution in which every present stage is the fulfilment of past preparations. Transformed into a secular theory of progress, the scheme of the history of salvation could seem to be natural and demonstrable.

The Christian understanding of history and time is not a matter of theoretical demonstration but a concern of faith, for only by faith can one "know" that the ultimate past and the ultimate future, the first and the last things, are converging on and represented in Jesus Christ as savior. No historian as such can possibly discover that Jesus is the Son of God and the second Adam[10] and that the history of his church is the core of all genuine history by being inspired by the Holy Ghost. And not only the "myth" of beginning and end[11] but also whatever is really historical in the biblical records presupposes the faith in revelation in order to be significant for judgment and salvation.[12] To the natural reason of an empirical historian it cannot but be incredible that our eternal happiness and the redemption of all creation should depend on an episode which happens to have happened in Palestine two thousand years ago. Empirically, the histories of Israel and of the Christian church are events like other events within a certain period of secular history but not phases in a history of salvation, preparing and fulfilling a central event.[13] On the other hand, the story of the central event, as presented in the Gospels, presupposes everywhere the unity and solidarity of the history of salvation from beginning to end. The particular story of Jesus Christ is, at the same time, the universal history of salvation. If modern Christians do not feel that the universal claim of such a particularity, that a temporal "once" claiming to be "for all," is a *scandalon,* it is due only to a lack of imagination and to the customary confusion of faith in Christ with Christian religion in general.

For a believer the redemptive aspect of history is not an aspect of secular history but the transcendent light which shines in the darkness of man's historical plight, and the story of Christ "a center of meaning at the edge of life's seeming meaningless-ness."[14] To walk in the line of the history of salvation means to renounce the highways of general happenings, glorious and spectacular or common and miserable. It is a narrow path of resolute renunciation, which gives direction and meaning to events—at least to some of them—by cutting across the many crossways of profane happenings. Seen in the perspective of the world's history, Jesus Christ is the founder of a new sect; seen with the eyes of faith, he is the *Kyrios Christos* and thereby the Lord of history. While the lords of the history of the world are Alexanders and Caesars, Napoleons and Hitlers, Jesus Christ is the Lord of the Kingdom of God and therefore of secular history only in so far as the history of the world hides a redemptive meaning. The particular stories of the world are but in-directly related to the narrow but universal history of salvation and in themselves incommensurate with it. Merely as a background and as empirical instruments in God's dealing with man are empires and world-historical persons drawn into the orbit of the biblical perspective of history in the Old and New Testament.

Behind the visible figures and happenings, mysterious powers are invisibly working as *archontes* or primary agents (Rom. 13:1; I Cor. 2:8). Since Christ these powers are already subjected and broken, but still they are powerfully alive. Invisibly, history has fundamentally changed; visibly, it is still the same, for the Kingdom of God is already at hand, and yet, as an *eschaton,* still to come. This ambiguity is essential to all history after Christ: the time is already fulfilled and yet not consummated.[15] The Christian times between Christ's resurrection and his reappearance are definitely the last times (I John 2:18; Matt. 12:28); but, as long as they last, they are penultimate times before the completion of the present, though hidden, Kingdom of Christ in the manifest Kingdom of God beyond historical times. On account of this profound ambiguity of the historical fulfilment where everything is "already" what it is "not yet," the Christian believer lives in a radical tension between present and future. He has faith and he does hope. Being relaxed in his present experience and straining toward the future, he confidently enjoys what he is anxiously waiting and striving for.[16]

To illustrate the relation between the "realized eschatology" and its future reality, we refer to O. Cullmann's comparison of the final *eschaton* with V-Day. In the course of a war the decisive battle may have been fought long before the real end of the war. Only those who realize the decisiveness of the critical battle will also be certain that victory is from now on assured. The many will only believe it when V-Day is proclaimed. Thus Calvary and the Resurrection, the decisive events in the history of salvation, assure the believer of the Day of the Lord in the ultimate future. On the levels of both secular and sacred history the hope in the future is grounded in the faith in an actual event which has come to pass. The tension between the crucial battle and the final V-Day extends over the whole interim period as the last, and yet not ultimate, phase of the war, for the ultimate issue is peace. The outcome of the crucial battle suggests that the end is already near, and yet it is still indefinitely remote, for one cannot safely foretell what exertions the enemy might be able to make to defer his final defeat.[17]

As an eschatological message of the Kingdom of God the theology of the New Testament is essentially unconcerned with the political history of this world. Neither the conflict with paganism nor the later antagonism between church and state characterizes the outlook of the New Testament, which is "primitive," that is, genuine and affirmative on account of the fact that early Christianity was not yet involved and established in the history of this world. The only antagonism which is not accidental but intrinsic to the message of the New Testament is that to Jewish futurism (expecting the Messiah in the future instead of recognizing him in the presence of Jesus) and to the apocalyptic *calculations* of the last events by Jews as well as by Christians.[18] In comparison with the amazing perseverance of the Jewish expectation, which is a faith of hope and waiting, the Christian hope is almost rational, for it rests on the faith in an accomplished fact.[19] The preliminary fulfilment of God's purpose in actual history assures the Christian believer of the final outcome. The Christians of the first generation believed in the eschatological victory and in the future manifestation of the Kingdom of God because they believed in the hidden presence of the Kingdom of the Crucified. The Christian faith, as expressed in the earliest creeds,[20] neither is concerned with an isolated future or past, nor can it be reduced to an existential "decision" in an ever present instant.[21] It comprehends the whole story of salvation, in the future and in the past but concentrated in Jesus Christ as the savior, "the same yesterday and today and forever" (Heb. 13:8).

Such a theological understanding of the history of mankind cannot be translated into world-historical terms and worked out into a philosophical system. World-historical establishments and upheavals hopelessly miss the ultimate reality of the Christian hope and expectation. No secular progress can ever approximate the Christian goal if this goal is the redemption from sin and death to which all worldly history is subjected. The history of salvation occasionally sheds some light also upon the history of the world, but the events of the world as such are neither the source nor the pattern of redemption. From the viewpoint of the New Testament, the significance of Tiberius and Augustus, of Herod and Pontius Pilate,[22] is determined not by their positions and actions but by their function within the divine purpose—hence Pontius Pilate's legitimate, though subordinate, place in the Christian creed. Jesus himself was born and crucified as a Roman citizen within a world-historical setting, but he never intended to make Rome and its empire Christian. Why, then, should a follower of Christ expect that any other empire should become Christianized? A "Holy Roman Empire" is a contradiction in terms. A Protestant will have no difficulty in agreeing with this statement, though he will hesitate to admit that it implies in principle also the theological impossibility of a "Christian democracy" and of a Christian civilization and history.[23] While the distinction between civilization and barbarism holds true on the historical level, the compound of a "Christian civilization" is as questionable as that of a civilized Christianity. As a history of the world, the empirical history after Christ is qualitatively not different from the history before Christ if judged from either a strictly empirical or a strictly Christian viewpoint. History is, through all the ages, a story of action and suffering, of power and pride, of sin and death. In its profane appearance it is a continuous repetition of painful miscarriages and costly achievements which end in ordinary failures —from Hannibal to Napoleon and the contemporary leaders. "Yea, they have not been planted; yea, they have not been sown; yea, their stock has not taken root in the earth; moreover, he bloweth upon them, and they wither, and the whirlwind taketh them away as stubble."[24] History is the scene of a most intensive life, which ends time and again in ruins. And it is awful, though in the spirit of the New Testament, to think that this reiteration of acting and suffering through all the ages should be required to complete the Passion of Christ.[25]

CONCLUSION

THE problem of history as a whole is unanswerable within its own perspective. Historical processes as such do not bear the least evidence of a comprehensive and ultimate meaning. History as such has no outcome. There never has been and never will be an immanent solution of the problem of history, for man's historical experience is one of steady failure. Christianity, too, as a historical *world* religion, is a complete failure.[1] The world is still as it was in the time of Alaric; only our means of oppression and destruction (as well as of reconstruction) are considerably improved and are adorned with hypocrisy.

The farther back we go from the philosophy of history of the eighteenth and nineteenth centuries to its original inspiration in biblical faith, the less do we find, with the exception of Joachim, an elaborate plan of progressive history. Hegel is more assertive than Bossuet, Bossuet more than Augustine and Orosius, Augustine more than St. Paul; and in the Gospels I cannot discover the slightest hint of a "philosophy of history" but only a scheme of redemption through Christ, and from profane history. The words of Jesus contain only one reference to the world's history; it separates strictly what we owe to Caesar from what we owe to God.[2] The most striking feature of the Christian tradition is this very dualism: in the Old Testament between the chosen people and the Gentiles; in the New Testament between the Kingdom of God and the standards of the world. The one, however, is a dualism within history, the other confronts the world from beyond its historical limits. St. Paul had, in a certain way, a theology of history because he understood the succession of Gentiles as a fulfilment of the religious history of the Jews. But he, too, was not concerned at all with secular history. Augustine developed the Christian theology of history on the two opposite levels of sacred and profane history; they meet sometimes, but they are separated by principle. Bossuet restated Augustine's theology of history with a greater emphasis on the relative independence of profane history and on its correlation with sacred history. He knew much more than St. Paul about the divine economy of secular history and therefore falls short of him. Voltaire and, unintentionally, Vico emancipated secular history from sacred history, subjecting the history of religion to that of civilization. Hegel translated and elaborated the Christian theology of history into a speculative system, thus preserving and, at the same time, destroying the belief in providence as the leading principle. Comte, Proudhon, and Marx rejected divine providence categorically, replacing it by a belief in progress and perverting religious belief into the antireligious attempt to establish predictable laws of secular history. Finally, Burckhardt dismissed the theological, philosophical, and socialistic interpretations of history and thereby reduced the meaning of history to mere continuity, without beginning, progress, or end. He had to overemphasize mere continuity because it is the poor remainder of a fuller notion of meaning. And, yet, the faith in history was to him, as to Dilthey, Troeltsch, and Croce, a "last religion." It was the futile hope of modern historism that historical relativism will cure itself.

The modern overemphasis on secular history as *the* scene of man's destiny is a product of our alienation from the natural theology of antiquity and from the supernatural theology of Christianity. It is foreign to wisdom and faith. Classical antiquity believed that human nature and history imitate the nature of the cosmos; the Old Testament teaches that man is created in the image of God; and the Christian teaching is focused on the imitation of Christ. According to the New Testament view, the advent of Christ is not a particular, though outstanding, fact within the continuity of secular history but the unique event that shattered once and for all the whole frame of history by breaking into its natural course, which is a course of sin and death. The importance of secular history decreases in direct proportion to the intensity of man's concern with God and himself. While we are overflooded with secular history but dried up religiously, the *Confessions* of Augustine do not contain the slightest hint at a serious interest in secular events as such. Christianity was thrown into the vortex of the world's history only willy-nilly; and only as a secularized and rationalized principle can God's providential purpose be worked out into a consistent system. As a transcendent principle, the will of God can never become the subject of a systematic interpretation, revealing the meaning of history in the succession and fortunes of states or even in the history of the church. In the Christian view, history is of decisive importance only in so far as God has revealed himself in a historical man. But different from the historical Socrates of Plato's dialogues, the historical Jesus of the Gospels is primarily not a historical teacher but God incarnate. Only we moderns who think of the faith in Christ in terms of "Christianity" and of Christianity in terms of history are inclined to call this revelation a "historical" one, implying thereby not only past actuality but also two thousand years of unrealized eschatology. Judged by the standards of the New Testament, God's revelation in a historical man is his self-disclosure in the "Son of Man," and the supreme test of his being the Son of God or a God-man is the Resurrection, by which he transcends the life and death of every conceivable historical man. For the believer, history is not an autonomous realm of human endeavor and progress but a realm of sin and death and therefore in need of redemption. Within this perspective the historical process as such could not be experienced as all-important.[3] The belief in the absolute relevance of history as such, which made the works of Spengler and Toynbee best sellers, is the result of the emancipation of the modern historical consciousness from the foundation in and limitation by classical cosmology and Christian theology. Both restrained the experience of history and prevented its growing into indefinite dimensions.

It was, in particular, the break with tradition at the end of the eighteenth century which produced the revolutionary character of modern history and of our modern historical thinking.

The political revolution in France and the industrial revolution in England and their universal effects upon the whole civilized world enhanced the modern feeling of living in an epoch when historical changes are all and everything. The philosophy of history has become a more fundamental concern than ever before, because history itself has become more radical. Not only have the innovations by natural science accelerated the speed and expanded the range of sociohistorical movements and changes, but they have made nature a highly controllable element in man's historical adventure. By means of natural science we are now, as never before, "making" history, and yet we are overwhelmed by it because history has emancipated itself from its ancient and Christian boundaries. With Vico divine providence has already become the natural law of history; and with Descartes nature has already become a mathematical project, serving man's mastery. Thus history now occupies a position which is analogous to that occupied by mathematical physics in the seventeenth century, and in consequence of it. To interpret sociopolitical history still in terms of ancient physics and cosmology or in terms of Christian ethics and theology seems to have become an anachronism for modern thinking on history.

There is only one very particular history—that of the Jews— which as a political history can be interpreted strictly religiously. Within the biblical tradition, the Jewish prophets alone were radical "philosophers of history" because they had, instead of a philosophy, an unshakable faith in God's providential purpose for his chosen people, punishing and rewarding them for disobedience and obedience. The exceptional fact of the Jewish existence could warrant a strictly religious understanding of political history, because only the Jews are a really historical people, constituted *as such* by religion, by the act of the Sinaitic revelation.[4] Hence the Jewish people could and can indeed understand their national history and destiny religiously, as a religious-political unity. The eternal law which the Greeks saw embodied in the regular movement of the visible heavens was manifested to the Jews in the vicissitudes of their history, which is a story of divine, though most irregular, interventions. God called Abraham from Ur; he brought up Israel out of Egypt; he gave the law at Sinai; he raised up David to be king; he punished his people by the rod of Assyria and Babylon; he redeemed them by the hand of Cyrus the Persian. And, most amazing, the strength of this faith in a divine moral purpose in history rose to a climax just when all empirical evidence was *against* it. When the Assyrian world power conquered the Near East, the prophets saw in the material ruin of Israel not a proof of the powerlessness of Jahveh but an indirect manifestation of his universal power. To Isaiah it was not Bel but Jehovah who triumphed in the fall of Judah.[5] Assyria itself was but an instrument in the hands of the God of Israel, which would be discarded when his purpose was accomplished. The very calamities of their national history strengthened and enlarged the prophetic faith in the sovereignty of the divine purpose; for He who sets empires in motion for judgment could use them for deliverance as well. The possibility of a belief in the providential ordering of world-historical destinies depends on this belief in a holy people of universal significance, because only peoples, not individuals, are a proper subject of history and only a holy people is directly related to the Lord as a Lord of history.

Christians are not a historical people. Their solidarity all over the world is merely one of faith. In the Christian view the history of salvation is no longer bound up with a particular nation but is internationalized because it is individualized. In Christianity the history of salvation is related to the salvation of each single soul, regardless of racial, social, and political status, and the contribution of the nations to the Kingdom of God is measured by the number of the elect, not by any corporate achievement or failure. From this it follows that the historical destiny of Christian peoples is no possible subject of a specifically Christian interpretation of political history, while the destiny of the Jews *is* a possible subject of a specifically Jewish interpretation. Even if we accept the traditional thesis that the Christian church of Jews and Gentiles is the successor of the chosen people, the Christian church would yet remain the mystical body of Christ, distinct from the historical character of the chosen people, which is a church in itself. Hence one has to conclude that a Jewish theology of secular history is indeed a possibility and even a necessity, while a Christian philosophy of history is an artificial compound. In so far as it is really Christian, it is no philosophy but an understanding of historical action and suffering in the light of the cross (without any particular reference to peoples and world-historical individuals), and, in so far as it is a philosophy, it is not Christian. The perplexing situation is that the attempt at a philosophy of history depends on the Hebrew-Christian tradition, while this very tradition obstructs the attempt to "work out" the working of God.

Since our preoccupation with history and historicity, we are inclined to believe that modern historical consciousness originates with Hebrew and Christian thinking, that is, with the eschatological outlook toward a future fulfilment. We, too, insisted throughout this study on the derivation of our historical sense from Hebrew and Christian futurism. But one has to distinguish, here as everywhere, between a historical source and its possible consequences. Granted that Hebrew and Christian eschatology has opened the horizon for our post-Christian understanding of the world's history, we must not transpose our modern and secular historical thinking into the "historical" consciousness of the Old and New Testaments. The story of the great Flood, the most conspicuous historical event in the Old Testament, tells us that, when the earth was filled with violence by man, God decided to destroy the whole human race, which he repented having made, with the exception of one single family. What else can this story teach than the radical disproportion between the history of the world and the succession of faith? Similarly, the message of the New Testament is not an appeal to historical action but to repentance. Nothing in the New Testament warrants a conception of the new events that constituted early Christianity, as the beginning of a new epoch of secular developments within a continuous process. For the early Christians the history of this world had rather come to an end, and Jesus himself was seen by them not as a world-historical link in the chain of historical happenings but as the unique redeemer. What really begins with the appearance of Jesus Christ is not a new epoch of secular history, called "Christian," but the beginning of an end. The Christian times are Christian only in so far as they are the last time. And, since the Kingdom of God is not to be realized in a continuous process of historical developments, the eschatological history of salvation also cannot impart a new and progressive meaning to the history of the world, which is fulfilled by having reached its term. The "meaning" of the history of this world is fulfilled against itself because the story of salvation, as embodied in Jesus Christ, redeems and dismantles, as it were, the hopeless history of the world. In the perspective of the New Testament the history of the world entered into the eschatological substance of its unworldly message only in so far as the first generations after Christ were still involved in it, but without being of it.

Thus, if we venture to say that our modern historical consciousness is derived from Christianity, this can mean only that the eschatological outlook of the New Testament has opened the perspective toward a future fulfilment—originally beyond, and eventually within, historical existence. In consequence of the Christian consciousness we have a historical consciousness which is as Christian by derivation as it is non-Christian by consequence, because it lacks the belief that Christ is the beginning of an end and his life and death the final answer to an otherwise insoluble question. If we understand, as we must, Christianity in the sense of the New Testament and history in our modern sense, i.e., as a continuous process of human action and secular developments, a "Christian history" is non-sense. The only, though weighty, excuse for this inconsistent compound of a Christian history is to be found in the fact that the history of the world has continued its course of sin and death in spite of the eschatological event, message, and consciousness. The world after Christ has assimilated the Christian perspective toward a goal and fulfilment and, at the same time, has discarded the living faith in an imminent *eschaton*. If the modern mind, concerned with the preservation and advance of the existing society, feels only the impracticability of such an eschatological outlook, it forgets that for the founders of the Christian religion, to whom the collapse of society was certain and imminent, it was, instead, practical good sense which dictated such concentration upon ultimate issues and a corresponding indifference toward intermediate stages of worldly happenings.[6]

The impossibility of elaborating a progressive system of secular history on the religious basis of *faith* has its counterpart in the impossibility of establishing a meaningful plan of history by means of *reason*. This is corroborated by common sense; for who would dare to pronounce a definite statement on the purpose and meaning of contemporary events? What we see in 1948 is Germany's defeat and Russia's victory, England's self-preservation and America's expansion, China's internal difficulties and Japan's surrender. What we cannot see and foresee are the potentialities of these facts. What became a possibility in 1943 and a probability in 1944 was not yet evident in 1942 and was highly improbable in 1941. Hitler could have been killed in World War I or in November, 1939, or in July, 1944, instead of finally killing himself. He could also have succeeded.

The apparent contingency of historical events has endless illustrations on a grand scale. Christianity, which seemed to Tacitus and Pliny an insignificant Jewish quarrel, conquered the Roman Empire; another quarrel, that of Luther, divided the Christian church. Such unpredictable developments, even when unfolded and established, are not solid facts but realized potentialities, and as such they are liable to become undone again. Christianity could have vanished from the history of the world as classical paganism did, could have succumbed to gnosticism, or could have remained a small sect. Christ himself, as a historical man, could have yielded to the temptation of establishing the Kingdom of God historically among the Jews and on earth. In the perspective of human wisdom and ignorance, everything could have happened differently in this vast interplay of historical decisions, efforts, failures, and circumstances.

It is true that, after it reaches a certain climax, the general course of historical destinies seems to be final and therefore subject to prognostication. Europe, too, had its "prophets"—Baudelaire and Heine, B. Bauer and Burckhardt, Dostoevski and Nietzsche. But none of them foresaw the real constellations and the outcome of Europe's agony. What they prognosticate is only the general pattern that history will probably follow. History, instead of being governed by reason and providence, seems to be governed by chance and by fate.

And yet, if we reduce the belief in providence to its genuine character, directing individuals and nations not visibly and consistently but in a rather cryptic and intermittent way, it agrees surprisingly well with that human skepticism which is the ultimate wisdom of Burckhardt's reflections on history. The human result, though not the motivation, of skepticism and faith in regard to the outcome of history is the same: a definite resignation, the worldly brother of devotion, in the face of the incalculability and unpredictability of historical issues. In the reality of that agitated sea which we call "history," it makes little difference whether man feels himself in the hands of God's inscrutable will or in the hands of chance and fate. *Ducunt volentem Fata, nolentem trahunt,* could easily be translated into terms of a theology which believes that God works not only through those who obey his will but also through those who perforce serve him against their will.

No one was more aware than Augustine of this coincidence of the pagan and the Christian reverence for fate and providence, respectively. Discussing the pagan view of fate, he distinguishes two types of fatalism: the one believing in horoscopes and based on astrology, the other based on the recognition of a supreme power.[7] Only the first, he says, is incompatible with the Christian belief; the latter may well agree with it, though the word *fatum* is an unfortunate expression for what is really meant: *sententiam teneat, linguam corrigat.* If fate means a supreme power not at our disposal, which rules our destinies, then fate is comparable to providential divinity.[8] There is indeed a common ground of fearful reverence and free submission to fate, or providence, in ancient antiquity and ancient Christianity, which distinguishes both of them from profane modernity and its belief in progressive manageability.

Neither genuine Christianity nor classical antiquity was profane and progressive, as we are. If there is any point where the Greek and the biblical views of history agree with each other, it is in their common freedom from the illusion of progress.[9] The Christian faith in the incalculable intervention of God's providence, combined with the belief that the world might at any moment come to a sudden end, had the same effect as the Greek theory of recurrent cycles of growth and decay and of an inexorable fate—the effect of checking the rise of a belief in an indefinite progress and an ever increasing manageability. Since both paganism and Christianity were religious, hence also superstitious,[10] they lived in the presence of incalculable powers and subtle dangers lurking in human achievements and gains. If the idea of progress had been presented to a Greek, it would have struck him as irreligious, defying cosmic order and fate. And when it was presented to a radical Christian of the nineteenth century, it had the same effect. Challenged by Proudhon's thesis that each of our progresses is a victory by which we crush providential divinity, Donoso Cortés answered with another *Civitas Dei*.[11]

If it is true that both the world of the Greeks and Romans and that of the Christians are religious, while the modern world is profane, then our foregoing statement that the world "still is as it was" needs some qualification. It is not the historical world but rather human nature which persists through all historical changes. There is, however, a world of difference between the city-state of the ancients, the Christian communities of the Middle Ages, and the states and cities in which we live. The communities of modern times are neither religiously pagan nor Christian; they are decidedly secular, i.e., secularized, and only so far, by derivation, are they still Christian. The old churches of modern cities are no longer the outstanding centers of the communal life but strange islands immersed in the business centers. In our modern world everything is more or less Christian and, at the same time, un-Christian: the first if measured by the standard of classical antiquity, the second if measured by the standard of genuine Christianity. The modern world is as Christian as it is un-Christian because it is the outcome of an age-long process of secularization. Compared with the pagan world before Christ, which was in all its aspects religious and superstitious and therefore a suitable object of Christian apologetics,[12] our modern world is worldly and irreligious and yet dependent on the Christian creed from which it is emancipated. The ambition to be "creative" and the striving for a future fulfilment reflect the faith in creation and consummation, even when these are held to be irrelevant myths.

Radical atheism, too, which is, however, as rare as radical faith, is possible only within a Christian tradition; for the feeling that the world is thoroughly godless and godforsaken presupposes the belief in a transcendent Creator-God who cares for his creatures. To the Christian apologists, the pagans were atheists not because they did not believe in any divinity at all but because they were "polytheistic atheists."[13] To the pagans the Christians were atheists because they believed in only one single God transcending the universe and the city-state, that is, everything that the ancients had consecrated. The fact that the Christian God has ruled out all the popular gods and protecting spirits of the pagans created the possibility of a radical atheism; for, if the Christian belief in a God who is as distinct from the world as a creator is from his creatures and yet is the source of every being is once discarded, the world becomes emancipated and profane as it never was for the pagans. If the universe is neither eternal and divine, as it was for the ancients, nor transient but created, as it is for the Christians, there remains only one aspect: the sheer contingency of its mere "existence."[14] The post-Christian world is a creation without creator, and a *saeculum* (in the ecclesiastical sense of this term) turned secular for lack of religious perspective.

That the Christian *saeculum* has become secular shows modern history in a paradoxical light: it is Christian by derivation and anti-Christian by consequence. Both aspects derive from the worldly success of Christianity and, at the same time, from its failure to make the world Christian. This failure can be explained in two different ways, either materialistically, when it indicates the "ideological" character of the Christian message, or religiously, when it indicates a fundamental proposition of the New Testament, viz., that the Kingdom of Christ is not of this world. Neither of these two interpretations, however, explains the curious mixture of our "Christian world," which lives by the hope in a better world and yet sets its hope on material production and welfare. The two great driving forces of modern history which, according to Burckhardt, are the striving for gain and the striving for power are in themselves insatiable, the more so as they become satisfied and connected with the eschatological hope in a final fulfilment.

The whole moral and intellectual, social and political, history of the West is to some extent Christian, and yet it dissolves Christianity by the very application of Christian principles to secular matters. The breaking-up of the *orbis terrarum* is everywhere the work of the Christian Occident. Europeans made the discoveries of the old Eastern and the new Western world, expanding their civilization with missionary zeal to the ends of the earth. Western explorers and travelers, diplomats and clergymen, engineers and businessmen, discovered and opened America, founded the British Empire, embarked on colonial politics, taught Russia how to become modernized, and forced Japan to open her land to the West. And while the spirit of Europe declined, her civilization rose and conquered the world. The question is whether this tremendous sweep of Western activity has anything to do with the nonsecular, religious element in it. Is it perhaps Jewish Messianism and Christian eschatology, though in their secular transformations, that have developed those appalling energies of creative activity which changed the Christian Occident into a world-wide civilization? It was certainly not a pagan but a Christian culture which brought about this revolution. The ideal of modern science[15] of mastering the forces of nature and the idea of progress emerged neither in the classical world nor in the East, but in the West. But what enabled us to remake the world in the image of man? Is it perhaps that the belief in being created in the image of a Creator-God, the hope in a future Kingdom of God, and the Christian command to spread the gospel to all the nations for the sake of salvation have turned into the secular presumption that we have to transform the world into a better world in the image of man and to save unregenerate nations by Westernization and re-education? There are in history not only "flowers of evil" but also evils which are the fruit of too much good will and of a mistaken Christianity that confounds the fundamental distinction between redemptive events and profane happenings, between *Heilsgeschehen* and *Weltgeschichte*.

EPILOGUE

THE attempt at elucidation of the dependence of the philosophy of history on the eschatological history of fulfilment and salvation does not solve the problem of our historical thinking. It rather poses a new and more radical problem, for it raises the question of whether the "last things" are really the first things and whether the future is really the proper horizon of a truly human existence. And, since the future exists only by anticipation, in the perspective and prospect of hope and fear, the question arises of whether man's living by expectation[1] agrees with a sober view of the world and of man's condition in it.

The Pandora myth, as told by Hesiod,[2] suggests that hope is an evil, though of a special kind, distinguished from the other evils which the box of Pandora contained. It is an evil which seems to be good, for hope is always hoping for something better. But it seems hopeless to look forward to better times in the future, since there is hardly a future which, when it has become present, does not disappoint. Man's hopes are "blind," i.e., unintelligent and miscalculating, deceptive, and illusory. And yet mortal man cannot live without this precarious gift of Zeus, as little as he can live without fire, the stolen gift of Prometheus. If he were without hope, *de-sperans,* he would despair, in "wan-hope."

The view most commonly held in antiquity was that hope is an illusion which helps man to endure life but which, in the last resort, is an *ignis fatuus.* On the other hand, St. Paul's verdict about pagan society was that it had no hope;[3] he meant a hope the substance and assurance of which is faith instead of illusion. The Christian faith hopes without the modern hope in a better *world* and without the ancient depreciation of the dubious gift of Zeus. Instead of accepting the Stoic maxim, *nec spe nec metu,* St. Paul asserts[4] that we are saved by hope—in fear and trembling. The promises of joy and triumph in which Scripture is

204

steeped cannot be separated from the new sense of suffering. "Mankind," says Léon Bloy, "began to suffer *in hope,* and this is what we call the Christian era!"

Who would be prepared to deny that the classic view is sober and wise, while the Hebrew and Christian faith, which erected hope into a moral virtue and a religious duty, seems to be as foolish as it is enthusiastic? Common sense, even theological common sense, will always insist that the early Christian expectation of an impending *eschaton* proved to be an illusion and will draw the conclusion that eschatological futurism is to be taken as a "myth," irrelevant for the "true," i.e., existential (Bultmann) or symbolical (Dodd) meaning of the New Testament message "for us."[5] But this illusion of the early Christians proved to be strangely persistent and quite independent of the rational probability or improbability of eschatological happenings. Time and again serious Christians expected the end of the world and its transfiguration in a near future,[6] the nearness of which is in direct proportion to the intensity of expectancy. One may wonder why common sense could never persuade the Christian sense of the future to discard its illusion. The only inference which hope and faith will draw from the fact that the world has lived on for two thousand years as if nothing had happened which warrants the imminence of a theological *eschaton* is that the end is delayed and therefore still coming. Hence hope and faith are justified in interpreting present events and catastrophes in the light of an *eschaton,* as a prefiguration of an ultimate outcome. The believer, too, will admit that the promises of the Old and New Testaments seem ever more jeopardized by the actual course of events; but his faith in things invisible cannot be invalidated by any visible evidence. Faithful hope does not eliminate the painful conflict between confidence and evidence; it rather enhances it. It is the same faith which creates and resolves the ultimate problem of a Christian and yet worldly existence.

If the last things were only the latest events in a continuous series of secular happenings, the hope in them would be indeed subject to disillusion. Only by their eschatological qualification, as redemptive events, can hope and faith in them be rightly maintained. The Christian hope is not a worldly desire and expectation that something will probably happen but a cast of mind based on an unconditional faith in God's redemptive purpose. Genuine hope is, therefore, as free and absolute as the act of faith itself. Both hope and faith are Christian virtues of grace. The reasons for such an unconditional hope and faith cannot rest on a rational calculation of their reasonableness. Hence hope can never be refuted by so-called "facts"; it can neither be assured nor discredited by an established experience. Hope is essentially confident, patient, and charitable. It therefore releases man from wishful thinking as well as from resignation. A mother who has an unconditional faith in her son is never wrong if, for the alien observer, the facts do not seem to justify her trust. It is rather the son who is wrong if he discredits his mother's faith. The question is therefore not the justification of absolute hope and faith by their relative reasonableness but whether such an unconditional hope and faith can be put into man instead of God and the God-Man. Hope is justified only by faith which justifies itself. Perhaps both grow only on the ruins of all-too-human beliefs and expectations, on the fruitful soil of despair of what is subject to illusions and deceptions.

If such unconditional faith seems to be fanciful to a modern mind, which prides itself on being "scientifically conditioned," the modern mind fails to see that the Christian message was *at all times* extreme and incredible to the natural reason of the well-balanced citizen. St. Paul was no less at odds with the skeptical wisdom of enlightened Romans than was Léon Bloy with that of enlightened Frenchmen. Natural reason will perhaps accept the hypothetical predictions of cosmic catastrophes and historical disintegrations, just as now, after the event, it accepts Kierkegaard's, Bauer's, Nietzsche's, and Dostoevski's amazing predictions of the end of Old Europe. Reason can even enjoy their power of foresight; for the fulfilment of prophecies, like that of scientific predictions, carries with it an invincible satisfaction. But reason will not accept the categorical, yet unfulfilled, proclamation of a veritable *eschaton* with last judgment and redemption.

Reason prefers to believe in the dependable continuity of the "historical process," the more dependable as the process continues in spite of, or rather because of, radical changes and transformations. This trust in historical continuity also determines our practical attitude in the face of catastrophes: they appear to be not final and absolute but temporary and relative. It is a cynical truth, but a truth nevertheless, that destructions are followed by reconstructions, and mass killings by higher birth rates. On the level of visible happenings it would indeed be unreasonable to expect, for instance, that atomic warfare will once and for all discontinue the process of civilization, that is, of man's appropriating the world through constructive destructions.

To be theoretically consistent, however, the trust in continuity would have to come back to the classical theory of a *circular* movement; for only on the basis of a circular, endless movement, without beginning and end, is continuity really demonstrable. But how can one imagine history as a continuous process within a *linear* progression, without presupposing a discontinuing *terminus a quo* and *ad quem,* i.e., a beginning and an end? The modern mind is not single-minded: it eliminates from its progressive outlook the Christian implication of creation and consummation, while it assimilates from the ancient world view the idea of an endless and continuous movement, discarding its circular structure. The modern mind has not made up its mind whether it should be Christian or pagan. It sees with one eye of faith and one of reason. Hence its vision is necessarily dim in comparison with either Greek or biblical thinking.

APPENDIX I

MODERN TRANSFIGURATIONS OF JOACHISM

Lessing's famous fragment on *The Education of the Human Race* is based on the idea of a progressive revelation ending in a third age, an idea which Lessing explicitly assimilates to the doctrine of the Joachites, though he undermines the faith in revelation and replaces it by education (§§ 1–4). The "elementary" books of the Christian revelation, or rather education, shall be superseded by a "new eternal gospel" (§§ 86 ff.), as promised in the New Testament; and "perhaps certain enthusiasts of the thirteenth and fourteenth centuries . . . have only erred in so far as they proclaimed its advent too early. . . . Perhaps this doctrine of three world-ages was not at all an empty whim of these men; and certainly they did not have any bad intentions when they taught that the new covenant would become as antiquated as the old one already was. Even so, they maintained the same economy of the same God, or, to let them speak my own language, the same plan for a common education of the human race. They only hastened it too much, believing that their contemporaries, who had just grown out of their childhood, could suddenly be made into adults, worthy of the third age, without proper preparation and enlightenment." The third age was conceived by Lessing as the coming reign of reason and human self-realization and yet as the fulfilment of the Christian revelation.

Lessing's influence was extraordinarily deep and far reaching. It affected the Saint-Simonian socialists in France; and even Comte's law of three stages was probably influenced by it, since Lessing's essay was translated by a Saint-Simonian when Comte was still a member of that group. Lessing's theory was then adopted by the German idealist philosophers, all of whom, in the attempt to rationalize the Christian doctrine, refer to the "spiritual" gospel of St. John as the most philosophical one. In Fichte's *Grundzüge des gegenwärtigen Zeitalters* the present age is one of complete sinfulness, preceding a final regeneration in a new age of the spirit, which corresponds to the millennial kingdom of St. John's revelation. Fichte rejects the living generation and his age as only Jewish prophets have done, expecting from this zero-point of history an ascending millennium and from death, resurrection. It has been rightly observed by K. Immermann (*Die Jugend vor fünfundzwanzig Jahren*) that the political radicalism beyond all measure which has characterized all the great movements of Western history since Charlemagne has its ultimate roots in the radicality of the Christian message, while it is foreign even to the most violent crises of ancient times.[1] To quote from a contemporary of Fichte: "The revolutionary desire to realize the Kingdom of God is the flexible starting point of progressive education and the principle of modern history."[2] And it does not make any difference that Fichte believed himself a Christian while he was denounced as an atheist on account of his criticism of revelation; for even atheism, in post-Christian times, draws its strength from the Christian faith in salvation.

The same is true of Hegel, who transformed the Christian religion into philosophy, an enterprise which can be interpreted (simply by quoting from Hegel) in two opposite ways: as an attack upon the Christian religion, though still in terms of theology, or as an apology, though in terms of philosophy.[3] This intrinsic ambiguity of every modern attempt to "realize" the Christian spirit beyond its original hope and faith appears at once when Hegel resolves to build his system and to make clear to himself "what can be meant by approaching God." The interesting document of this resolve is a letter to Schelling,[4] in which he encourages his friend to embarrass as much as possible the theologians (whose "very existence" proves to him this necessity), in the attempt to extinguish the conflagration of dogmatics; but then he goes on to say: "May the Kingdom of God come and our hands not be idle." Inspired by this Christian principle, he made the most comprehensive attempt of modern times to realize the Kingdom of God on earth in the realm of the spirit, thereby provoking the criticism of Marx, who saw in Hegel's realization only an idealistic evaporation of every real existence, except in the "spirit," that is, ideologically.

The most profound and original attempt to establish the reign of the spirit philosophically is that of Schelling, in the thirty-sixth lecture of his *Philosophy of Revelation*.[5] Schelling, like Joachim, refers to St. Paul (I Cor. 13:8 ff.) and to St. John as the apostles of the future, in order to justify his elaboration of a spiritual religion of the human race; for "only thus can Christianity remain the religion of the Germans" after the Reformation. And many a listener to his Berlin lectures of 1841 had the impression that he was watching the rise of a "new stage of consciousness" and the birth of a "new religion." Schelling's thesis was that the work of Christ could only lay foundations but could not survive in its contemporary settings. He is "the last God," terminating the gods of antiquity, and in place of himself he proclaims the Spirit which is independent of the ecstatic gifts of the apostolic age. Christianity after Christ is no longer conditioned by the tension between a new and supernatural message and the cosmic powers of paganism but is free to develop into a completely self-conscious human knowledge. When Christianity entered the history of the world, it had to adopt the general conditions and laws of this world, i.e., the law of change and development. It had to unfold the primitive seed which Christ had sown in the earth. The progress of the Christian religion, therefore, consists not merely in its being spread over the earth but rather in developing the partial *gnosis* into a universal scientific knowledge. It would have been against the spirit of Christ if the Christian religion had remained in the prehistorical state of the primitive church. It had to grow into a historical world religion. Hence the only question is whether the New Testament provides for such future stages of providential development.

The result of Schelling's exegesis is that the development is already indicated in the New Testament itself by the outstanding rank and different character of three apostles—Peter, Paul, and John. The first laid the foundation of a continuous succession, but historical succession does not mean a repetition of the same fundament. It demands, rather, a new principle of constructive continuation as represented first by James and then by Paul and finally by John. Corresponding to Moses, Elijah, and John the Baptist, who consummates the Old Testament, Peter, Paul, and John represent the three stages of the Christian church. All three reflect the trinity of the one God. Peter is the apostle of the Father, Paul of the Son, while John is the apostle of the Spirit who is leading to the full truth of the future. The first represents the age of Catholicism, the second that of Protestantism, the third the perfect religion of mankind. In a footnote Schelling expresses his surprise and delight at having found his own scheme anticipated and justified by Joachim, as he later learned from Neander's *History of Christian Religion and Church*.

It is well known how deeply Russian thinkers of the nineteenth century have been influenced by Hegel and Schelling. It is therefore not surprising to find many parallels among them, for instance, in Krasinsky's *Third Realm of the Holy Spirit* and in Merezhkovsky's *Third Testament Christianity*. What is less well known, however, is that the title, *Das dritte Reich,* of a most influential book by the Russo-German writer, A. Moeller van den Bruck, derives from the author's acquaintance with Merezhkovsky. It is pathetic to think that the first German Reich, the Holy Roman Empire, lasted about one thousand years; the second, that of Bismarck, not quite half a century; and the third, which was supposed to last forever, a dozen years! The fact that the Third Reich still accepted the traditional Christian chronology instead of starting a new and secular time-reckoning with itself, like the French, the Fascist, and the Russian revolutions, is due to compromise and dishonesty.

The last attempt to re-evaluate the whole course of history radically was made by Nietzsche when he dated his *Ecce Homo,* "On the first day of the year one (September 30, 1888, of the false chronology)," thus dividing the course of history once more into an old and a new dispensation, the first being Christian, the second post-Christian and anti-Christian by a reversion to classical paganism. What seems to be an ambitious fancy of a solitary writer is, however, a crucial problem; for one cannot ignore the question of whether our traditional time-reckoning is grounded in historical experience. To divide the time of secular history into an old and a new age, before and after Christ, would be justified only if Christianity had brought about a new world. Originally, however, Christianity did not claim to change the world. It proclaimed a new heaven and earth, implying the end of this world. But the world went on and still exists as before. It is the world which has maintained itself, not the Christian expectation of its end. If, nevertheless, we still maintain the Christian frame of reference in our historical maps and thinking, this can be done thoughtfully only if we also maintain the Christian expectation which was its principle; for the significance of the Christian distinction of historical time into B.C. and A.D. does not depend on an expedient division of secular periods, subject to constant revisions, but on an absolute eschatological turning-point which affected the very belief in a continuous history of the world. In the nineteenth century the imminence of such a decisive turning-point was realized not by professional theologians but by men like Kierkegaard, Marx, and Nietzsche. It was Nietzsche who ventured to write a countergospel called *Zarathustra.* The key to a systematic understanding of it is the first speech, "On the Three Metamorphoses," represented by the allegorical figures of a camel, a lion, and a child. But what else is the "Thou shalt" of the camel than the law of the Old Testament; the "I will" of the lion than the partial freedom of the second dispensation; and the "I am" of the cosmic child than the perfect freedom of being reconciled with God or the world, respectively?

While we do not intend to overwork such possible affiliations into a one-dimensional history of ideas, they certainly demonstrate one thing: the amazing vitality not only of Joachim's vision but, in general, of the Christian tradition and its power of motivation. The mere fact that Christianity interprets itself as a *new* Testament, superseding an *old* one and fulfilling the promises of the latter, necessarily invites further progress and innovations, either religious or irreligious and antireligious—hence the derivation of the secular irreligions of progress from the eschatology of the church, together with their theological pattern.

The fact that the result of such a derivation usually distorts and perverts the original intention of the historical source does not contradict the "law" of history but rather confirms it; for the rule of historical developments is that the ways by which ideas become effective are beyond man's intention. History always achieves more and less than what has been intended by the authors of a movement. The great path-makers of history prepare the way for others just because they do not walk that way themselves. Thus Rousseau prepared the way for the French Revolution, although he would not have recognized his ideas in Robespierre; Marx prepared the way for Lenin and Stalin, although he would not have recognized his ideas in contemporary Russia; Nietzsche prepared certain basic ideas of Italian and German fascism, although he would not have recognized his "Will to Power" in Mussolini and Hitler.

Similarly and more generally, the Christian scheme of history and the particular scheme of Joachim created an intellectual climate and a perspective in which alone certain philosophies of history became possible which are impossible within the framework of classical thinking. There would be no American, no French, and no Russian revolutions and constitutions without the idea of progress and no idea of secular progress toward fulfilment without the original faith in a Kingdom of God, though one can hardly say that the teaching of Jesus is manifest in the manifestoes of these political movements. This discrepancy between the remote results and the meaning of the initial intentions shows that the scheme of derivation by secularization cannot be equated with a homogeneous causal determination. Hence one cannot charge the initiators of a movement with personal responsibility for its historical results. In history "responsibility" has always two sides: the responsibility of those who teach and intend something and the responsibility of those who act and respond. But one cannot establish a direct responsibility of an intention for provoking this or that response. Between the latter and the former there is no simple equation but also no independence—both together produce historical results, which are, therefore, ambiguous and never definite in their potential bearing and meaning. Christianity might ultimately be "responsible" for the possibility of its own secularization, including its non-Christian consequences, but the original proclamation of a Kingdom of God certainly did not intend to make the world more worldly than it was for the pagans.

APPENDIX II

NIETZSCHE'S REVIVAL OF THE DOCTRINE OF ETERNAL RECURRENCE

In 1884, after the completion of *Zarathustra*, Nietzsche wrote in a letter from Venice: "My work has time, I do not want to be misjudged as though I were concerned with the particular task of the present time. Fifty years hence a few men will probably realize what I have done. For the time being it is not only difficult but (according to the laws of historical perspective) simply impossible to discuss me publicly without remaining infinitely behind the truth." "Fifty years hence" fell exactly in 1934, and at that time Nietzsche had indeed become a matter of public discussion and world-wide significance. His thought has an exoteric and an esoteric aspect, the one called "neo-paganism,"[1] the other "eternal recurrence."

Strange—if not absurd—as it may seem to us, to Nietzsche himself the doctrine of eternal recurrence was the fundamental issue of his philosophy. Like the Christian gospel, which was a stumbling block to the Jews and foolishness to the Greeks, Nietzsche's gospel of eternal recurrence is a stumbling block and foolishness to those who still believe in the religion of progress. Whether foolish or wise, the doctrine of eternal recurrence is the key to Nietzsche's philosophy, and it also illuminates his historical significance because it revives the controversy between Christianity and paganism.

Nietzsche's doctrine is a definite answer to a definite problem, which can be discovered in his earliest thought. He treats this problem for the first time at the age of eighteen—twenty years before *Zarathustra*—in two papers written at college on "Fate and History" and "The Freedom of the Will and Fate."[2] At the beginning he confesses that it will be extremely difficult to establish a standpoint from which to judge our traditional Christian interpretation of life. Such an attempt, he says, may well be the task of a lifetime, for how can we discard with impunity the authority of two thousand years? It would appear youthful frivolity to embark without a compass upon a sea of doubt in search of a new continent.[3] Why not cling to history and natural science instead of indulging in vague specu-

214

lations on the Christian or non-Christian meaning of life? But we cannot avoid the fundamental question of man's significance in the totality of the world, of the meaning of human will and history within the non-human universe; for is history not very casual and contingent as compared with the eternal revolution of the heavenly bodies and its cosmic necessity? Are the events of history perhaps only the dial-plate indicating the ever self-repeating movement of a hand which has no inner relation to the indicated events? Or is there an eternal cycle, comprising human decisions as well as natural occurrences? Can we conceive humanity as an inmost circle within the circle of cosmic fate, so that the hidden spring in "the great clock of being"[4] is humanity? To conceive, however, such a synthesis of the free will which creates history with universal fate or necessity, the philosopher would have to transcend the all-too-human standpoint and look at things from beyond humanity. It is the standpoint which Nietzsche eventually found in his conception of the superman Zarathustra, "six thousand feet beyond man and time." At first, however, he states the antinomy between Will and Fate. "In the freedom of the will lies the principle of emancipation and separation from the embracing totality of being, while fate reintegrates the emancipated will into the whole of being. At the same time fate also evokes the power and freedom of willing as a countermovement to the stubbornness of necessity. Absolute freedom would transform man into a creator-God, absolute necessity into an automaton."[5] Apparently, this problem could be solved only "if free will were the highest potency of fate."

A year later Nietzsche wrote an autobiographical sketch in which he formulated once more the problem to which the will to eternal recurrence became the answer. After a short description of his Christian-Protestant background, he discusses the stages by which man has outgrown everything which once sheltered him; and then he asks the question: "But where is the ring which will at last encompass him? Is it the *World* or is it *God?*" Interpreted in terms of Nietzsche's mature philosophy, this alternative means: Is the ultimate standard and pattern of our existence the classical view of the world as an eternal cosmos, revolving in periodic cycles, or is it the Christian view of the world as a unique creation out of nothing, called forth by the omnipotence of a non-natural God? Is the ultimate being a divine cosmos, recurrent like a circle in itself, or a personal God, revealing himself not primarily in nature but in and to humanity under the sign of the cross?

Twenty years later Nietzsche had definitely decided that it is the world which redeems our contingent existence, reintegrating the Christian ego (which "since Copernicus has fallen from the center toward an x") into the order of cosmic necessity, i.e., into the eternal recurrence of the same. The first explicit announcement of this new doctrine occurs in *The Joyful Wisdom* (§§ 341 and 342) under the title "The Heaviest Burden" and in connection with the complementary announcement of "The Death of God" (§ 343). "This life, as thou livest it now, as thou hast lived it, thou needst must live it again, and an infinite number of times; and there will be in it nothing new; but every grief and every joy, every thought and every sigh, all the infinitely great and the infinitely little in thy life must return for thee, and all this in the same sequence and the same order. And also this spider and the moonlight through the trees, and also this moment and myself." Here the idea is introduced, however, not as a metaphysical doctrine but as an ethical imperative: to live *as if* "the eternal hourglass of existence" will continually be turned, in order to impress on each of our actions the weight of an inescapable responsibility.

In *Zarathustra,* in which eternal recurrence is the basic inspiration, it is not presented as a hypothesis but as a metaphysical truth. Zarathustra pretends to reveal "the highest kind of being"; in conformity with the abiding truth of being, Zarathustra is also a "plan of a new way of life." The characteristic subtitle which Nietzsche had planned for his chief work and which he also used in the various plans for the *Will to Power,* is "Midday and Eternity." Midday is to be understood as noontide, as the supreme instant of fulfilment, the climax and crisis in which the vision of eternity becomes once and for all decisive. The experience of this eternal instant is described as an ecstatic inspiration,[6] in which all being becomes speech in the most appropriate similes. Thus Zarathustra's parables are not intended as mere poetry but as a metaphysical language,[7] renewing the old literary form of the didactic poem and of gnomic wisdom.

What led Zarathustra to his crucial experience is briefly this: a conversion and rebirth to a new "great healthiness" out of an equally great sickness or despair, a sickness unto death. The prophet (*Wahr-sager*) of modern nihilism, whose counterpart is the prophet of eternal recurrence (the latter is the exact reverse of the first), describes the sickness of modern man thus: "I saw a great sadness come over mankind. The best turned weary of their works. A doctrine appeared, a faith ran beside it: all is empty, all is alike, all hath been. . . . To be sure we have harvested; but why have all our fruits become rotten and brown? What was it fell last night from the evil moon? In vain was all our labor, poison hath all our wine become, the evil eye hath singed yellow our fields and hearts. Arid have we all become. . . . All our fountains have dried up, even the sea hath receded. All the ground trieth to gape, but the depth will not swallow! Alas, where is there still a sea in which one could be drowned? so soundeth our plaint across shallow marshlands!"[8] The critical time in which out of sickness great health is born is referred to as "the highest time"[9] in the double sense of despair, when time is running out, and of blessed climax.[10] Preceding the stillness of supreme blessedness is the ghostly stillness of despair.[11] The dialectic of despair and redemption, of depth and height, of darkness and light, is finally overcome in an "abyss of light," the time of which is a "standstill of time." Hence the decisive instant of noontide is neither short nor long but a timeless *nunc stans,* or eternal. In it the despair announced by the prophet of nothingness is turned into the bliss announced by Zarathustra, the prophet of the highest kind of being. Instead of despairing that all is alike and in vain, Zarathustra rejoices in the freedom from all-too-human purposes in the eternal recurrence of all things, whose time is an ever present circle, while the time of ordinary hopes and fears, of regret and expectation, is a straight line into an endless future and past.[12] The discovery of this *circulus vitiosus deus* is to Nietzsche "the way out of two thousand years of falsehood," liquidating the Christian Era, when man believed in a progressive history determined by an absolute beginning and end, by creation and original sin at the one end, by consummation and redemption at the other end— both eventually secularized and trivialized into the modern idea of an indefinite progress from primitive backwardness to civilized progressiveness.

Over against this modern illusion resulting in "the last man,"[13] Zarathustra proclaims the eternal recurrence of life in its unmoralized fulness of creation *and* destruction, of joy *and* suffering, of good *and* evil. While he is still convalescent, his animals say: "Everything goeth, everything returneth; eternally rolleth the wheel of existence. Everything dieth, everything blossometh forth again; eternally runneth the wheel of existence. Everything breaketh, everything is integrated anew; eternally buildeth itself the same house of existence. All things separate, all things again greet one another; eternally true to itself remaineth the ring of existence. Every moment beginneth existence, around every Here rolleth the ball There. The middle is everywhere. Crooked is the path of eternity."[14] Remembering, however, his sickness unto death, Zarathustra is not yet prepared to accept the idea that even the meanest type of man will recur again and again, until his animals persuade him to reconcile himself with his particular fate to proclaim this redeeming doctrine. Now he is indeed the superman, a man who had overcome himself by accepting voluntarily what cannot be otherwise, thus transforming an alien fate into his proper destiny. From now on he lives by the experience of a perfect noontide, when "the world is perfect" and time has flown away into the well of eternity.[15] He is now a "blesser and yea-sayer." "This, however, is my blessing: to stand above everything as its own heaven, its round roof, its azure bell and eternal security. . . . For all things are baptized at the font of eternity and beyond good and evil. . . . This freedom and celestial serenity did I put like an azure bell above all things when I taught that over them and through them no Eternal Will 'willeth.' "[16] Eventually, he dedicates to the higher man his dithyramb on all Eternity:

"O man! Take heed!
What saith deep midnight's voice indeed?
I slept my sleep—,
From deepest dream I've woke, and plead:—
The world is deep,
And deeper than the day could read.
Deep is its woe—,
Joy—deeper still than grief can be:
Woe saith: Hence! Go!
But joys all want eternity—,
—Want deep, profound eternity!"[17]

This "drunken song" repeats the two songs on eternity at the end of the third book. They express the final unqualified "Yes and Amen" to all being as such, also embracing and justifying the existence of man. By accepting with an "ultimate will"—willing backward the past as well as forward the future—eternal necessity as "the highest constellation of being," the original contradiction between free will or history and fate or nature seems to be solved.

"Shield of necessity!
Supreme star of Being!
which no desire reaches,
which no 'Nay' defiles,
eternal 'Yea' of Being,
I am thy 'Yea' eternally:
for I love thee, Eternity!"[18]

218

Zarathustra's soul is "the most fated soul which out of joy flingeth itself into chance."[19]

Not only does eternal recurrence answer the problem of Nietzsche's first writings; it is also the fundamental thought in his latest work. Indeed, the description of Zarathustra's "soul" is identical in structure with the "world" of Dionysos as described in the last aphorism of the *Will to Power*. Both represent the highest kind of being, and the last disciple of the philosopher Dionysos is also the prophet of eternal recurrence.[20] And just as the *Will to Power* has as its critical motive and aim the transvaluation of all Christian values (the *Antichrist* being the first book of the *Will to Power*), so Zarathustra is the most elaborate countergospel to the Christian gospel and its theological presuppositions, for the doctrine of eternal recurrence counteracts the doctrine of creation with all its moral consequences.[21] Dionysos, as well as Zarathustra, is against Christ. Zarathustra's friends celebrate his memory in utter blasphemy by the festival of the donkey,[22] the symbol of stupidity, who repeats time and again nothing but "ye-a."

Eternity, as the eternal Yea or self-affirmation of being which repeats itself in periodic cycles, remains, throughout, the leitmotiv of Nietzsche's intellectual passion. In a letter written after the onset of insanity he confesses that, though he would have preferred to remain a simple professor, he had no choice but to sacrifice himself as "the buffoon of the new eternities." The new eternity which Nietzsche rediscovered by his being an Antichrist is the old eternity of the cosmic cycle of the pagans.

If there is such a thing as a "history of ideas," then the idea of eternal recurrence is an amazing example, considering Nietzsche's revival of this classic idea after two thousand years of Christian tradition.[23] Of course, the idea itself did not persist and reappear like an old relic by chance excavation; rather, the historical situation again became controversial. It is contemporary Christianity which evoked in Nietzsche the revival of an idea that was basic for pagan thinking. Placed at the final stage of an evaporated Christianity, he had to search for "new sources of the future," and he found them in classical paganism. The death of the Christian God made him understand again the ancient world. It is of secondary importance that he knew that world through his professional studies as a classical philologist. Many scholars were familiar with the doctrine of eternal recurrence in Heraclitus and Empedocles, Plato and Aristotle, Eudemos and the Stoics; but only Nietzsche perceived in it creative possibilities for the future, in opposition to a Christianity which was reduced to moral values.[24] Reviving the idea of eternal recurrence, Nietzsche was true to his own insight[25] that there is a definite pattern of possible philosophies which is filled in time and again; for it is not so easy to be modern beyond the great alternative of the classical and the Christian schemes.

Nietzsche did not realize, however, that his own *contra Christianos* was an exact replica in reverse of the *contra gentiles* of the Church Fathers. Not only the doctrine of eternal recurrence, which was discussed by Justin, Origen, and Augustine, but all the general topics of Christian apologetics against pagan philosophers recur in Nietzsche's philosophy, with the viewpoints interchanged. If one compares the arguments of Nietzsche with those of Celsus and Porphyry, it is not difficult to see how little has been added to the ancient arguments, except the Christian pathos of being "Antichrist" instead of being a philosopher. To Celsus as well as to Nietzsche the Christian faith is crude and absurd. It destroys the rationality of the cosmos by an arbitrary initiative. The Christian religion to both is a subversive revolt of uneducated, obstinate people who have no sense for aristocratic virtues, civic obligations, and ancestral traditions because they are low, vile, and ignorant. Their God is shamelessly inquisitive and all too human, "a God of all dark corners," and a staff for the weary. If the only thing which really matters is the salvation of the soul of each individual, "why then show any public spirit, why be grateful for one's origin and one's forbears?" says Nietzsche, like Celsus. Those "holy anarchists" called "Christians" made it their piety to weaken the *imperium Romanum* until even Teutons and other barbarians were able to become master of it.[26] Nietzsche's *Antichrist* is a repetition of the old complaint that Christians are *hostes humani generis,* mean people of bad breeding and taste. This historical identity of the ancient and modern attacks against Christianity indicates the lasting significance of the first and the historical importance of the second, though the first had been forgotten until Nietzsche resumed it.

On account, however, of the changed conditions, the idea of eternal recurrence did not simply recur the same but was greatly and fatally changed. It was Nietzsche's noble passion to sing a new song of the "Innocence" of cyclic being and becoming—on the level of a Christian "experience." Thus *Zarathustra* is from cover to cover a counter*gospel* in style as well as in content. Far remote from being genuinely pagan, Nietzsche's neo-paganism is, like that of D. H. Lawrence,[27] essentially Christian, by being anti-Christian. In spite of his criticism of the traditional humanistic approach to Greek culture, he was less of a classical pagan than Winckelmann and Goethe were. Too deeply marked by a Christian conscience, he was unable to achieve that "transvaluation of all values" which Christianity once had effected against paganism; for, though he intended to revert modern man to the ancient values of classical paganism, he was so thoroughly Christian and modern that only one thing preoccupied him: the thought of the *future* and the *will* to create it.

Zarathustra, "the victor over God and Nothingness" (the latter deriving from the death of the first), is "the redeeming man of the future." Nietzsche's whole philosophy is one great "Prelude of a Philosophy of the Future."[28] No Greek was concerned with man's distant future. All their myths, genealogies, and histories re-presented to them their past as an ever present foundation. Also un-Greek is Nietzsche's conception of his philosophical system, the *Will to Power,* which rests on an absolute concept of will. He applies it even to the eternal recurrence of the cosmos, which is beyond will and purpose. To the Greeks the cyclic motions of the heavenly spheres manifested a universal rational order and divine perfection; to Nietzsche the eternal recurrence is "the most frightful" conception and "the heaviest burden"[29] because it bears upon and conflicts with his will to a future redemption. To the Greeks the eternal recurrence of generation and corruption explained temporal changes in nature as well as in history; to Nietzsche the willed acceptance of eternal recurrence requires a standpoint "beyond man and time." The Greeks felt awe and reverence for fate; Nietzsche makes the superhuman effort to will and to love it. Thus he was unable to develop his vision as a supreme and objective order, as the Greeks did, but introduced it as a subjective ethical imperative. The theory of eternal recurrence becomes with him a practical device and a "hammer," to pound into man the idea of an absolute responsibility, substituting that sense of responsibility which was alive as long as men lived in the presence of God and in the expectation of a last judgment.

But, since the will does not move in a circle but in a straight line and in an irreversible direction, the crucial problem of Zarathustra becomes the "redemption"[30] of the will from its one-dimensional structure. Yet how can the will integrate itself with the cyclic law of the cosmos, where every movement of advance is, at the same time, one of return? Nietzsche's answer is: The will must redeem itself from itself by also willing backward, i.e., by accepting voluntarily what it did not will, the whole past of all that is already done and existent—in particular, the fact of our own existence, which nobody had produced by his will. All this is entirely un-Greek, not classic, not pagan, but derived from the Hebrew-Christian tradition, from the belief that world and man are created by God's purposeful will. Nothing is more conspicuous in Nietzsche's godless philosophy than the emphasis on being creative and willing, creative by willing, like the God of the Old Testament. To the Greeks, human creativeness was an "imitation of nature."

Nietzsche undoubtedly achieved the metamorphosis from the Christian "Thou shalt" to the modern "I will," but hardly the crucial transformation from the "I will" to the "I am" of the cosmic child, which is "innocence and forgetfulness, a new beginning and a self-rolling wheel."[31] As a modern man he was so hopelessly divorced from any genuine "loyalty to the earth" and from the feeling of eternal security "under the bell of heaven" that his great effort to remarry man's destiny to cosmic fate, or to "translate man back into nature," could not but be frustrated. Thus, wherever he tries to develop his doctrine rationally, it breaks asunder in two irreconcilable pieces: in a presentation of eternal recurrence as an objective fact, to be demonstrated by physics and mathematics, and in a quite different presentation of it as a subjective hypothesis, to be demonstrated by its ethical consequences.[32] It breaks asunder because the will to eternalize the chance existence of the modern ego does not fit into the assertion of the eternal cycle of the natural world.

Nietzsche was not so much "the last disciple of Dionysos" as the first radical apostate of Christ. As such, however, he was what the "last pope" called him: "the most pious of the godless." When he created the figure of the last pope, who is "out of office" after the death of God, he understood himself perfectly well as a religious figure. Zarathustra and the pope understand each other because both are dedicated and consecrated but not profane. Toward the end of their conversation the old pope says to Zarathustra: " 'O Zarathustra, thou art more pious than thou believest, with such an unbelief! Some God in thee hath converted thee to thine ungodliness. ... Nigh unto thee, though thou professest to be the ungodliest one, I feel a hale and holy odour of long benedictions: I feel glad and grieved thereby. Let me be thy guest, O Zarathustra, for a single night. Nowhere on earth shall I now feel better than with thee!' 'Amen! So shall it be,' said Zarathustra with great astonishment."[33]

ACKNOWLEDGMENTS

The author expresses thanks to the following publishers and authors for permission to make use of material from their publications:

Columbia University Press for the quotations from *Seven Books of History against the Pagans* by IRVING W. RAYMOND

Cornell University Press for the quotation from the translation by BERGIN and FISCH from VICO's *New Science*

Harcourt Brace and Company for the quotation from *Murder in the Cathedral* by T. S. ELIOT

International Publishers for the quotation from *Feuerbach* by FRIEDRICH ENGELS

Charles H. Kerr and Company for the quotations from *A Contribution to the Critique of Political Economy* by KARL MARX

Monsignor Ronald A. Knox and Sheed and Ward, publishers, for the quotation from *God and the Atom*

The Macmillan Company for the quotation from *The Idea of Progress* by J. B. BURY, from *The Eternal Gospel* by R. JONES, and from *The Joyful Wisdom* and *Thus Spake Zarathustra* by FRIEDRICH NIETZSCHE

Pantheon Books, Incorporated, for the quotations from *Force and Freedom* by J. BURCKHARDT

Random House, Incorporated, for the quotation from *Capital and Other Writings* ("Modern Library" edition) by KARL MARX

Charles Scribner's Sons for the quotation from *The Will to Freedom* by J. N. FIGGIS

Westminster Press for the quotation from *Eyes of Faith* by PAUL S. MINEAR.

For permission to make use of his previously published articles, "Nietzsche's Doctrine of Eternal Recurrence," *Journal of the History of Ideas,* June, 1945; and "The Theological Background of the Philosophy of History," *Social Research,* March, 1946, the author is indebted to the editors of these journals.

Last, but not least, the author is grateful for much valuable help given him by his colleagues, Matthew Spinka and Paul Schubert, and by E. W. Wilcock, in the preparation of the manuscript.

KARL LÖWITH

HARTFORD, CONNECTICUT
July 1948

224

NOTES

PREFACE

1. "Salvation" does not convey the many connotations of the German word *Heil,* which indicates associated terms like "heal" and "health," "hail" and "hale," "holy" and "whole," as contrasted with "sick," "profane," and "imperfect." *Heilsgeschichte* has, therefore, a wider range of meaning than "history of salvation." At the same time, it unites the concept of history more intimately with the idea of *Heil* or "salvation." *Weltgeschichte* and *Heilsgeschichte* both characterize the events as worldly and sacred, respectively. In the German compound nouns history is conceived not as an identical entity, related only externally to world and salvation but as determined either by the ways of the world or by those of salvation. They are opposite principles of two different patterns of happenings. This difference does not exclude, but rather implies, the question of their relation (see G. van der Leeuw, *Religion in Essence and Manifestation* [London, 1938], p. 101).

2. See F. M. Powicke, *History, Freedom, and Religion* (London, 1940), p. 34.

3. *The Joyful Wisdom,* § 357.

4. *Dialogues concerning Natural Religion,* I and XII.

INTRODUCTION

1. When Troeltsch and Dilthey endeavored to "overcome" the dogmatic presuppositions of the theology and metaphysics of history, their actual standard of judgment was their dogmatic belief in the absolute value of history as such.

2. See H. Kohn, "The Genesis of English Nationalism," *Journal of the History of Ideas,* Vol. I (January, 1940); H. D. Wendland's article on "The Kingdom of God and History," in *The Official Oxford Conference Books,* III (Chicago and New York, 1938), 167 ff. The secular messianism of Western nations is in every case associated with the consciousness of a national, social, or racial vocation which has its roots in the religious belief of being called by God to a particular task of universal significance. This holds true for England and the United States as well as for France, Italy,

Germany, and Russia. Whatever form the perversion of a religious vocation to a secular claim may assume, the abiding significance in these
secularizations is the religious conviction that the world lies in evil and
has to be saved and regenerated.

3. See Augustine *Confessions* xi.

4. Herodotus i. 1; Thucydides i. 22 and ii. 64; Polybius i. 35 and vi.
3, 9, 51, 57. Cf. Karl Reinhardt, "Herodots Persergeschichten," *Geistige
Überlieferung,* ed. Ernesto Grassi (Berlin, 1940), pp. 138 ff.; C. N.
Cochrane, *Christianity and Classical Culture* (New York, 1940), chap. xii;
R. G. Collingwood, *The Idea of History* (Oxford, 1946), pp. 17 ff.

5. See W. von Humboldt, *Politischer Briefwechsel* (Berlin, 1935),
Letter 77 of April, 1807.

6. J. Burckhardt, *Force and Freedom: Reflections on History* (New
York, 1943), pp. 90 f.; *Griechische Kulturgeschichte,* in *Gesamtausgabe*
(Basel, 1929 ff.), IX, 247 ff. Only on this modern assumption that history
is a story of "liberty" does the ancient belief in a preordained and predictable future become an absurdity. Thus Collingwood (*op. cit.,* pp. 54, 120,
220) asserts that the philosophy of history *must* end with the present and
must dismiss eschatology as an "intrusive" element because nothing else
has happened which could be ascertained; and that "whenever historians
claim to be able to determine the future in advance of its happening, we
may know with certainty that something has gone wrong with their fundamental conception of history." But what if history is not such a simple story
of free action within a given situation but a story of human action and
suffering with a natural and fatal or supernatural and providential pattern? How much deeper did Léon Bloy penetrate into the problem of
history when he said that the possibility of proving that history has an
architecture and meaning would require "l'holocauste préalable du Libre
Arbitre, tel, du moins, que la raison moderne peut le concevoir," viz., as
bound up with arbitrariness and divorced from necessity and therefore
unable to understand how a man may accomplish with freedom an act of
necessity (*Textes choisies,* ed. A. Béguin [Fribourg, 1943], pp. 71 f.).

7. *Democracy in America,* Introd.

8. *The Decline of the West* (New York, 1937), I, chap. iv, 117 ff.; cf.
chap. xi.

9. *Ibid.,* I, 38; II, 292 ff. Cf., below, Appen. II.

10. *Jahre der Entscheidung* (Munich, 1933); English trans., *The Hour
of Decision* (New York, 1934).

11. A. J. Toynbee, *A Study of History* (London, 1934-39), IV, 23 ff.

12. *Ibid.*, V, 16 and 188 ff.; VI, 174, n. 4.
13. *Ibid.*, VI, 169 ff.
14. A. J. Toynbee, *Civilization on Trial* (Oxford University Press, 1948), p. 236.
15. *Ibid.*, p. 242.
16. *Ibid.*, p. 237.
17. *Ibid.*, p. 238.
18. *Ibid.*, p. 239.
19. *Ibid.*, p. 240.
20. *A Study of History*, I, 339 ff.
21. *Ibid.*, I, 34 and 169 ff.; cf. Spengler, *op. cit.*, I, 15 ff.
22. See the plan (Part XII) of the whole work.
23. *A Study of History*, I, 196 ff.
24. *Ibid.*, VI, 534 ff.
25. *Ibid.*, pp. 324 ff.
26. *Civilization on Trial*, pp. 235 f.
27. That this is the fundamental quest of the modern historical consciousness of men like A. Comte, A. de Tocqueville, E. Renan, and F. Nietzsche has been stated most frankly by A. de Tocqueville when, in the Introduction to *Democracy in America*, he asks himself the question: "Où allons-nous donc?" With reference to Nietzsche's incisive criticism of historical antiquarianism, E. Troeltsch (*Der Historismus und seine Probleme* [Tübingen, 1922], pp. 495 and 772) formulated the task of the philosophy of history as "Überwindung der Gegenwart und Begründung der Zukunft." How remote is such a definition of the task and problem of history from the classical *historein* and how familiar to the Christian idea of history as a history of judgment and fulfilment!
28. Hermann Cohen, *Die Religion der Vernunft aus den Quellen des Judentums* (Leipzig, 1919), pp. 307 ff., 293 ff.; cf. *Logik der reinen Erkenntnis* (Berlin, 1902), pp. 131 ff. Within the Christian church the thesis that historical thinking is the product of prophetism has found its fullest application in the prophetical historism of Joachim of Floris.
29. Cf. E. Benz, "Die Geschichtstheologie der Franziskanerspiritualen," *Zeitschrift für Kirchengeschichte*, LII (1933), 118 ff.

CHAPTER I

1. See Vladimir G. Simkhovitch, "Approaches to History," *Political Science Quarterly*, Vols. XLIV and XLV (1929 and 1930), containing a critical discussion of the historicogenetic method by which new beginnings,

breaks, and changes are looked at with an a priori scheme of mere continuity—as if the actual aim of a new historical effort could be understood by going backward to its antecedents. See also R. E. Fitch, "Crisis and Continuity in History," *Review of Religion,* Vol. VIII (March, 1944).

2. Letters of February 28 and March 5, 1846, to H. Schauenburg (*J. Burckhardts Briefe,* ed. F. Kaphahn [Leipzig, 1935]).

3. See letters of April 26, 1872; April 13, 1882; and July 24, 1889, to F. von Preen.

4. See J. H. Nichols' Introduction to the translation of Burckhardt's *Force and Freedom: Reflections on History* (New York, 1943), p. 75.

5. Letter of April 21, 1872, to A. von Salis.

6. Letter of December 26, 1892, to F. von Preen.

7. Letters of January 14 and 30, 1844, to W. Beyschlag.

8. See my article: "Can There Be a Christian Gentleman?" *Theology Today,* April, 1948.

9. *Reflections on History,* pp. 233, 243, 248 ff.

CHAPTER II

1. *Marx-Engels Gesamtausgabe* (Frankfurt, 1927), I. Abt., I/1, pp. 5 ff.

2. *A Contribution to the Critique of Political Economy* (Chicago, 1904), p. 13.

3. From *The German Ideology,* in the English translation of *Capital, The Communist Manifesto, and Other Writings* ("Modern Library" [New York, 1932]), pp. 1 f.

4. *Die Revolution von 1848 und das Proletariat,* in K. *Marx als Denker, Mensch und Revolutionär* (Berlin, 1928), p. 41.

5. The following quotations are from the *Communist Manifesto* in the English translation of the "Modern Library," pp. 321 ff.

6. *A Contribution* ..., p. 11.

7. *Ibid.,* p. 12.

8. Cf. M. Weber, *Gesammelte Aufsätze zur Soziologie und Sozialpolitik* (Tübingen, 1924), pp. 505 ff.; A. J. Toynbee, *A Study of History* (London, 1934–39), V, 178 f., 581 ff.; N. Berdyaev, "The Russian Revolution," *Vital Realities* (New York, 1932), pp. 105 ff.

9. *A Contribution* ..., pp. 310 f.

10. See L. Feuerbach's Preface to the first edition of the *Essence of Christianity* (English trans.; New York, 1855); *Briefwechsel und Nachlass,* ed. K. Grün (Leipzig, 1874), I, 406 ff.; cf. also F. Engels, *L. Feuerbach*

and the Outcome of Classical German Philosophy (New York, 1941), p. 56; S. Kierkegaard, Attack upon Christendom (Princeton, 1944).

11. Marx-Engels Gesamtausgabe, I. Abt., I/1, pp. 242 f.

12. Ibid., pp. 607 ff.

13. Ibid., I. Abt., II, pp. 426 f.

14. Fourth Thesis on Feuerbach, in F. Engels, L. Feuerbach . . . , p. 83.

15. Letter of July 27, 1871, to Kugelmann.

16. Marx-Engels Gesamtausgabe, I. Abt., I/1, p. 304.

17. F. Engels, L. Feuerbach . . . , p. 77.

18. For a more detailed analysis of Marx and Hegel see my book, Von Hegel bis Nietzsche (Zürich, 1941); cf. also S. Hook, From Hegel to Marx (New York, 1935); and H. Marcuse, Reason and Revolution (Oxford University Press, 1941).

CHAPTER III

1. Lectures on the Philosophy of History, trans. J. Sibree (London, 1900), pp. 75 ff.

2. Ibid., pp. 21 ff.

3. In a conversation with the historian Luden, Goethe says: "Even if you were able to interpret and investigate all sources, what would you find? Nothing but one great truth which has long been discovered and for whose confirmation one does not need to seek far; the truth, namely, that in all times and in all countries things have been miserable. Men have always been in fear and trouble, they have pained and tortured one another; what little life they had, they made sour one to the other. The beauty of the world and the sweetness of existence which the beauty of the world offered them, they were not able to esteem or to enjoy. Only to a few life became comfortable and enjoyable. Most people, after having played the game of life for a time, preferred to depart rather than to begin anew. That which perhaps gave or gives them some degree of attachment to life was and is the fear of death. Thus life is; thus it always was; thus it will always remain. That is, after all, the lot of man. What further witness is needed?" (Goethes Gespräche, Gesamtausgabe, ed. F. von Biedermann [2d ed.; Leipzig, 1909], I, 434 ff.).

4. Briefe von und an Hegel, ed. Karl Hegel (Leipzig, 1887), I, 13; Lectures on the Philosophy of History, p. 340; Introduction to Lectures on the Philosophy of Religion, trans. E. B. Speirs and J. B. Sanderson (London, 1895).

5. Lectures on the Philosophy of History, p. 16; see also p. 477.

6. *Ibid.,* p. 34; *Encyklopädie der philosophischen Wissenschaften,* ed. Bolland, No. 209, *Zusatz.* The most impressive description of the working of the *List der Vernunft* is contained in a letter of July 5, 1816, on Napoleon (*Briefe von und an Hegel,* pp. 401 ff.).

7. Transposed into the materialistic pattern, Hegel's "cunning of reason" becomes the ultimate driving force of the class struggle, working in and behind the conscious interest and "individual whims of all kinds." It produces the lasting results which are amazingly foreign to the transient intentions (see F. Engels, *L. Feuerbach and the Outcome of Classical German Philosophy* [New York, 1941], pp. 48 ff.).

8. See J. Plenge, *Hegel und die Weltgeschichte* (Münster, 1931).

9. See, besides the *Lectures on the Philosophy of History* (ed. Lasson), pp. 200, 779, Hegel's letter to a Baltic baron, which is quoted in K. Rosenkranz, *Hegels Leben* (Berlin, 1844), pp. 304 ff. The most elaborate prognostication of Russia's rise and final struggle with Germany is that of Hegel's pupil, Bruno Bauer, *Russland und das Germanentum* (Charlottenburg, 1853). See also Napoleon's *Mémorial de Sainte-Hélène,* entry of November, 1816; and Tocqueville's famous comparison of Russia's and America's potentialities, at the end of the first part of his *Democracy in America.*

CHAPTER IV

1. J. B. Bury, *The Idea of Progress* (New York, 1932), pp. 22, 73; cf. W. R. Inge, *The Idea of Progress* (Oxford, 1920) and *The Fall of the Idols* (London, 1940); A. Salomon, "The Religion of Progress," *Social Research,* December, 1946.

2. Modern man still has hope in progress, but no faith in his pilgrimage. As R. A. Knox put it: "Those who had lost the sense of religious certainty enrolled themselves under the banner of optimism; the world's future occupied their thoughts instead of a future world, and, by a kind of inverted Confucianism, they fell to worshipping their grandchildren. With this optimistic agitation . . . the leaders of religion have . . . too readily associated themselves" (*God and the Atom* [American ed.; New York, 1945], p. 59). Cf. Reinhold Niebuhr's statement: "Modern Christianity was pathetically eager to disavow the most . . . distinctive insights of Biblical faith for the sake of sharing the faith of secular culture in the idea of progress. This faith is now becoming discredited and disillusion follows in its wake. Liberal Christianity is involved in this disillusionment. Having sought to make a success story of the Biblical history of a crucified saviour

. . . it finds itself unable to cope with the tragic experience of our day" ("The Impact of Protestantism Today," *Atlantic Monthly*, February, 1948).

3. A comprehensive and penetrating study on Proudhon has recently been published by H. de Lubac, *Proudhon et le christianisme* (Paris, 1945), in particular, chaps. ii and iv. Cf., also, the essay on Proudhon in A. L. Guérard, *French Prophets of Yesterday* (London, 1913), pp. 172 ff.

4. See Kant's essay of 1784, *Idee zu einer allgemeinen Geschichte in weltbürgerlicher Absicht*, and his review of Herder's *Ideen zur Philosophie der Geschichte der Menschheit*. Cf. also R. G. Collingwood, *The Idea of History* (Oxford, 1946), pp. 93 ff.

5. *Système des contradictions économiques ou philosophie de la misère* (1846), Prologue.

6. *Ibid.*, chap. viii, which contains Proudhon's solution of the problem of providence.

7. *Ibid.*

8. *Idée générale de la révolution au XIXᵉ siècle*, cited by De Lubac, *op. cit.*, p. 185.

9. This work was posthumously published in two volumes under the title *La Bible annotée*.

10. "Dans l'ignorance où je suis de tout ce qui regarde Dieu, le monde, l'âme, la destinée; forcé de procéder comme le matérialiste, c'est à dire par l'observation et l'expérience, et de conclure dans le langage du croyant, parce qu'il n'en existe pas d'autre; ne sachant pas si mes formules, malgré moi théologiques, doivent être prises au propre où au figuré ... : la rigueur de la dialectique exigeait que je supposasse, rien de plus, rien de moins, cette inconnue qu'on appelle Dieu. Nous sommes pleins de la Divinité, *Jovis omnia plena;* nos monuments, nos traditions, nos lois, nos idées, nos langues et nos sciences, tout est infecté de cette indélébile superstition hors de laquelle il ne nous est pas donné de parler ni d'agir, et sans laquelle nous ne pensons seulement pas" (*Système* ... , Prologue, chap. iii).

11. *Ibid.*, chap. viii; cf. G. Sorel, *Matériaux d'une théorie du prolétariat* (Paris, 1921), p. 241, n. 1: "Proudhon's definitions are heavily charged with theological reminiscences. One can rightly say that, if Rousseau owes much to sentimental Christianity, Proudhon is an inheritor of French theology. It is not impossible that the renascence of the study of Proudhon, which one notices nowadays, will contribute to bring the mind of the layman back to theology."

12. See E. Rosenstock-Huessy, *The Christian Future or the Modern Mind Outrun* (New York, 1946), p. 70.

13. See A. Harnack, "Der Vorwurf des Atheismus in den ersten drei Jahrhunderten," *Texte und Untersuchungen zur Geschichte der altchristlichen Literatur,* N.F. (1905), XIII, 4.

14. *Système* ... , Prologue.

15. See De Lubac, *op. cit.,* chap. vi, sec. 3.

16. *Correspondance* (Paris, 1875), X, 187 f. and 205 f. (letters of October 27 and 29, 1860); cf. *De la création de l'ordre dans l'humanite,* chap. i, sec. 3, and chap. ii, sec. 4.

17. In the "Personal Preface" of 1842 to the last volume of the *Cours de philosophie positive,* Comte admits that he avoided reading Vico, Kant, Herder, and Hegel for the sake of the consistency and purity of his own conception. Imposing upon himself for twenty years this "cerebral hygiene," he found it "at times inconvenient, but more often wholesome."

18. This work was based upon a course of lectures delivered between 1826 and 1829. Later on, Comte wished to change its title to the more appropriate one of a "System" of positive philosophy. I quote from the condensed English translation by H. Martineau, *The Positive Philosophy of A. Comte* (2 vols., 2d ed.; London, 1875), correcting, however, the translation where it is unnecessarily free and supplementing it occasionally from the complete French edition in six volumes by E. Littré (Paris, 1864). Among the many books on Comte, see in particular the theological study by H. de Lubac in *Le Drame de l'humanisme athée* (Paris, 1945), pp. 135 ff., and R. L. Hawkins, *A. Comte and the United States* (Cambridge, 1936).

19. *The Positive Philosophy* . . . , II, 154. Apart from this attempt at a naturalistic explanation, Comte accepts, however, Bossuet's restriction of universal history to the history of the Christian Occident, in spite of his criticism of Bossuet's theological foundations: "If Bossuet was guided by literary principle in restricting his historical estimate to one homogeneous and continuous series, it appears to me that he fulfilled not less successfully the philosophical conditions of the inquiry. Those who would produce their whole stock of erudition and mix up with the review such populations as those of India and China and others that have not aided the process of development, may reproach Bossuet with his limitations: but not the less is his exposition, in philosophical eyes, truly universal. Unless we proceed in this way, we lose sight of all the political relations arising from the action of the more advanced on the progress of inferior nations. . . . When we have learned what to look for from the *élite* of humanity, we shall know how the superior portion should intervene for the advantage of the inferior; and we cannot understand the fact, or the

consequent function, in any other way: for the view of coexisting states of inequality could not help us. Our first limit then is that we are to concentrate our sociological analysis on the historical estimate of the most advanced social development" (II, 151 f.). This remarkable insight into the methodical priority of that civilization which is in principle "progressive" (by being Christian) implies an attack upon Voltaire's criticism of Bossuet (see below, chap v).

20. *The Positive Philosophy* . . . , I, 13; II, 58, 430 f.

21. *Ibid.*, II, 72 ff.; French ed., IV, 264, 272 ff., 278.

22. *The Positive Philosophy* . . . , I, 20.

23. *Ibid.*, II, 442, 386.

24. *Ibid.*, I, 22.

25. *Ibid.*, II, 58, 407.

26. *Ibid.*, p. 430.

27. French ed., IV, 293.

28. *The Positive Philosophy* . . . , I, 3.

29. *Ibid.*, pp. 13 f.

30. Comte's belief in progressive positivism is, of course, no longer shared by "the best minds" of the Old World, but it still prevails in the New World, the constitution of which is a product of eighteenth-century beliefs.

31. The term "sociology" was used for the first time by Comte with regard to Condorcet's work, in order to designate "social physics" as that positive science which deals with the fundamental laws of social phenomena. "Positive philosophy" is thus synonymous with "sociological philosophy" (*The Positive Philosophy* . . . , II, 442; cf. French ed., IV, 185 n.).

32. According to Comte, they are France, Italy, Germany, England, and Spain. Eventually, however, the salvation by positivism will extend to the whole of the white race and at length to the whole of mankind (*The Positive Philosophy* . . . , II, 409 ff., 464, 467).

33. *Ibid.*, I, 13; cf. French ed., IV, 16.

34. *The Positive Philosophy* . . . , II, 11 ff.; cf. French ed., IV, 51, about the limits of tolerance.

35. *The Positive Philosophy* . . . , II, 3; cf. French ed., IV, 17.

36. *The Positive Philosophy* . . . , II, 44.

37. Pascal, *Pensées et opuscules*, ed. Léon Brunschvigg (Paris, 1909), p. 80.

38. *The Positive Philosophy* . . . , II, 47 ff.

39. French ed., V, 231.

40. See on Bossuet: *ibid.*, IV, 204; V, 8, 187, 418; VI, 251. On De Maistre: *ibid.*, IV, 64, 135, 138. As to Comte's identification of Catholic philosophy with that of De Maistre and Bonald, cf. H. de Lubac's critical remarks, *Le Drame de l'humanisme athée,* 2d part.

41. *The Positive Philosophy* . . . , II, 218 ff., 242, 352; French ed., V, 241.

42. *The Positive Philosophy* . . . , II, 252. In his old age Comte tried, indeed, to bring about a provisional alliance with Catholicism by making definite proposals to the general of the Jesuits.

43. Cf. the classical studies of Fustel de Coulanges, *La Cité antique,* and of Sir H. J. Maine, *Ancient Law.*

44. *The Positive Philosophy* . . . , II, 226.

45. *Ibid.,* pp. 241 ff., 249.

46. *Ibid.,* pp. 151 f. (cf. French ed., V, 8 and 247 f.).

47. *The Positive Philosophy* . . . , II, 244, 374.

48. *Ibid.,* pp. 45 n., and 285; cf. French ed., V, 243 f.

49. *The Positive Philosophy* . . . , II, 270.

50. *Ibid.,* pp. 17, 283.

51. Louis de Bonald once defined the deist as a man who in his short existence had not had time to become an atheist. In a note (French ed., V, 379) Comte characterizes his own position by saying that atheism, though representing the nearest approximation to positivism, is yet, because of its sheer negativism, more remote from the positive system than is the Catholic one. It would therefore be wrong to confound atheism, i.e., "the most negative and transient phase of Protestantism," with positivism, which does not condemn religious beliefs but gives them a rational and positive justification.

52. *The Positive Philosophy* . . . , II, 283.

53. *Ibid.,* p. 284.

54. *Ibid.,* p. 285.

55. *Ibid.,* p. 7.

56. To appreciate the complete reversal of Comte's viewpoint see J. N. Figgis, *Civilization at the Cross Roads* (London, 1912).

57. "There is no science which, having attained the positive stage, does not bear marks of having passed through the others. Some time ago it was . . . composed, as we can now perceive, of metaphysical abstractions; and, further back in the course of time, it took its form from theological conceptions. We shall have only too much occasion to see . . . that our most advanced sciences still bear very evident marks of the two earlier

periods through which they have passed" (*The Positive Philosophy* ... , I, 3).

58. *Ibid.*, I, 51; II, 55; cf. French ed., IV, 227 f.

59. French ed., IV, 279.

60. *The Positive Philosophy* ... , II, 457.

61. *Op. cit.*, pp. 61 ff.

62. French ed., IV, 504 n.; *The Positive Philosophy* ... , II, 463.

63. *The Positive Philosophy* ... , II, 393; cf. also p. 464, on the superiority of the Christian over the classical education.

64. *Ibid.*, p. 388.

65. See H. de Lubac, *La Drame de l'humanisme athée*, pp. 247 ff.

66. French ed., IV, 504 ff.; cf. *The Positive Philosophy* ... , II, 375.

67. *The Positive Philosophy* ... , II, 7.

68. *Ibid.*, pp. 276, 396.

69. French ed., IV, 514.

70. *The Positive Philosophy* ... , II, 274 f., 375. Similar instances of progressive optimism could be given from H. Spencer, who did not doubt that evil "must" disappear and that man "must" become perfect by progressive development.

71. *Ibid.*, p. 462.

72. *Ibid.*, pp. 124 ff.

73. *Ibid.*, pp. 128 f.

74. *Ibid.*, p. 463.

75. It is not for lack of "social ethics" but on account of a genuine Christian insight that Kierkegaard insisted throughout his whole work on the ultimate irrelevance of "world history" as compared with the absolute relevance of the religious story of each individual. Even Catholic thinkers agree with him in this respect (see T. Haecker, *Der Christ und die Geschichte* [Leipzig, 1935], pp. 98 and 101 ff.; Knox, *op. cit.*, p. 123).

76. A. Comte, *A General View of Positivism* (London, 1865), p. 112.

77. *Ibid.*, p. 350.

78. See L. Feuerbach, *The Essence of Christianity* (New York, 1855), Introd., chap. ii.

79. Cf. De Lubac's conclusion, *Le Drame de l'humanisme athée*, p. 277.

80. We quote from the English translation: *Outlines of an Historical View of the Progress of the Human Mind* (London, 1795).

81. *Ibid.*, p. 4. Compared with the millennarist conceptions of progress of the early Socialists (in particular, of Fourier), the Saint-Simonians, Condorcet, and Comte appear cautious rationalists.

82. A universal scientific language is to complete the progress as initiated by alphabetical writing; it will render error "almost impossible" (*ibid.*, pp. 10, 351, 363 f., 366).

83. *Ibid.*, pp. 14 f.

84. *Ibid.*, pp. 356 f.

85. *Ibid.*, p. 349.

86. *Ibid.*, pp. 349; see also pp. 326 f.

87. *Ibid.*, pp. 344 ff.

88. *Ibid.*, pp. 367 ff.

89. *Ibid.*, pp. 325 f.

90. *Ibid.*, pp. 347; see also pp. 172 ff.

91. *Ibid.*, p. 355.

92. *Ibid.*, pp. 186 ff.; see also pp. 206 f.

93. *Critical Miscellanies, First Series* (New York, 1897), pp. 88 ff.

94. Already Condorcet had occasionally reflected upon the possibility of a new civilized barbarism due to a too progressive rate of population; as a remedy he proposed birth control (*Outlines of an Historical View . . .*, p. 344).

95. *Diary of a Writer*, August, 1880.

96. From *Tolstoi's Flucht und Tod*, ed. R. Fülöp-Miller and F. Eckstein (Berlin, 1925), p. 103.

97. A. J. Toynbee, *A Study of History* (London, 1934–39), I, 46.

98. *Discours sur les avantages que l'établissement du christianisme a procuré au genre humain; discours sur les progrès successifs de l'esprit humain.* Besides these two essays, Vol. II of Turgot's *Œuvres* (Paris, 1844) also contains a *Plan de deux discours sur l'histoire universelle* and *Pensées et fragments.* Like Comte and Cordorcet, Turgot knew himself greatly indebted to Bossuet's *Discourse on Universal History*, which he intended to "re-write" (see *Œuvres*, II, 626 n.). Cf. the interesting comparison of Turgot's view with that of Bossuet by G. Sorel, *Les Illusions du progrès* (Paris, 1927), chap. v, sec. 1.

99. Turgot, *Œuvres*, II, 598.

100. *Ibid.*, p. 675.

101. *Ibid.*, p. 594.

102. *Ibid.*, p. 595.

103. *Ibid.*, p. 633.

104. *Ibid.*, p. 632; cf. (pp. 55 f., 62, 125 ff., 142) the corresponding descriptions of Bossuet, Vico, and Hegel. This sense of human blindness in action is common to Christianity and antiquity. But in the Christian ex-

perience it is not due to the blindness of fortune but is inherent in the nature of man. If man's will were not at variance with the will of his creator, no history at all would happen. On the other hand, what really happens in history is that God's providential wisdom, mercy, and judgment direct man's passions toward a final end—with or without his consent (cf. Collingwood, *op. cit.*, pp. 46 ff.).

105. Turgot, *Œuvres*, II, 628.

CHAPTER V

1. See the great work of Paul Hazard, *La Crise de la conscience européenne* (Paris, 1935).

2. Frederick's letter of October 26, 1740, to Voltaire (*Letters of Voltaire and Frederick the Great,* selected and translated by R. Aldington [New York, 1927]).

3. Frederick's letter of June, 1738, to Voltaire.

4. Voltaire's letter of August 3, 1775, to Frederick.

5. Frederick's letter of May 5, 1767, to Voltaire.

6. Frederick's letter of February 10, 1767, to Voltaire.

7. See the essay of W. Kaegi, "Voltaire und der Zerfall des christlichen Geschichtsbildes," *Corona,* Vol. VIII (1937–38).

8. *Essai sur les mœurs et l'esprit des nations* (*Œuvres complètes* [1792], XXII, 194 f.). Author's translation of all quotations from the *Essai.*

9. *Essai* ... (*Œuvres,* XXII, 166). Cf. in Voltaire's *Dictionnaire philosophique,* the article "Juifs."

10. *Essai* ... (*Œuvres,* XXII, 49, 76 f., 120, 167, 175, 189; XXIII, 104).

11. *Dictionnaire philosophique,* article "Histoire."

12. *Essai* ... (*Œuvres,* XXII, 75 f., 179 ff.). After Voltaire, only Gibbon had an equally far-reaching influence in freeing history from religious interpretation.

13. Cf. Frederick's remarkable criticism of Voltaire's deism in his letter to Voltaire of December 25, 1737.

14. Cf. the article "Homme" in the *Dictionnaire philosophique,* which shows that Voltaire's belief in progress was, after all, soberly tempered by biblical skepticism.

15. How far remote Newton's conception of celestial mechanics was from Voltaire's antireligious understanding is shown by the fact that Newton also wrote a book on the prophecies of Daniel.

16. Cf. *Dictionnaire philosophique,* article "Bien, tout est bien." The

argument of Candide recurs in D. Hume's *Dialogues concerning Natural Religion,* Part X.

17. See Kant's physical treatise *On the Causes of Earthquakes* (1756), which was prompted by the earthquake of Lisbon.

18. Cf. Kant's essay *Über das Misslingen aller philosophischen Versuche in der Theodizee.* What this classical refutation really proves is, however, only the impossibility of a *philosophical* attempt at a theodicy. On religious grounds the problem of a theodicy may perhaps be insoluble also, but it cannot be disposed of as irrelevant (cf. T. Haecker, *Schöpfer und Schöpfung* [Leipzig, 1934], chap. i).

19. See *Essai* ... (*Œuvres,* XXIII, 4 [*Avant-propos*]) and *Remarques pour servir de supplément* (*Œuvres,* XXIX, 155); cf. the article "Histoire" in the *Dictionnaire philosophique.*

20. Article "Histoire."

21. See a most instructive article by H. Weiss, "The Greek Conceptions of Time and Being in the Light of Heidegger's Philosophy," *Philosophy and Phenomenological Research,* December, 1941.

22. A typical instance of the confusion of religious progress with the religion of progress is E. F. Scott's chapter on progress in his book *Man and Society in the New Testament* (New York, 1946). He tries to do justice to both: as a modern man to the modern mind and as a New Testament scholar to the teachings of Jesus, to the belief in progress, and to the faith in Christ. He holds that the modern conception of progress has "enriched" that of the New Testament by "the emphasis it lays on man's own activity." In spite of this emphasis on man's activity, "pressing forward" and improving his earthly conditions, Scott cannot help understanding the question of Jesus: "What can it profit a man if he gain the whole world and lose his soul" in its unquestionable meaning: that religious progress refers to the inward condition of each individual soul and that it cannot be measured by the various kinds of progress of the world, in knowledge and comforts, health, and wealth (pp. 261, 279 f.). And yet he ventures to say that the New Testament teaches "everywhere" that man must accept the earthly life "in all its advanced conditions," which he naïvely supposes will help us toward a "clearer and more genuine faith" (p. 270), since the material and the spiritual interests "must go together." All improvements on the material side of life, like better housing and food, have a "religious nature" (pp. 271, 276). In consequence of this pre-established harmony between progress and religion, Scott comments on the foregoing reference to Jesus' distinction between the world and man's soul by saying that it would be

"foolish to deny that much is gained by wealth, security, and control of natural forces." They give "tremendous advantages even in the pursuit of the higher life," and the quest for them may sometimes be a "paramount duty," though we should not forget that the earliest Christians were "far in advance of us as Christian men"—obviously without our modern improvements! Confirming his own remark that no phrase has wrought such confusion as that of "religious progress," Scott confuses throughout this chapter the modern religion of progress with religious progress, to reach the conclusion that, "while religion is necessary to progress, it is no less true that progress is necessary to religion" (p. 269), a formula which sounds as smooth as it is wrong; for all modern progress has been achieved quite independently of, if not against, the faith in salvation through Christ, and the faith in Christ was, for eighteen hundred years, quite independent of all our recent improvements.

23. See V. Solovyof, *The Justification of the Good,* trans. N. A. Duddington (New York, 1918), pp. 191 ff. There the lack of spiritual progress is strikingly proved from the perfection as achieved in Christ. Nobody can doubt, Solovyof argues, that there is an amazing progress in the short period from Socrates' natural wisdom to the radiant manifestation of triumphant spirituality in Christ. But who would dare to assert a similar spiritual advance in the much longer period after Christ and, for instance, compare Spinoza and Kant or Luther and Fox with Christ? The fact, however, that history did not produce other persons still more perfect proves that the perfection of Christ cannot be understood as the natural product of Jewish and pagan historical evolution and that the Kingdom of God cannot be a product of Christian history. Only the revelation of a God-Man, but no Man-God, only absolute but no relative perfection, can explain why it is that after Christ there is progress in all spheres of life, except in the fundamental sphere of personal spiritual power.

CHAPTER VI

1. We refer occasionally to the first, untranslated edition (*La Scienza nuova prima*) as "*SNI,*" and generally to the last edition (*La Scienza nuova seconda*) as "*NS.*" Both have been edited most carefully by F. Nicolini (Bari, 1931, and 3d ed., 1942). Our quotations from the English translation by T. G. Bergin and M. H. Fisch (Cornell University Press, 1948) are cited by the numbered paragraphs. The most comprehensive presentation of Vico's thought is B. Croce's *The Philosophy of G. Vico,* translated by R. G. Collingwood (New York, 1913). See also F. Amerio, *Introduzione allo studio di Vico* (Torino, 1947). Two other very valuable studies

are R. Peters, *Der Aufbau der Weltgeschichte bei Vico* (Berlin, 1929), and "Augustinus und Vico," which appeared in the series "Geist und Gesellschaft," Vol. III: *Vom Denken über Geschichte* (Breslau, 1928). English monographs on Vico are: R. Flint, *Vico* (London, 1884), and the more popular one by H. P. Adams, *The Life and Writings of Vico* (London, 1935). For further references see Appen. IV in Croce's book. A revised and enlarged commentary by F. Nicolini, which was at first published together with his edition of Vico's *Scienza nuova seconda* (3 vols., 1911–16), is in preparation.

2. Marx, who knew the *New Science,* found in it in embryo Wolf's *Homer,* Niebuhr's *History of the Roman Emperors,* the foundations of comparative philology, and "many a gleam of genius." Cf. the article by M. Lifshitz, on Vico in *Philosophy and Phenomenological Research,* March, 1948.

3. See Croce, *op. cit.,* pp. 272 f.

4. *NS,* § 1096.

5. *Ibid.,* § 385.

6. See A. Koyré, *Entretiens sur Descartes* (New York, 1944).

7. For a detailed treatment of Vico's theory of knowledge see Croce's work, chaps. i and ii and Appen. III. See also Amerio, *op. cit.,* chaps. ii, iv, v.

8. *SNI,* § 40.

9. *NS,* § 331. See also E. Auerbach's stylistic interpretation of this phrase in "Sprachliche Beiträge zur Erklärung der Scienza von G. Vico," *Archivum Romanicum,* XXI (1937), 173 ff.

10. *NS,* § 331.

11. *Ibid.,* §§ 346 and 148. Cf. Auerbach's analysis of Vico's concept of nature (*op. cit.,* pp. 177 ff.).

12. *NS,* § 349.

13. *Ibid.,* §§ 7 and 390; cf. *SNI,* § 23. See E. Auerbach, "G. Vico und die Idee der Philologie," in *Homenatge a Antoni Rubio I Lluch* (Barcelona, 1936).

14. *NS,* § 2.

15. See Croce, *op. cit.,* pp. 115 ff.

16. *SNI,* § 8; *NS,* § 1110.

17. *NS,* § 12. Consecrated marriage and burial are the most humanizing early institutions, so much so that, according to Vico's etymology, *humanitas* comes from *humando,* "burying."

18. *NS,* § 250.

19. *Ibid.,* §§ 179 and 1110.

20. *Ibid.*, §§ 339, 379, 385.

21. *Ibid.*, § 382.

22. *Ibid.*, §§ 132–36.

23. *Ibid.*, § 630.

24. *Ibid.*, § 343.

25. *Ibid.*, § 342.

26. *Ibid.*, § 348.

27. See Peters, *op. cit.*, chap. vii.

28. *NS*, §§ 5, 130, 335, 342, 345, 1109.

29. *SNI*, § 9; *NS*, §§ 136, 310.

30. Cf. in Vico's *De antiquissima Italorum sapientia* (*Opere*, Vol. I, ed. G. Gentile and F. Nicolini [Bari, 1914]), chap. viii, where it seems as if fortune, chance, and fate were altogether reducible to providence.

31. Croce, *op. cit.*, pp. 28 f. and 115 ff.

32. *Ibid.*, p. 116.

33. *NS*, § 2. Italics are ours.

34. *Ibid.*, § 132.

35. *NS*, § 1108. Italics are ours.

36. *Ibid.* Cf. Croce's summary of this dialectic (*op. cit.*, p. 118): "Men thought they were escaping the threats of the thundering sky by carrying their women into caves to satisfy their passions out of God's sight: and by thus keeping them safely secluded they founded the first chaste unions and the first societies; marriage and the family. They fortified themselves in suitable places with the intention of defending themselves and their families: and in reality, by thus fortifying themselves in fixed places they put an end to their nomadic life and primitive wanderings, and began to learn agriculture. The weak and disorderly, reduced to the extremity of hunger and mutual slaughter, to save their lives took refuge in these fortified places, and became servants to the heroes: and thus without knowing it they raised the family to an aristocratic or feudal status. The aristocrats, feudal chiefs or patricians, their rule once established, hoped to defend and secure it by the strictest treatment of their servants, the plebeians: but in this way they awakened in the servants a consciousness of their own power and made the plebeians into men, and the more the patricians prided themselves on their patriciate and struggled to preserve it, the more effectively they worked to destroy the patrician state and to create democracy."

37. *NS*, § 629.

38. *Ibid.*, § 630.

39. *Ibid.*, § 376.

40. Cf. *ibid.*, § 391.

41. *Ibid.*, §§ 13, 365, 377 ff., 391.

42. *Ibid.*, §§ 385 and 948. Italics are ours.

43. *Ibid.*, §§ 1049 and 1055.

44. *Ibid.*, § 1099.

45. See *Social Contract*, Book IV, chap. viii.

46. *NS*, § 366.

47. *Ibid.*, §§ 13, 54, 165 ff., 295 f., 313, 365, 1110.

48. *Ibid.*, §§ 1047 ff.

49. *Ibid.*, § 31.

50. *Ibid.*, §§ 348 f.

51. *Op. cit.*, pp. 133 and 143 f.

52. Similar to Croce's liberal compromise between recurrence and pro-gression is the Marxist solution of M. Lifshitz (*op. cit.*, p. 414). Lifshitz is convinced that in the process of the Communist revolution "the return of human affairs" will become simply "the natural pulsation of the social organism."

53. *NS*, §§ 1089 ff.

54. *Ibid.*, § 241; cf. also § 243.

55. *Ibid.*, § 1106.

56. Peters, *op. cit.*, p. 139.

57. *NS*, § 1106.

58. *SNI*, §§ 41 and 8.

59. See B. Labanca, *G. Vico e i suoi critici cattolici* (Naples, 1898).

60. Croce (*op. cit.*, p. 196) observes that it is not impossible that Spino-za's biblical criticism suggested to Vico his criticism of the Homeric poems.

CHAPTER VII

1. *Sermon sur la providence*, in *Sermons choisis de Bossuet* (Paris, n.d.). Cf. the first and last chapters of the *Discours sur l'histoire universelle;* we quote from the English translation: *An Universal History from the Begin-ning of the World to the Empire of Charlemagne*, by James Elphinston (Dublin, 1785).

2. *Sermon sur la providence*, from *Sermons choisis*.

3. *Ibid*.

4. Cf. *Discours*, Part III, chap. v, on Alexander the Great; and III, vi, on Roman virtue.

5. *Ibid.*, I, x; II, xxiii; cf. also Eusebius *Dem. evang.* viii. 2.

6. *Discours*, I, xii.

7. *Ibid.,* II, i, xx, xxi; III, i.
8. *Discours,* English trans., pp. 318 f.
9. *Ibid.,* p. 320.
10. *Ibid.,* pp. 404 f.
11. Cf. Léon Bloy's criticism of Bossuet, *Textes choisis,* ed. A. Béguin (Fribourg, 1943), pp. 70 and 92.
12. *Discours,* English trans., pp. 198 ff.
13. *Ibid.,* pp. 266 ff. Cf. *Sermon sur le véritable esprit du christianisme, Sermons choisis.*
14. *Sermon sur la vertu de la croix de Jésus-Christ, Sermons choisis.*

CHAPTER VII

1. The most penetrating studies are those of H. Grundmann, *Studien über Joachim von Floris* (Leipzig, 1927); E. Buonaiuti, *Gioacchino da Fiore: I Tempi, la vita, il messaggio* (Rome, 1931); also his introductions to the critical editions of the *Tractatus super quatuor evangelia* (Rome, 1930) and the *Scritti minori* (Rome, 1936); E. Benz, "Die Kategorien der religiösen Geschichtsdeutung Joachims," *Zeitschrift für Kirchengeschichte,* 3. Folge, I (1931), 24–111, and *Ecclesia spiritualis* (Stuttgart, 1934). A short English monograph is H. Bett, *Joachim of Flora* (London, 1931). A very valuable "critical survey" of the literature on Joachim, by George La Piana, appeared in *Speculum,* Vol. VII (1932). The following presentation is based chiefly on the admirable studies of H. Grundmann and E. Benz. A critical edition of the chief works of Joachim (*Concordance of the Old and New Testament, Exposition of the Apocalypse, Psalterium of Ten Strings,* all of them printed in the early sixteenth century) has not yet appeared. The only translation which I was able to locate is the rather free and selected rendering by the French writer, E. Aegerter, *Joachim de Flore, l'évangile éternel* (Paris, 1928). The chief sources for Joachim's thesis of three dispensations are the *Introduction* and chap. v of the *Exposition of the Apocalypse,* and *Concordance . . . ,* Book V, chap. lxxxiv. Joachim's idea can be traced back to the Montanist heresy of the second century (cf. Tertullian *On Monogamy* xiv; *On the Veiling of Virgins* i). An orthodox criticism of Joachim's heretical thesis is found in St. Thomas, *Summa theol.* ii. 1, qu. 106, a.4. Cf. E. Benz, "Thomas von Aquin und Joachim de Fiore," *Zeitschrift für Kirchengeschichte,* LIII (1934), 52 ff.
2. Rev. 14: 6–7.
3. *The Eternal Gospel* (New York, 1937), pp. 3 f. Jones accepts the idea of an Eternal Gospel in general but not "the fierce comfort of an apocalyp-

tic relief expedition from the sky." Thus he dismisses Joachim, after a few introductory pages, to present his own ideas of an "endless revelation" of a "spiritual reality," revealing God "in the moral victories of history," though he realizes that it is a precarious undertaking to endeavor to show that secular history is a revelation of God and that there are glimpses of an Eternal Gospel in it.

4. It would be worth while to re-examine, together with the religious function of imagination, the methodical relevance of allegorical interpretation which has been used since the earliest times. It is remarkable that the most critical of all modern church historians, F. Overbeck, came to the startling conclusion that the allegorical interpretation of Scripture "is theology itself" (*Christentum und Kultur* [Basel, 1919], pp. 90 f.). The necessity of allegorical interpretation, in the widest sense, depends ultimately on the fact that the basis of the Christian doctrine and of the church is a *historical* document which has to be "interpreted" spiritually in order to prove its *truth*. Substituting for history and truth the more fashionable distinction between facts and values does not solve the problem of their relations. It only dissolves definite scriptural meanings into indefinite "spiritual values," which may be found anywhere.

5. *Concordance . . . ,* Preface.

6. II Cor. 3:17; Rom. 8:1–11; Galatians, chap. 4. It is a long way from the Greek concepts of spirit and freedom to the New Testament concepts and from there to their modern, emancipated meanings. To Paul *pneuma* is a mysterious infusion of grace, transforming man into a pneumatized being; *eleutheria* is the freedom of such a pneumatized being from death and sin, through voluntary obedience. Hence Christian liberty can never be opposed to authority and obedience. The question is only which kind of authority and obedience makes really free. Joachim, too, did not question the authority of the Father, of the Son, *and* of the Holy Spirit. But, while to Augustine perfect freedom is impossible within an earthly existence, Joachim expected the full freedom of the spirit within future history.

7. I Cor. 13:9–10; cf. Rom. 13:12; I Cor. 13:12; John 16:12.

8. See E. Frank, *Philosophical Understanding and Religious Truth* (New York, 1945), chap. vi. In its rationalistic form the most consistent "spiritualization" of the New Testament "letter" is Kant's *Religion within the Limits of Reason Alone*. Distinguishing the "pure religion of reason" or "moral faith" from "ecclesiastical faith" based on historical revelation, Kant interprets the whole history of Christianity as a gradual advance from a religion of revelation to a religion of reason, by which the Kingdom of

God becomes realized as an "ethical state on earth." Consequently, Kant has no scruples in asserting that in the entire known history of the church the present period, i.e., the Enlightenment, is the best one (see English trans. by T. Greene [Chicago, 1934], p. 122). It is the most advanced expression of the Christian faith for the very reason that it eliminates the irrational presupposition of faith and grace.

9. See E. Benz, "Die Kategorien...," p. 100, and *Ecclesia spiritualis,* pp. 434 and 460 ff., with reference to the endeavor of the Joachites to interpret the history of the church strictly religiously as a commentary on the significant figures and events of the New Testament. Cf. H. Grundmann's penetrating analysis of Joachim's exegetical method and its historical antecedents (*op. cit.,* pp. 18–55; also Buonaiuti, *op. cit.,* pp. 189 ff.). What is amazing in Joachim's interpretation is not that it is "the maddest flight of allegorical exposition and apocalyptic fancy" (H. Bett) but the degree of discipline by which Joachim succeeds in establishing a Christian logic of history through the concordance of the most important events in the history of the church with the literary succession of the New Testament figures and visions.

10. See E. Kantorowicz, *Kaiser Friedrich II* (Berlin, 1927; English trans., New York, 1931). This work was widely read by the German youth of the twenties, as it assured them of the messianic mission of "the Secret Germany"—until the secret became unveiled and profaned in Hitler's Third Reich. Frederick, excommunicated by the church, crowned himself in Jerusalem, assuming the messianic title of a *Dominus mundi.*

11. See Benz, *Ecclesia spiritualis,* pp. 387 ff., and the biographies of Cola di Rienzo by Gabriele d'Annunzio, *La Vita di Cola di Rienzo* (Milan, 1912), and P. Piur, *Cola di Rienzo* (Vienna, 1931). The interpretation of St. Francis as the *novus dux* is derived from Joachim. The spiritual origin of the title *dux* is Matt. 2:3–6. The transposition of the spiritual title of St. Benedict and St. Francis to that of a political leader persisted in Italy up to the *Duce* of our time. In the 1920's a Fascist pamphlet was published by a Catholic priest on *St. Francis and Mussolini,* elaborating, rather laboriously, the concordance between the reconstructive achievements of both. There the message of Mussolini is called a *messaggio francescano,* and two opposite pages show the reproductions of a painting by Giotto representing St. Francis preaching to the birds and a photograph of Mussolini caressing his lioness!

12. I Cor. 7:29 ff.; cf. John 17:10 ff.; Rom. 7:14 ff.

13. See Benz, *Ecclesia spiritualis,* pp. 404 and 432 ff., on the theology of history of Petrus Aureoli.

14. With Joachim resurrection became a historicotheological category. Since the life, death, and resurrection of Jesus Christ are the pattern of his body in the church, the historical church, too, must live, decay, and revive.

15. Applying this principle to the controversial question of poverty and property, the church argued against the Franciscan Spirituals that, if primitive Christianity had demanded absolute poverty as the most perfect state, the present state of affairs would indeed contradict the law of progression. Hence the church ventured to prove that the possession of *temporalia* has always been legitimate.

16. Grundmann, *op. cit.,* pp. 96 ff.

17. That Christianity is the very opposite of a religion fit for the world was understood from Paul and Tertullian up to Rousseau (*Social Contract,* Book IV, chap. viii, on "Civic Religion"), Kierkegaard (*Attack upon Christendom* [Princeton, 1944], pp. 102 f., 111, 127), and Nietzsche (*The Antichrist,* ed. O. Levy [London and New York, 1913–24], pp. 130, 186, 221 f.).

18. More orthodox than the theologians of the nineteenth century, Feuerbach clearly restated the fundamental difference between the Christian and the pagan world conceptions by the criterion of creation (*The Essence of Christianity* [English trans.; New York, 1855], chaps. x, xi, xvi [German ed., chaps. xi, xii, xvii]).

19. E. Renan rightly observed that the most surprising thing is that Protestantism did not spring into existence three centuries earlier ("Joachim de Flore et l'évangile éternel," *Revue des deux mondes* [1866]; English translation in: *Leaders of Christian and Antichristian Thought* [London, n.d.], pp. 129–205). In a certain way, however, the reform as intended by the Joachites was a much more radical break with the established church than was the reform achieved by Luther, for Luther never questioned the Old and New Testament "letter" but made its importance even more literal. As to his failure to desecularize the church see Christopher Dawson, *The Judgment of the Nations* (New York, 1942), pp. 100 ff.

20. See Kierkegaard's Preface to "That Individual" in *The Point of View* (Oxford University Press, 1939), pp. 109 f.

21. See below Appen. I.

CHAPTER IX

1. We quote from the English translation of the *City of God* by M. Dods ("Nicene and Post-Nicene Fathers of the Church," Vol. II [Buf-

falo,1887]) but take the liberty of revising this translation wherever it seems necessary.

2. *City of God* xi. 4; *Conf.* xi. 4. The argument is slightly different on account of the varying emphasis either on the well-ordered character of the changes or on change as such. In the second case heaven and earth proclaim that they were created because they are subject to change and what is mutable cannot be eternal. The presupposition is the classical thesis that what is perfect and divine is exempt from change.

3. *Conf.* xi. 5.

4. St. Francis' famous *Canticle of the Sun* is a praise of the Lord of Creation and not to be confounded with any pagan or pantheistic sentiment (cf. Matthew Arnold's essay on "Pagan and Christian Religious Sentiment," *Essays Literary and Critical* ["Everyman's Library" ed.], pp. 127 ff.).

5. Cf. Cicero *De natura deorum* ii. 2, 5, 7, 8, 11–15, 17, where the divinity of the world is directly inferred from its own cosmic structure and nature.

6. Augustine's concept of time as related to motion and change (*City of God* xi. 6) is a Greek discovery (Aristotle *Physics* iv. 10–14). The Christian revolution in the comprehension of time occurs with Augustine's question "where" time is originally at home. His answer is: in the invisible distention of the human mind (its attention, presenting presence; its remembrance, presenting past; its expectation, presenting future) but not outside in the universe, i.e., in the motions of the heavenly bodies, which are the visible pattern of the classical concept of motion and time (see Augustine *Conf.* xi. 24 and 28 ff.).

7. *City of God* xi. 6; cf. *Conf.* xi. 13.

8. Augustine follows the chronology of Eusebius, who reckoned 5,611 years from the creation to the taking of Rome by the Goths.

9. *City of God* xii. 10 and 12. The following discussion is based on xii. 10–13 and 17–20; xi. 4 and 6.

10. In the Christian perspective no intrinsic reliability of the cosmos can be assumed except through the reliability of the will of God, who says, as it were, every morning to the sun: "Do it again!" (see G. K. Chesterton, *Orthodoxy* [New York, 1909], chap. iv).

11. *City of God* xii. 20.

12. *Ibid.*

13. *Ibid.* xii. 17. A theoretical solution of the antagonism between the theory of eternal motion and the doctrine of creation has been attempted by

St. Thomas within his general endeavor to reconcile Aristotle's *Physics* with Genesis, while the Averroists opposed the eternity of motion to the doctrine of creation (*Summa theol.* i, qu. 46; *Summa contra Gentiles* ii. 34; *On the Eternity of the World.* Cf. also Giles of Rome, *Errores philosophorum,* ed. J. Koch, trans. J. O. Riedl [Milwaukee: Marquette University Press, 1944]).

14. Cf. Rom. 4:17, where the power of creating is even secondary to that of resurrecting.

15. Ps. 12:8. The modern versions (King James, American Revised, Goodspeed, Moffatt) translate the "circle" of the Latin, Greek, and Hebrew texts by a meaningless "on every side," "to and fro," and "around us"! After Nietzsche's revival of the cyclic theory, a radical attempt to refute it on purely ethical grounds was made by O. Weininger in a most interesting essay on "The Irreversibility of Time," in *Über die letzten Dinge* (Vienna, 1907). The main sources for the classical view of eternal recurrence are: Heraclitus, Frags. 30, 31, 51, 63, 67, 88; Empedocles, Frag. 115; almost all the myths in Plato; Aristotle *Met.* xii. 8, *On the Heavens* i. 3 and 14, and *Problems* xvii. 3; Eudemus, Frag. 51; Nemesius *De nat. hom.* 38, 147; Marcus Aurelius xi. 1; Seneca *Ep. ad Lucilium* 24. The main sources for the Christian discussion of it are, besides Augustine: Justin *Dialogue with Trypho* i, Introd.; Origen *Against Celsus* iv. 67, v. 20, and *De principiis* ii. 3.

16. Rom. 8:24 f. The Christian hope, far from being the natural gift of a cheerful temperament, is a religious duty, not the least when things are hopeless. It is, like faith and charity, a mystical virtue of grace, while all pagan virtues are reasonable ones (see G. K. Chesterton, *Heretics* [New York, 1906], chap. xii). For a modern version of the Christian doctrine of hope see the great poem "L'Espérance" by C. Péguy, in *Men and Saints* (New York, 1944).

17. See H. Scholz, *Glaube und Unglaube in der Weltgeschichte* (Leipzig, 1911); E. Troeltsch, *Augustin, die christliche Antike und das Mittelalter* (Munich and Berlin, 1915); H. Grundmann, *Studien über Joachim von Floris* (Leipzig, 1927), pp. 74 ff.; cf. also J. B. Bury, *The Idea of Progress* (New York, 1932), p. 21.

18. St. Thomas *Summa theol.* ii. 2, qu. 1, a.7. The *articuli fidei* cannot develop historically, for they are in themselves perfect and timeless. They can only become explicated.

19. See W. Nigg, *Das ewige Reich* (Zürich, 1944), pp. 123 ff., and the much more penetrating study of J. Taubes, *Abendländische Eschatologie* (Bern, 1947). Cf. also Grundmann, *op. cit.,* pp. 70 ff., with reference to

Joachim's attitude toward the traditional, in particular, the Augustinian, scheme of history; and E. Lewalter, "Eschatologie and Weltgeschichte bei Augustin," *Zeitschrift für Kirchengeschichte,* Vol. LIII (1934). The most explicit treatment of the relation between history and eschatology is to be found in two letters of Augustine (Nos. 197 and 199) to Bishop Hesychius.

20. See Goethe's remarkable note in the *Westöstlicher Divan* ("Israel in der Wüste"), that "the proper, unique and deepest theme of all history" is the conflict between faith and unbelief. But this note is remarkable also for its modern modification of the Christian faith into a faith "of whatsoever form." In the last analysis, epochs of faith are to Goethe all epochs that are "productive."

21. *City of God* iv. 34; v. 12, 18, 21; xvi. 43; xvii. 16; xviii. 45 ff. Cf. the theological interpretation of the history of the Jews by Bossuet, *Discours sur l'histoire universelle,* Part II, chap. xx; and by Newman, *A Grammar of Assent* (New York, 1898), chap. x, sec. 2.

22. *City of God* v. 21.

23. *Ibid.* v. 17.

24. See the study on Augustine by Scholz, *op. cit.;* John Figgis, *The Political Aspects of Augustine's City of God* (London and New York, 1921); F. W. Loetscher, "Augustine's City of God," *Theology Today,* Vol. I (October, 1944).

CHAPTER X

1. We quote from the English translation by Irving Woodworth Raymond, *The Seven Books of History against the Pagans* (New York, 1936). Orosius' work was officially approved by a papal bull in 494 and was henceforth used as a textbook of history and quoted throughout the Middle Ages by men like Otto, bishop of Freising (*The Two Cities: A Chronicle of Universal History to the Year 1146 A.D.* [New York, 1928]). Alfred the Great made an Anglo-Saxon version of Orosius. Only from Dante on was the Augustinian pattern of history weakened by the followers of Joachim.

2. Orosius, *op. cit.,* pp. 208 f.

3. *Ibid.,* p. 392.

4. *Ibid.,* p. 64.

5. *Ibid.,* p. 393.

6. Cf. G. Boissier, *La Fin du paganisme* (Paris, 1894), II, 397 ff.

7. Orosius, *op. cit.,* p. 33.

8. *Ibid.,* pp. 318 f.

9. *Ibid.,* p. 82.

10. *Ibid.*, pp. 30 f.

11. *Ibid.*, p. 74.

12. E. Peterson, *Der Monotheismus als politisches Problem* (Leipzig, 1935).

13. Orosius, *op. cit.*, pp. 120, 263, 310 ff.

14. *Ibid.*, pp. 104, 152.

15. *Ibid.*, pp. 139 f.

16. *Ibid.*, p. 90.

17. *Ibid.*, p. 205.

18. *Ibid.*, p. 140.

19. Eph. 2:2; 6:12.

20. Orosius, *op. cit.*, p. 393.

21. *Ibid.*, p. 167.

CHAPTER XI

1. As an amateur in the field of New Testament studies I present this outline with great hesitation. It relies mainly on O. Cullmann's *Christus und die Zeit* (Zollikon-Zürich, 1946), which seems to me the most illuminating and consistent interpretation of the Christian view of the history of salvation. One may object that Cullmann's exposition is a philosophical construction rather than a faithful exegesis. In defense of his exposition and of my own adoption of it I would, however, say that a constructive exegesis cannot but be a "construction," i.e., explicating, complementing, and reinforcing the fragmentary indications and implications of the "letter" in the "spirit" of the whole context. It thus unfolds the theological logic of the New Testament. Among the Fathers of the Church this logic has been developed most clearly by Irenaeus as a history of salvation. As such the understanding of history cannot but be "dogmatic." In recent times the justification of a dogmatic treatment of the historical substance of the New Testament has indirectly been given by A. Schweitzer, who has shown that the action and message of the historical Jesus remain unintelligible if separated from their dogmatic-eschatological presuppositions (*Geschichte der Leben Jesu Forschung* [2d ed., 1913], chap. xxi). Schweitzer's distinction between empirical, or natural, and dogmatic, or eschatological, history corresponds to our distinction between *Weltgeschichte* and *Heilsgeschichte*.

2. See the profound and lucid interpretation of Romans, chaps. 9–11, by Erik Peterson, *Die Kirche aus Juden und Heiden* (Salzburg, 1933).

3. O. Cullmann, *Koenigsherrschaft Christi und Kirche im Neuen Testament* (Zollikon-Zürich, 1946), pp. 35 f.; cf. also *Christus und die Zeit*, pp. 99 ff.

4. Origen *Against Celsus* iv. 23.

5. See, e.g., Shailer Mathews, *Spiritual Interpretation of History* (1916), and S. J. Case, *The Christian Philosophy of History* (1943).

6. See P. S. Minear, *Eyes of Faith* (Philadelphia, 1946), pp. 142 f.

7. Cf. K. Barth, *Kirchliche Dogmatik*, III, Part I (1945), 64.

8. See Aristotle *Physics* iv. 10, and Hegel's paraphrase of the Aristotelian analysis of time in the *Jenenser Logik, Metaphysik und Naturphilosophie*, ed. G. Lasson (Leipzig, 1923), pp. 202 ff.; *Encyklopädie der philosophischen Wissenschaften*, §§ 253 ff. As Aristotle and Hegel show, the distinction of a "before" and "after" does not exclude the theory that the *whole* time might move in a circle instead of progressing irreversibly toward a future goal.

9. Cf. Minear, *op. cit.*, pp. 97 ff.

10. Cf. Kierkegaard's analysis of Jesus as a "sign" (*Training in Christianity* [1941], pp. 124 ff.).

11. See C. H. Dodd, *History and the Gospel* (London, 1938), p. 168; *The Apostolic Preaching and Its Developments* (London, 1936), Appendix on "Eschatology and History." More consistent than Dodd is Bultmann, who applies the *Entmythologisierung* not only to the beginning and end but to the whole temporal frame of the New Testament (*Offenbarung und Heilsgeschehen* [1941], pp. 28 ff.).

12. Cf. Cullmann, *Christus und die Zeit*, pp. 81 ff.

13. *Ibid.*, pp. 115 ff.

14. See R. Niebuhr, "The Impact of Protestantism Today," *Atlantic Monthly*, February, 1948, p. 60.

15. This point has been most carefully elaborated by W. G. Kümmel, *Verheissung und Erfüllung* (Basel, 1945).

16. See P. Althaus, *Die letzten Dinge* (4th ed., 1933), pp. 44 f.

17. Cullmann's illustration (*Christus und die Zeit*, pp. 72 f.) also sheds some light on the question of the relevance of the deferment of the last things. Cullmann compares the chronological mistake of the early Christian expectation with a premature prediction of V-Day. In both cases, he says, the deceptive expectation of a *near* end rests on the positive conviction that the *decisive* event has already taken place. Against M. Werner he argues (p. 75): "It is not as if the faith in a fulfilment which has already taken place in Jesus Christ is a 'substitute' for the unfulfilled expectation of the nearness of the Kingdom of God; on the contrary, this faith has produced the intense expectancy of the first." But one may wonder whether the conviction in the decisiveness of a past event can be maintained if the

final fulfilment as promised by it is indefinitely delayed. It may be that one or three years of future warfare will not shake such confidence, but what about a hundred or a thousand years? A too long-delayed V-Day cannot but discredit the conviction in the decisiveness of the battle which has taken place. Hence the many laborious attempts to come to terms with the *Naherwartung* of the New Testament, at the price of giving up its temporal frame of reference as a mere frame—for example, Althaus (*op. cit.,* pp. 263 ff.), who separates the "erroneous form of temporal nearness" from its "essential" significance, i.e., to provoke an ever watchful "readiness" in the face of an "ever present possibility" of a last day. The *eschaton,* he says, is "essentially" near, i.e., "always quite near," i.e., "in principle" near—though not in fact! We have, therefore, to conceive the end of history "quite in the same way" as we should conceive the imminence of death, i.e., not with reference to external signs of approaching old age but as something which may happen at any moment. Althaus does not realize that there is an essential difference between the last term of individual life and that of history. The indefiniteness of the time *when* death will occur does not exclude, but rather implies, the certainty *that* it will occur, for this certainty rests on the empirical evidence that man is mortal, in principle *and* in fact. In the case of the end of history the faith in the sheer factuality of the coming of the Kingdom of God is, however, not independent of the temporal question, and the uncertainty of its *when* may very well shake the conviction that there will be a last day at all. The confidence in a theological *eschaton* stands or falls with faith alone. And whenever hope and faith were intensely alive, Christian believers felt sure that the last things were imminent, while to a merely hypothetical readiness (as if a last day were coming) the corresponding kind of expectation is what Althaus calls *Fernerwartung,* i.e., no genuine expectancy at all.

18. Mark 13:3 ff. and 28 ff.; Matt. 24:26 f. and 36; Luke 17:20 f.; Acts 1:6 f.; I Thess. 5:1 ff.

19. Cf. Althaus, *op. cit.,* pp. 44 ff., on hope and faith; Kierkegaard, *Edifying Discourses,* I (1943), 6 ff.

20. O. Cullmann, *Die ersten christlichen Glaubensbekenntnisse* (Zollikon-Zürich, 1943).

21. Overemphasizing with Kierkegaard the ever *present* situation of being challenged by Jesus Christ, here and now, to a final commitment, Bultmann's existential interpretation of the Christian eschatology minimizes the fact that the *Christian* "decision" depends on the hope in a *future* fulfilment. Such dependence of the eschatological attitude on the reality of a

future *eschaton* is essential also for the anticipation of death, which deter-mines Heidegger's analysis of finite existence and which serves Bultmann as an illustration of the existential meaning of the future Kingdom of God (*Jesus*, chap. ii, § 4). Both Heidegger and Bultmann insist that the "true" futurity of the human and divine *eschaton*, respectively, lies in the instant of our decision. They ignore the fact that neither death nor the Kingdom of God could ever provoke a decision, and even less a radical change in man's conduct and attitude, unless they were expected as real events in the future. Following Kierkegaard's thesis of "appropriation" of the objective truth by an existing individual concerned with that truth, Heidegger and Bultmann go so far in appropriating the imminence of death and the King-dom of God, respectively, as to annul their essential remoteness and given-ness. Cf. the penetrating criticism of Althaus on Bultmann's existential eschatology (*op. cit.*, pp. 2 ff.) and Cullmann's criticism of Kierkegaard's concept of existential "contemporaneity" (*Christus und die Zeit*, pp. 128 and 148).

22. Luke 3:1; 2:1.

23. Cf. John Baillie, *What Is a Christian Civilization?* (New York, 1945). For an extreme Protestant view of world history see Luther (Wei-mar ed.), XV, 370, and *Letters*, V, 406.

24. Isa. 40:24.

25. Col. 1:24.

CONCLUSION

1. See N. Berdyaev, *The Meaning of History* (New York, 1936), pp. 198 ff.; F. Overbeck, *Christentum und Kultur* (Basel, 1919), p. 72.

2. Cf. V. G. Simkhovitch, *Toward the Understanding of Jesus* (New York, 1927), as an outstanding attempt at a historicopolitical interpretation of the antihistorical and antipolitical meaning of the message of Jesus.

3. Cf. G. Krüger, *Die Geschichte im Denken der Gegenwart* (Frankfurt, 1947).

4. See F. Rosenzweig, *Der Stern der Erlösung* (Berlin, 1921), II, 212 f.; III, 48 ff., which is perhaps the most penetrating contemporary interpreta-tion of the exceptional character of Jewish history and destiny.

5. Cf. Berdyaev, *op. cit.*, chap. v; C. H. Dodd, *History and the Gospel* (London, 1938), pp. 32 f.

6. A. N. Whitehead, *Adventures of Ideas* (New York, 1933), p. 19.

7. *City of God* v. 1 and 8; Minucius Felix *Octavius* xi and xxxvi; *Summa theol.* i, qu. 116.

8. To Boethius (*De consolatione philosophiae* iv. 6), fate and providence

are but two aspects of the same truth. See also the interesting discussion on "Providence Miscalled Fortune," by Thomas Browne, in *Religio medici*. Browne distinguishes the operation of God's providence in nature and history. In nature the way of providence is open and intelligible; to foresee its effects is not prophecy but prognostication. But God's providence is more obscure, "full of Meanders and Labyrinths," in directing the operation of personal and national history, where unexpected accidents slip in and unthought-of occurrences intervene. This we often miscall "fortune" or "chance," though it reveals, if well examined, the hand of God. Those who hold that all things are governed by fortune would not err if they did not persist there. The Romans who erected a temple to fortune thereby acknowledged, "though in a blinder way," something of divinity. Similarly, Schelling: "Fate, too, is providence … as providence is fate. … To extricate oneself from fate there is only one means: to surrender oneself to providence. This was the mood of that period of the deepest transformation when fate vindictively struck everything which was beautiful and glorious in antiquity" (*Werke*, I. Abt., V, 429). See also the profound analysis of pagan fate in Kierkegaard, *The Concept of Dread* (Princeton, 1944), chap. iii, § 2, pp. 86 ff.

9. Cf. J. B. Bury, *The Idea of Progress* (New York, 1932), pp. 18 ff.

10. In all modern definitions, superstition is judged by rational standards; accordingly, superstitions are nothing but "irrational." Actually, however, superstitions (*Aberglaube*) are primitive modes of religious beliefs. As such, they were understood by a classical pagan philosopher as well as by a great Christian believer. Plutarch (*Moralia* ["Loeb Classical Library" (New York, 1928)], II, 455 ff.) defines the superstitious man as one who is perversely affected with the thoughts of God. While the atheist sees no gods at all, the superstitious only mistakes them. W. Blake ("Notes on Lavater," quoted by A. Gilchrist, *Life of W. Blake* ["Everyman's Library"], p. 55) remarks: "No man was ever truly superstitious who was not truly religious as far as he knew. True superstition [as distinct from hypocrisy] is ignorant honesty and this is beloved of God and man."

11. *Ensayo sobre el catolicismo, el liberalismo y el socialismo considerados en sus principios fundamentales* (Madrid, 1851), II, 3. English trans., *An Essay on Catholicism, Authority, and Order* (New York, 1925).

12. Cf. Augustine *City of God* iv. 8; vi. 9.

13. See above, n. 13 to chap. iv; cf. also E. Frank, *Philosophical Understanding and Religious Truth* (New York, 1945), p. 32; O. Spengler, *The Decline of the West* (New York, 1937), Vol. I, chap. xi, pp. 408 ff.

14. See my article: "Heidegger: Problem and Background of Existen-

tialism," *Social Research*, September, 1948.

15. See Descartes, *Discourse on Method*, Part VI.

EPILOGUE

1. The emphasis upon the future has found its most thorough explication in Heidegger's *Sein und Zeit*, in spite of his rejection of theological transcendence. The *Dasein* is constantly ahead of itself by taking care of and providing for its worldly existence. It is determined by an all-pervading *Vor-struktur*. To exist authentically means to anticipate resolutely the ultimate end of one's own existence, i.e., one's death. Since existence knows of no other *eschaton* than death, the prevalent mode of existential anticipation is not hope but dread.

2. See K. von Fritz, "Pandora, Prometheus, and the Myth of the Ages," *Review of Religion*, March, 1947.

3. Cf. Dante, *Inferno*, IV, 42; see also W. R. Inge, *The Idea of Progress* (Oxford, 1920), pp. 26 ff.

4. Rom. 8:24. See the profound analysis of hope by G. Marcel, *Homo viator* (Paris, 1944), pp. 39 ff.; cf. *The Philosophy of Existence* (New York, 1949), pp. 16 ff., and Kierkegaard, *Edifying Discourses*, I (1943), 30 ff.

5. See the pertinent criticism of Dodd's and Bultmann's reinterpretations of the futurist realism of the New Testament eschatology by W. G. Kümmel, *Verheissung und Erfüllung* (Basel, 1945), pp. 86 ff.; cf. also R. N. Flew, *Jesus and His Church* (1938), p. 32; and O. Cullmann, *Christus und die Zeit* (Zürich, 1946), pp. 33 ff., 82 f.

6. See W. Nigg, *Das ewige Reich* (Zürich, 1944).

APPENDIX I

1. Cf. Donoso Cortés, *Ensayo sobre el catolicismo, el liberalismo y el socialismo considerados en sus principios fundamentales* (Madrid, 1851), Book III on "Heresy and Revolution." Like Comte, Donoso Cortés derives the modern revolutions from "the great heresy of Protestantism," recognizing, however, that these modern revolutions draw their particular strength and destructive passion from the adoption of Christian principles: "All of them wear the raiment of the Gospel." They are such dangerous "heresies" because they spring from the orthodox faith in a final solution and salvation.

2. F. Schlegel, *Athenäumsfragmente*, No. 222.

3. Cf. my book *Von Hegel bis Nietzsche* (Zürich, 1941), pp. 53 ff., 219 ff., 447 ff.

4. See, above, n. 4 to chap. iii. A comparative analysis of Hegel's philos-

ophy of "spirit" with Joachim's prophecy is contained in J. Taubes, *Abendländische Eschatologie* (Bern, 1947), pp. 90 ff.

5. *Werke*, II. Abt., IV, 294 ff.; see also E. von Hartmann, *Religion des Geistes; Ausgewählte Werke*, VI, 2.

APPENDIX II

1. See John N. Figgis, *The Will to Freedom or the Gospel of Nietzsche and the Gospel of Christ* (New York, 1917), pp. 309 ff.

2. Nietzsche's *Jugendschriften* (not translated) (Musarion ed., 1923), I, 60.

3. Cf. in Nietzsche's later writings the symbol of Columbus, e.g., *The Dawn of Day*, § 575; the poem "The New Columbus"; *The Will to Power*, § 957.

4. See the recurrence of this metaphor in *Zarathustra*, ed. O. Levy, pp. 176 and 270; *The Joyful Wisdom*, § 341.

5. Cf. the restatement of this antinomy in *Zarathustra*, pp. 191, 246.

6. *Ecce Homo*, pp. 101 ff.

7. *Ibid.*, pp. 102 f. and 108; cf. *The Twilight of the Idols*, p. 111; *The Genealogy of Morals*, Preface.

8. *Zarathustra*, pp. 160 f.; cf. also p. 268.

9. *Ibid.*, p. 156.

10. Correspondingly, two opposite sounds are heard at that time: the cry of distress of the higher man (pp. 291 ff.) and the deep stroke of the clock at the great noontide, which is also a midnight (pp. 390 ff.) in which all things become eternalized.

11. *Zarathustra*, pp. 225, 175.

12. *Ibid.*, pp. 187 ff.

13. *Ibid.*, p. 12.

14. *Ibid.*, p. 266.

15. *Ibid.*, pp. 336 ff.

16. *Ibid.*, pp. 200 f.

17. *Ibid.*, p. 398.

18. *Ruhm und Ewigkeit* (Part 4).

19. *Zarathustra*, p. 255; cf. *Ecce Homo* on Zarathustra, No. 6; *The Twilight of the Idols*, No. 49; *Lieder des Prinzen Vogelfrei: An Goethe*. Accordingly, Nietzsche describes personal coincidences of his life, e.g., the completion of *Zarathustra* with the death of Richard Wagner, as "sublime chances," manifesting necessity or fate.

20. *The Twilight of the Idols*, p. 120; *Ecce Homo*, p. 73.

21. One of the most conspicuous implications of the belief in creation, according to all Christian ethics and in contradistinction to all classical

ethics, is the unconditional condemnation of suicide as an insurrection against the creator. On a purely moral basis no valid argument can be advanced against the possible dignity of suicide (cf. Augustine *City of God* i. 16–27).

22. *Zarathustra*, pp. 384 ff.; cf. *Ecce Homo*, p. 60. It is interesting to note that the adoration of an ass was a popular charge léveled against the early Christians (see Tacitus *Hist.* v. 3, 4; Tertullian *Apol.* 16; Minucius Felix *Octavius* ix; cf. also P. Labriolle, *La Réaction païenne* [Paris, 1934], pp. 193 ff.).

23. The idea reappeared sporadically throughout the Middle Ages in the Aristotelian theology, e.g., of Siger de Brabant; and no less a writer than Dante (*Paradiso*, XXXIII, 137 ff.) imagined the Trinity as three revolving circles into which the image of man had to be fitted miraculously. Superseding the absolute beginning and end of the Christian drama of creation and consummation, man is finally redeemed by co-revolving with the love-inspired universe! A similar blending of the Christian and the classical world views characterizes the prologue to Goethe's *Faust*. In modern philosophy the idea of eternal recurrence is discussed, e.g., by Hume (*Dialogues concerning Natural Religion,* Part VIII), Fichte (*The Vocation of Man,* Part III, chap. iv), and, most seriously, by Schelling (*The Ages of the World* [New York, 1942], pp. 119, 153).

24. Nietzsche, says J. N. Figgis (*op. cit.,* pp. 305 f.), "is a standing witness that, even if you throw over the whole creed, you are no nearer to your end; you will have made ridiculous what was always hateful. . . . The very last thing that will attract is a Christianity with the supernatural left out, and all the old moral ideals intact."

25. *Beyond Good and Evil,* § 20.

26. Cf. *The Antichrist,* pp. 130, 145, 186, 205, 221 f.

27. Cf. D. H. Lawrence, *Phoenix: The Posthumous Papers of D. H. Lawrence* (New York, 1936), pp. 724 ff., 731 ff.; and *The Man Who Died* (London, 1931); cf. also D. Brett, *Lawrence and Brett* (Philadelphia, 1933), p. 288.

28. This is the subtitle of *Beyond Good and Evil.*

29. *The Joyful Wisdom,* § 341.

30. *Zarathustra,* Part II, chap. xlii, on "Redemption."

31. *Ibid.,* pp. 25 ff.

32. For a more detailed discussion of the theoretical difficulties of Nietzsche's doctrine see my book *Nietzsches Philosophie der ewigen Wiederkunft des Gleichen* (Berlin, 1935), pp. 82 ff., 99 f.

33. *Zarathustra,* p. 319.

INDEX

PHOENIX BOOKS
in Philosophy